AF655466

RING THE VICTOR", *published in "Harper's Weekly" February 1882.*

RKG Snooker

RKG CUE SPORTS ARCHIVES

REPORTS & SCORES: WORLD AM. BILLIARDS C'SHIP. (3); REPORT LONDON SNOOKER FINAL (11); REPORTS AUSTRALIAN BILLIARDS & SNOOKER C'SHIPS (9/13) B.A. & C.C. TEAM SNOOKER DRAW (15) etc., etc.

THE Billiard Player

1/-

THE OFFICIAL JOURNAL OF THE GAME
Incorporating
"BILLIARDS AND SNOOKER"

JANUARY 1959
NO. 457

PROPRIETORS:—THE BILLIARDS ASSOCIATION & CONTROL CLUB LTD.

WORLD AMATEUR BILLIARDS C'SHIP TITLE GOES TO INDIA

LESLIE DRIFFIELD
(England)
who finished 2nd and missed recapturing the world title by 136 points.

TOM CLEARY
(Australia)
who, not quite at his best, yet revealed his rare artistry.

WILSON JONES (India)
who won all 5 matches in the Championship, made the highest break, 501, and achieved his great ambition of winning the world title.

WILFRED AXIAK
(Malta)
who put up a fine show at his first appearance in the World Championship.

CHANDRA HIRJEE
(Indian Champion)
who, rather disappointed expectations, but played cultured billiards

From Archives : It was a great news in Billiards for India

RKG

CUE SPORTS COMPENDIUM

RKG

CUE SPORTS COMPENDIUM

Publisher
Ravindra Kumar Gupta

Editor
Yashbir Sharma

Layout & Designing
Shamim Nida

RKG Publishers
CREATIVE PUBLISHING

7-B, Dr. C.V. Raman Road,
New Friends Colony, Near Gurudwara,
New Delhi - 110 065.

E-mail: rkghospitalities2007@gmail.com

www.rkgpublishers.com

First Edition 2015

Second Edition 2018

Front Cover Photos :

In ascending order - Walter Lindrum, Joe Davis, Wilson Jones, Steve Davis, Efren Reyes, Stephen Hendry, Ronnie O'Sullivan, Pankaj Advani

Printed at

Kaveri Print Process Pvt. Ltd.,
Patparganj Industrial Area, Delhi - 110 092

Disclaimer Clause

Articles, Data, Facts, Photos etc. wherever appearing in the book is taken from various sources like Cue Sports-Magazine (2000-2005), Wikipedia & other related websites. While every precaution has been taken by editor to provide the readers with accurate, upto date, factually correct data & useful information but the editor and publisher do not assume and hereby disclaim any liability to any person, party, or group for any loss, damage, or disruption caused by errors or omissions, inadvertently whether such errors or omissions result from negligence, accident, or any other cause. The book is to give helpful information on Cue Sports to the readers and are not meant to defame, purge, humiliate, and cause any inconvenience or injury to anyone or group of persons or company.

© All rights reserved. No part of this publication may be reproduced, stored in a retrieval system or transmitted in any form or by any means, electronic, mechanical, photocopying, recording or otherwise without the prior written permission of the publisher.

RKG

CUE SPORTS COMPENDIUM

CONTENTS

Section 1 BILLIARDS

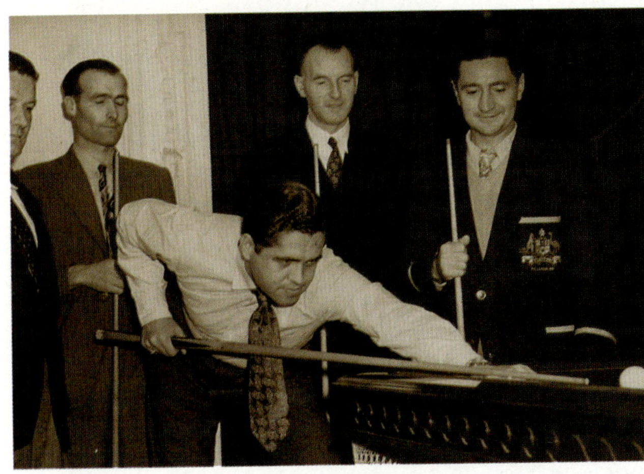

Section 2 SNOOKER

Section 3 POOL AND OTHER CUE SPORTS GAMES

From the Publisher's Desk

Since my childhood age of 16, I developed the passion for Cue Sports because it is an elite game & requires lot of concentration, mind application and professional skills. I have completed 50 golden years since I started playing this game and from last 25 years, I am dedicatedly promoting this game.

I formed the Delhi Billiards & Snooker Association in the year 1977 & organized the World Amateur Billiards Championships in 1981 & 1985 on behalf of the association which were met with rip roaring success.

After leaving DBSA, I sponsored four International & National tournaments in Mussoorie, Agra & New Delhi from 1998 to 2003. The purpose of sponsoring such tournaments was to give players the exposure & opportunity to showcase their skills on a suitable platform and also to win the prize money.

After a gap of a decade I started sponsoring the RKG International Masters Series in 2013 in which leading players of India got the opportunity to match their expertise with world's best. Currently I am sponsoring the RKG 1st Pro-Open Snooker Series which consists of Four Zonal Tournaments in Delhi, Ahmedabad, Chennai and Kolkata. The Grand Finale is at NSCI Mumbai. For both the above two series the organising part was and is being taken care by Yasin Merchant with his team.

During the period 2000-2005 I have also started the Cue Sports monthly magazine for the lovers of this game as through which they can cherish the articles & expert views from legend players of Cue Sports and at the same time to give players the exposure they deserve as the print media were neglecting the Cue Sports. Infact even till now the print media is not covering the Cue Sports fairly.

With the objective of increasing the awareness about the game, I have recently launched a world class website **www.rkgsnooker.com** for more detailed analysis and coverage of Cue Sports. It will be packed with all the information, photographs and the happenings of various tournaments, so necessary for the up-liftment of this game.

I acknowledge my team who burnt the mid-night oil in compiling this compendium ably with Graphic Designer Shamim Nida for letting his imagination run amuck, Sunil Gandhi for data collection and proof reading, Kanhaiya for checking and Yashbir Sharma for writing various articles and leading the team in making this book.

I have made a blue print for cue sports and any idea or suggestion to improve it further will act as a catalyst. At the various prize distribution ceremonies, the speakers are magniloquent in delivering speeches, raving about the help extending to this sport. But, I mean it.

In the end I would like to request the readers to send their valuable comments which will be helpful for me in continuing this crusade...

RAVINDRA KUMAR GUPTA

From the Editor's Desk

Dear Readers,

I am glad to bring out this Compendium book comprising of articles, photos, data etc. in three sections of Billiards, Snooker, Pool and other games. All the great legends and present stalwarts of Cue Sports are portrayed in this book.

As I write this piece with all humility and deep sense of gratitude towards the kind benevolence of One and only, Ravindra Kumar Gupta, who made me an author way back in 1974, gave the honour of editing cue sports and subsequently condescended to oversee this compendium.

I clearly remembered the rainy day six years ago when Ravindra called me in the morning to come to his house to discuss something very special. I immediately reached and was pleasantly surprised to get the idea of conceiving the Cue Sports book with interesting and unique features. The dummy was made about five years ago but the same could not be finalised at that time.

In this book apart from saga of veterans and present stars from Billiards, Snooker, and Pool, we have added very interesting and little known games of Cue Sports like Carom Billiards, Cricket, Slosh, Shuffle Pool and Skittles on the advice of Ravindra. In the last part of the book some very invaluable and distinctive photo gallery of famous World personalities is exhibited.

I have taken utmost precaution and care while trying to cover famous international and national players in this book, but due to constraint of space, many famous current and legend players could not be covered who were also the masters of this game.

I am beholden to irrepressible graphic designer Shamim Nida, who lent the myriad of colours of various hues and sizes.

The main object of publishing this book is to create more awareness of this game in young players and kids by giving information about legend and current champions (from India and Abroad) who have taken Cue Sports to greater heights.

RKG's imprint can be seen on every page. The idea is to make this book for posterity.

YASHBIR SHARMA

BILLIARDS

Section - 1

Page

A POTTED HISTORY OF ENGLISH BILLIARDS

Although doubts have been voiced about the origins of snooker, it is generally accepted that the game came into being in India in 1875. Billiards is a far older game with an even more clouded history, but Louis XI of France is recorded as having a fledgling billiard table in the 15th Century.

The word 'billiard' is believed to be derived from 'ball' words such as pila (Latin), billa (Medieval Latin) and bille (French), as well as 'stick' words like bille (Old French), billette (French) and billart (Old French). Shakespeare was one of the first recorded users of the word in his line: "Let's to billiards, come Charmian," in Anthony and Cleopatra (act 11, sceneV). Other early writers who refer to billiards are Ben Johnson in his simile: "smooth as a billiard ball" in 1637, and Charles Cotton in his book The Compleat Gamester of 1674.

Billiards reputedly began life as a lawn game similar to croquet before being brought indoors and onto a table by the aristocracy. At first two balls were pushed

Son of the first recognised champion of English billiards John Roberts Senior (1823-1893), junior waseasily the most commanding figure the game has ever known, both on and off the table. For years he was able to give a third of the game start to any opponent, and won the professional billiards championship on eight occasions, the last in 1885.

He played in front of royalty many times and did countless world tours, including India, where Maharajah of Jaipur made him, for one months play in a year, a courts billiard player for life, on an annual salary of £500 with expenses. It is likely that John Roberts first came into contact with snooker, during one of these Indian tours.

with a mace, a stick flattened and curved at one end, but in around 1670 players began to use the thin end of the mace more often. By about 1800, the transformation from mace to cue was complete.

In the early years, billiards kept in touch with its 'grass roots' by using hoops and posts, but they died out by the end of the 18th Century. During this century, English billiards also became distinct from the continental version. The French, closely followed by the British, introduced a red ball into play and the British incorporated cannons into their point scoring. The French took a different route and abandoned pockets altogether to concentrate solely on cannons. To this day continental billiards is still played on pocketless tables.

GREAT VICTORIANS IN BILLIARDS

John Roberts Jr.

John Roberts Junior stands out as one of the great Victorians in the world of sport. He was to billiards what W.G.Grace was to cricket, and had billiards continued its popularity, Roberts would be as well known today as his illustrious contemporary.

John Roberts Jr.

A late nineteenth century game between John Roberts Jr. and Edward Diggle.

Roberts was a showman, immaculately dressed, a legacy he has passed down to today's bow tied players. The other side of the coin however, was to behave as a law unto himself in everything connected with billiards.

Portrait of John Roberts Jr.

He invented the top of the table game at billiards, which combines pots and cannons around the billiard (black) spot. This obviously put him in good stead when he played snooker, as this report from the New World Of Billiards of June 1908 clearly demonstrates.

It was Tom Reece incidentally who made a billiard break of 499,135 UNFINISHED against a certain hapless Joe Chapman in 1907. For over 5 weeks he had the two object balls suspended on either jaw of the top pocket, with endless scoring with the anchor cannon at 2 points a time.

London's gentry would pop in from their clubs to see an hour or so, on their way home. Imagine the poor referee having to get dressed each day in his best bib and tucker, and stand there counting the score, hour after hour. Reece also had a cruel sense of humour and would turn to his opponent and ask sarcastically, "what kind of chalk are you using?" or "how are you finding the table?"

Getting back to John Roberts Junior, in 1908 he was obviously still a force to be reckoned with, although time was beginning to take its effect. The story goes that Charles Dawson was playing him after receiving a considerable start, when one of Roberts' supporters asked the referee who he thought would win. The referee replied he thought Dawson would. "Well he can't", replied the supporter, "nobody will ever beat Roberts". The referee then suggested that Roberts was not so young as he used to be and that Anno Domini might beat him. "Oh", said Roberts backer, "I didn't mean by any of your foreign players, I meant by an Englishman."

Needless to say, Anno Domini did finally beat Roberts, and the master cueman of his generation, died in his 72nd year on the 23rd December 1919.

W. J. Peall

Never mind 'pot as many balls as you can,' how about, 'how many times,without interruption, can you pot the black off its spot?'

Well a contemporary of John Roberts Jr. was W. J. Peall, whose claim to fame was his ability at billiards, to pot the red off its spot endlessly, when the rules allowed no limit to this form of scoring. His highest run was a break of 3,304.

His big advantage was that he was only a little over 5 feet tall, and stood virtually upright at the table, and so did not suffer with the aching back, which any repetitive shot normally gives. He was also one of the country's earliest motorists, and achieved some notoriety, when he fell foul of the law, by being one of the first caught speeding in a police 'radar' trap.

'On Saturday 14th September 1901, William J Peall was summoned, at Reigate, for driving a motor car near Redhill at a speed greater than twelve miles an hour. This was the result of a trap set by police in order to catch motorists and cyclists. The police sergeant deposed that on Saturday, August 18th, he timed the defendant as

having driven his car 176 yards in eighteen seconds, which worked out at twenty miles per hour. Under cross-examination he admitted that a mistake had been made in the measurements, and the distance was only 158 yards, which reduced the pace, and he also stated that to time the car he was standing behind a hedge some twenty five yards from the end of the 158 yards, and took the start when the car was passing the brow of the hill some 200 yards away, and the finish opposite a gate. He admitted the gate was fully ten feet wide, and was very uncertain as to what part of the gate he timed the car to, also that his watch was not a stop watch. When asked if he had anyone to corroborate his evidence, another constable was called, who stated that what the first witness had said was correct, but, on being cross examined, admitted that he was hiding in a field some yards further on, and could not see the car coming at all.Mr Peall then elected to give evidence on oath, and maintained that the sergeant could not at all check the times with an ordinary watch, and that it was impossible to tell when a car came by a spot 200 yards away, also that he was very indefinite as to where the measurements ended. As to the second constable's evidence, he might have been a hundred miles away for all he knew, and the defendant asked that his evidence not to be taken into account. The defendant stated he had witnesses to prove his defence, but, without giving him time to call them, the Bench imposed a fine of £2 and costs.

One could say that Mr.Peall was rather hard done by.

In 1937, Peall presented the Royal Automobile club with a quite magnificent trophy, which he won as Billiards champion in 1892, which now sits proudly at their centre in Pall Mall London, and is awarded yearly for the best performance in the Club's International Rally.

W.J.Peall died at the ripe old age of 98 in 1952.

George Gray

The Australian George Gray seemed certain to dominate the second decade of the 20th century through his mastery of in-offs. With a total command of a relatively limited range of shots and the concentration needed to repeat them. By gauging the strength and direction of the shot so well, he could make the red travel up the table and back off the top cushion to within an inch of its previous position.

With composition balls and Rileys cushions of his own selection he could make a thousand break almost at will.

Once at Manchester his opponent and also his road manager George Nelson wanted to catch a train home to his family for the weekend. The last train on Saturday was 9.15 pm but the session did not end until 10.00 so Nelson made sure Gray was in play at 9.00 and left to catch his train secure in the knowledge that he would play out time.

Willie Smith

Willie Smith, formerly a linotype operator from Darlington, only entered the Billiards Championship twice, and won it on both occasions. The first was in 1920, against that wonderful touch player Claude Faulkiner, and then in 1923 he regained the title from Tom Newman. Willie was possibly the best non-specialised, all round billiard player of all time. He played the game the average club player could identify with,

making shots they would attempt. The only difference was that Willie usually got them.

Willie's best break was one of 2743, which must have taken great strength and concentration, as there were no quick repetitive close cannon shots in his game.

His reasons for not entering the championship more often were due to his constant wrangles with the governing body, a phenomenon which is still repeated in many sports today.

Like many old-time Billiards professionals, Willie never really took to snooker, but almost reluctantly played the 22 ball game to earn a living. When asked

Willie Smith and Claude Falkiner

in 1980 if he enjoyed watching the World Snooker Championships on television, he replied he would enjoyed it a lot more if they changed the rules. "Which rules?" he was asked. "All of them," he replied.

THE SKETCH.

WILL THEY MEET, AND WITH WHAT RESULT?

FRED LINDRUM AND GEORGE GRAY

Joe Davis

Although born in the coal mining village of Whitwell, Derbyshire, on April 15th 1901, Joe was fortunate that his parents soon moved to the Queens public house at Whittington Moor, near Chesterfield, which housed a full size billiard table. Another fortunate coincidence was that the room had a 3 inch false floor, which allowed Joe to reach the table at a very young age. He made his first billiard century break at 11 years of age, and became local amateur Billiards champion at 13.

At the outbreak of the First World War, with his father being called up to serve his country, Joe was taken under the wing of Ernest Rudge, who owned a Billiards hall in Chesterfield. From there, Joe was used to "field the balls" for all the leading players of the day, witnessing what could be done on the table, which encouraged him greatly.

Early reports of his professional career gave a clear indication of his potential, and the success which was to follow. There were new, quite distinctive features in Joe's cue action, which held him in good stead when he turned his attention to snooker. For example, his method of sighting right down over the cue and his ultra rigid stance, were both considered worthy of note in the billiard press of 1923. Tom Newman remarked some years later, when Joe was getting the better of him in the billiards championships, that it was Joe's potting which made the difference, as much as 3000 points over a fortnights play.

Joe's first win over Tom Newman for the Professional Billiards Championship came in 1928 and his only defeat in the event was against Walter Lindrum in 1933 and 1934. Although quite capable of making century breaks, Walter never took to snooker. If he had maybe the record books would read differently today.

In 1924, Joe together with two billiard traders , first put forward the idea of a Professional Snooker Championship to the Billiards Association and Control Council, to complement the Amateur Championship which started in 1916. The idea was met with a marked lack of enthusiasm. The secretary of the governing body, the BA&CC, commented, " The suggestion will receive consideration at an early date, but it seems a little doubtful whether snooker as a spectacular game is sufficiently popular to warrant the successful promotion of such a competition."

At a meeting on September 1st 1926 however, it was finally agreed and in1927, the first professional championship was held.

There was 10 contenders for this first title, most of them far better known for their prowess at billiards; Tom Newman and Melbourne Inman being the most notable. Perhaps the relatively low entry was something to do with the 10 Guineas (£10.50) entry fee demanded, half of which was to go towards the purchase of a suitably impressive trophy. As the first prize was a mere £6-10s (£6.50), no player made a fortune on the championship, but the title, trophy and prize money were duly won by Joe Davis. He beat Tom Dennis 20-11 in the final held at Camkins Rooms in Birmingham, making a top break of 57.

The following year, the championship was played on a challenge basis, with one player coming through to compete with the champion. Joe Davis successfully defended his title in 1928 against Fred Lawrence, winning 16-13.

The 1929 final was a repeat of the first tournament, Davis beat Dennis, this time by a margin of 19-14 and increased the top championship break to 61. The same pair also met in the 1930 final, with the same result over more frames: the winning margin was 25-12 and Joe's top break a championship record of 79.

With this record, it seemed almost inevitable that the only entrants for the 1931 championship were, yes, Joe Davis and Tom Dennis! It was staged in a back room at a Nottingham pub owned by Dennis. However home advantage did not help

Dennis who lost 25-21. The following year saw three entrants for the championship, which was still run on a challenge basis. The New Zealander Clark McConachy won through to meet Joe, who together with Walter Lindrum and Tom Newman, were travelling the country, billed as the "Big Four" billiard players.

It was another famous billiard player, the great "all rounder" Willie Smith, who challenged Joe for the title in 1933 and again in 1935, while Tom Newman was the finalist in 1934. Joe won each time increasing the championship record break to 110 in 1935.

The whole basis of the championship changed in 1936, when it took on the regular knockout format that we know today. This new structure attracted 12 entrants, one of whom was the Australian Horace Lindrum, nephew of the great Walter Lindrum. Horace and Joe made it to the final, with Horace leading 27-24 at on stage, before the maestro, with his now customary final burst, turned the game round to win 34-27. Spectators crowded into Thurstons in Leicester Square, as snooker could at last be said to have overtaken billiards in popularity as a spectator sport.

Horace Lindrum featured again in the 1937 final, losing to Joe by the slightly smaller margin of 32-39. In 1938 and 1939, Sidney Smith won through to assume the runners up position. Joe beat him 37-24 in 1938 and 43-30 in 1939. Smith however, could take comfort from the fact that he had already won a place in the record books by cueing the worlds first total clearance, scoring 133 in a seperate event.

Fred Davis, Joe's younger brother, fought through some tough earlier rounds, to narrowly lose to Joe by the odd frame in the 1940 final.

The second world war prevented the staging of the world championship, just as it disrupted all sporting life. But in 1946, Joe Davis was back to take the title for the 15th consecutive time over 20 years, by beating Horace Lindrum, in a closely fought final. The result was 78-67 and during this tournament, held at London's Royal Horticultural Hall, Joe made a total of six century breaks and raised the championship record break to 136. There upon he retired from future World Professional Championships.

On his retirement, many people in the game thought that Joe should have kept the trophy. Fortunately for today's champions, this did not take place, as a close circle of Joe's friends bought an exact replica, which was presented to him in 1947.

Joe wanted to retire undefeated, and probably saw his brothe Fred, as his main threat. Incredibly, over a series of games, Fred was the only one to beat Joe on level terms.

In 1947, Joe along with Sidney Smith and Bob Jelks, became a director of Leicester square Hall, formerly Thurstons. Ted Lowe was managing director. Joe of course was the top attraction at this new venue, and in 1955, against Willie Smith, did the ultimate, the first officially recognised break of 147. At this venue and others Joe raised large sums of money for various charities, and in 1968 was awarded the OBE.

It warms the heart today to think that Joe saw some of the benefits of his labours. This must have been evident to him during the 1978 Embassy World Snooker Championship, while watching his younger brother Fred playing his semi-final match. As Joe took his seat at the crucible, the packed audience rose as one to applaud him. Sadly, before the final Joe was taken ill and the man who for one whole generation embodied everything good about the game, died a few months later.

Walter Lindrum

LINDRUM, FREDERICK WILLIAM (1888-1958) and WALTER ALBERT (1898-1960), Billiards prodigies, were the only sons of Frederick William Lindrum, billiardist, and his wife Harriet, née Atkins. Fred was born on 6 February 1888 at South Melbourne and Walter on 29 August 1898 at Kalgoorlie, Western Australia. The boys received only brief formal education, Fred at Kalgoorlie, Walter in New South Wales at St Francis Boys' and the Albion Street Superior Public schools, Paddington.

Their paternal grandfather, Frederick William (Fred I) (d.1880), had arrived in Adelaide from Plymouth Devon, England, as a child in 1838, later established a vineyard at Norwood and was a hotelkeeper in Adelaide and at Victor Harbor. In 1862 he was a billiard-saloon proprietor; and on 17 September 1865 in Adelaide, the day his son (Fred II) was born, he defeated the visiting 'world champion' John Roberts senior (presumably in a handicap match).

Fred II played billiards from childhood. In 1886 he moved to Melbourne and next year won the native-born Australian championship. But by 1892 (in a pattern to be repeated by later Lindrums) he had sunk from the top competitive ratings and within a few years moved to Western Australia where he opened a billiard-room

at Kalgoorlie and conducted a bookmaking business. He spent peripatetic years at Donnybrook, Perth, Kalgoorlie and Broad Arrow before moving to Sydney in 1909 and finally, in 1912, to Melbourne. There, at 317 Flinders Lane, he ran the Lindrum billiard-hall until his death on 11 April 1943. According to Walter, from 1909 to 1912 his father was the greatest billiard player in the world but 'only ... my brother Fred and myself knew it. He passed over public matches to coach the two of us'.

The elder son (Fred III) was obviously his father's first choice. Left-handed, he was trained for convenience as a right-handed player. (Ironically, his brother, having injured his right hand, learned a left-handed game). In Perth, where he helped his father to manage a Billiards-room, Fred won tournaments in 1904 and 1905 and next year became Western Australian champion. He went on to win the Australian title in Sydney in 1908. The year 1911 saw the peak of his career when in a successful defence against the English professional Tom Reece he made breaks of 830, 840 and 1239—the last an Australian record. The most elegant of players, a great showman, Fred took to the drink and after a disastrous English tour in 1911-12 never again looked a world-class competitor. While technically retaining the Australian championship (until 1934) he was soon eclipsed by Walter.

Fred died on 22 October 1958 at South Yarra. On 28 July 1913 he had married Augusta Hewett (d.1932) at Fitzroy. He was survived by his son from this marriage and by his second wife Dorothy Anne Jane, formerly Dyer, née Graham, whom he had married on 7 April 1948.

Walter was probably driven to excel by his need to match or surpass his brother in his father's eyes: significantly, his assumption of a billiardist's career followed hot on the heels of Fred's failure. World War I, however, obscured his rise, and though after it he racked up major successes against English visitors it was not until the 1929-30 season that he went to England and immediately won recognition as the best billiard player ever seen.

On this first tour Lindrum carried almost all before him, and made sixty-seven of what his nephew Horace was to call with perhaps understandable pique his 'highly scientific but somewhat mechanical thousands at billiards'. Lindrum himself effectively encouraged this view with a modest insistence that billiard champions are not born but made, an insistence reinforced by endless, perhaps exaggerated, reminiscences of dedicated practice from early childhood. It is generally said, too, that Lindrum owed his pre-eminence to 'nursery cannons' (close cannons barely moving the balls): but Lindrum's closest rivals also, necessarily, mastered this art and, though Lindrum's largest competitive break of 4137 on 19-20 January 1932 consisted of nearly two-thirds of such cannons, it was probably a more virtuoso insistence on that play by

the New Zealander Clark McConachy which led, as McConachy wished, to a change in the rules in September. Tom Newman wrote in 1929: 'It is the greatest injustice you can do to Walter Lindrum to write him down as a "scoring machine". Nothing could be more unlike him. He is showing you everything the game beautiful can show'.

Praise like Newman's—and it was chorused—must have been sweet to Lindrum's ears; but conflicting trade interests, always a major determinant in professional billiards, kept him that first season from playing for the 'world championship'. Coming back for the next season, he won an international tourney, a round-robin in which he gave 7000 start to the others and which ended in a play-off between Newman and Lindrum. This was perhaps the peak of Lindrum's career—but the tournament had been so successful that the annual world championship was abandoned.

Lindrum was also to miss the championship in his third northern season which he spent mostly on a North American exhibition tour. He finally won the cup, from Joe Davis, in May 1933 in his fourth international season and, to the consternation of the Billiard Association and Control Council (the English governing body), insisted on defending it in Australia. In 1934 in Melbourne he retained it against Davis and McConachy and in 1938 against McConachy, without the sanction of the B.A.C.C. In 1950, by which time, even in its strongholds, English billiards had given way to snooker, he refused McConachy's challenge and returned the cup to England.

It was not really the rule changes that ended Lindrum's record-breaking progress. He in fact made four breaks of over 3000—the highest 3752—against Fred in 1940-41 under the revised baulk-line rule. But he seems to have found competition an unwelcome strain, and having achieved the pinnacle in English billiards was content to stop, leaving pre-eminence in snooker to Davis. Nothing came of attempts to arrange matches under hybrid rules with the American champion Willie Hoppe. In later life, Lindrum deployed his skill to raise money for charities. He was appointed M.B.E. in 1951, and C.B.E. in 1958.

Lindrum married Rose Coates on her death-bed on 23 August 1929 in Sydney. His second marriage, to Alicia Hoskin on 9 April 1933 in London, ended in divorce in 1955. Childless, Lindrum died intestate of coronary vascular disease at Surfers Paradise, Queensland, on 30 July 1960; he was buried in Melbourne general cemetery after a funeral service at St Paul's Cathedral. His third wife Beryl Elaine, formerly Russell, née Carr, whom he married on 21 July 1956, survived him.

Lindrum was the author of several books on billiards. He was featured on the 1981 Australian 60-cent postage stamp and a technical school scholarship was founded in his memory in 1963. The cuttings, letters and telegrams on display at the Lindrum Billiard Centre in Melbourne reveal the astonishing range—probably owing something to his Freemasonry—of his acquaintances.

Fred and Walter's sister Violet was also a skilled player. Her son Horace Norman William Morrell (1912-1974) changed his name to Lindrum and became world snooker champion.

History of Billiards in India

Billiards, the three-ball game, arrived at the Indian shores in the 1920s largely due to the efforts of M. M. Begg. Begg, a character actor of yesteryears, played a pivotal role in the foundation of the Billiards and Snooker Federation of India and subsequently represented the country in world championships. The Federation took root in Calcutta in the year 1926 and since then Calcutta remains the stronghold of the Federation except for a brief period of four years, when it was housed in Bombay.

Despite being one of the few sports to churn out a healthy number of Indian world champions, the game of biliards is yet to catch the fancy of the Indian masses. Widely considered an elitist game, an Indian victory in billiards does not lead to a mass hysteria as a triumph in games like Cricket does.

Notwithstanding the slow progress, billiards in India has been played with the highest quality, a fact embodied by a bevy of world-class performers. Back in 1958, Wilson Jones put up a masterly performance to become the first Indian to win the coveted World Amateur Billiards Championship held in Calcutta. Since then, players of the caliber of Michael Ferreira and Geet Sethi have kept the Indian tricolour flying high in the international arena. The advent of double world champion Pankaj Advani and a horde of talented youngsters augurs well for the future of billiards in India.

Spurred by recent achievements in the world stage, a number of State Billiards Associations have made ardent efforts to tap the abundant talent pool in the country. The Karnataka State Billiards Association (KSBA) has been in the forefront of organizing tournaments as well as conducting coaching camps for international championships. The KSBA has earned plaudits for putting in place a state-of-the-art infrastructure that is regarded as one of the best in the world. It's high time now other state bodies followed suit and replicate the success of the KSBA.

BILLIARDS IN INDIA

In a cricket-obsessed country like India, cue sports like billiards have had to toil hard to gain mass acceptance. This, despite the fact that over the years India has been a force to reckon with in world billiards competitions. An impressive assembly of great champions like Wilson Jones, Michael Ferreira and Geet Sethi has underlined the powerhouse status of the country.

In India, the progress of biliards has been stymied by the popular notion that the game is elitist in nature and is the prerogative of the affluent class. Because of such a mindset, bravura performances of our champions have failed to spur the youngsters to follow a career in billiards and snooker.

But, of late, billiards has been able to catch the fancy of the masses courtesy the dazzling performances of prodigies like Pankaj Advani. The media too, for a change, has started to provide substantial coverage to billiards and other cue sports. The Billiards and Snooker Federation of India, the apex body, needs to play a proactive role in popularizing the game.

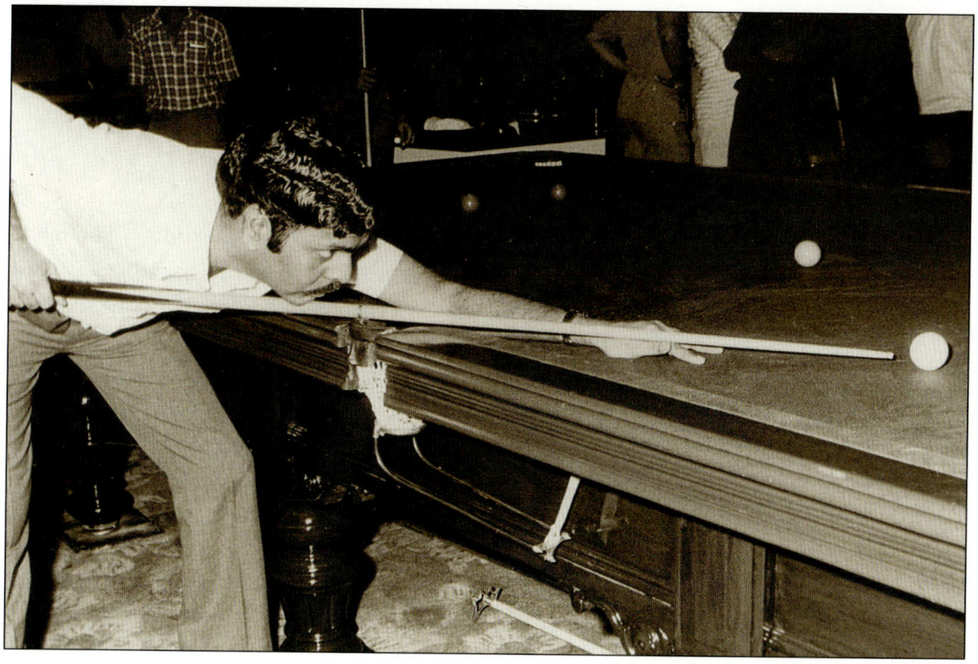

as the BSFI and the other state Billiards associations. The clubs are also an integral part of the management of Billiards in India and they are serving the purpose of increasing the popularity of Billiards in India. They are also providing the Billiards lovers with an opportunity to play the game.

BILLIARDS TOURNAMENTS IN INDIA

Billiards is considered among the few games where India has got considerable success in the international arena. The game came to India during the first half of the twentieth century and it being run and managed by the Billiards and Snooker Federation of India (BSFI), at the moment. The BSFI and several other state Billiards associations in India are working relentlessly for the well being of the game in India and they are organising a number of tournaments every year. The main objective behind organising the Billiards tournaments in India is to spread the game all over the country and also to bring up new talents to represent India in various international events.

The Billiards tournaments in India are organised at various levels like senior, junior, sub-junior etc and they are organised at both the state and national level. Apart from that, the BSFI and the other Billiards associations also play host to several international Billiards tournaments including the World Championships in India. The tournaments are mainly held in the major cities like Kolkata, Delhi, Mumbai, Bengaluru, Chennai etc. and players from all over the country take part in them. The organisers of the Billiards tournaments in India follow the rules and regulations identified by the BSFI, while organising the tournaments.

The Billiards tournaments in India have so far proved to be quite fruitful for Billiards in India. It can be said that because of these tournaments only, India has seen such a huge number of world class Billiards players so far. The players like Wilson Jones, Michael Ferreira, Geet Sethi, Pankaj Advani etc. honed their skills and excellence on the Billiards board in these tournaments only. So, in this way, the Billiards tournaments are playing a vital role for the total development of Billiards in India.

MANAGEMENT OF BILLIARDS IN INDIA

In India, the game of Billiards is being run and managed by a large number of associations spread all over the country. The national governing body for Billiards in India is the Billiards and Snooker Federation of India (BSFI) and it is being assisted by many state level associations. The BSFI and all the other associations are working with the common objective of a better management of Billiards in India and for spreading the game in all parts of the country. They are also working to develop the entire condition of the game in India.

Management of Billiards in India The apex body for Billiards in India and the most integral part of management of Billiards in India, the Billiards and Snooker Federation of India (BSFI) started its journey in Calcutta (Kolkata) in the year 1926. M. M. Begg was one of the pioneers for establishing the BSFI. Since its inception, the BSFI has taken a lot of initiatives to improve the condition of Billiards in India. It has conducted various training programmes throughout the country, organised different tournaments at both the state and national levels for the seniors and juniors, etc. The BSFI has also roped in former great Billiards players like Michael Ferreira, Geet Sethi etc for advising it about the formation of national championships. They are advising the BSFI about how to improve the total condition of Billiards in India, as well.

Apart from the BSFI, there are also several state level Billiards associations in India that are working for the better management of Billiards in India. The state associations are mainly working to spread the game into their respective states and also to bring up new talents from the grass route level. They are also conducting various training programmes and organising several tournaments for facilitating the upbringing of the young and talented players in their states. They are assisting the BSFI in various activities, as well. Some of the major State Billiards associations in India include the Delhi Billiards & Snooker Association, the Andhra Pradesh Billiards & Snooker Association, the Bihar State Billiards Association, the Gujarat State Billiards Association, the Jharkhand State Billiards & Snooker Association, the Karnataka State Billiards Association, the Kerala State Billiards Association, the Madhya Pradesh Billiards & Snooker Association, the Billiards & Snooker Association of Maharashtra, the Punjab Billiards & Snooker Association, the Tamil Nadu Billiards & Snooker Association, the Tripura Billiards & Snooker Association, the Uttar Pradesh Billiards & Snooker Association, etc.

There are several Billiards clubs in India that are working with the same objective

Most of the Billiards tournaments in India are mainly 9 ball tournaments. However, there are some 8 ball tournaments organised in India, as well. There are some tournaments that are for both Billiards and Snooker. Some of the most notable Billiards tournaments in India include the All India 9 Ball Pool League, Mumbai; the CCI Platinum Jubilee Open Snooker Tournament, Mumbai; the All India Junior Open Snooker Tournament, Mumbai; the All India Open 9 Ball Pool Championship, Mumbai; the Snooker Sangram - I Frame Knockout Snooker Handicap Tournament; the 8 & 9 Ball Karnataka State Ranking Pool Tournament, Bengaluru; the All India Invitational Snooker Championship; the Snooker Tournament, New Delhi, etc.

TERMS OF BILLIARDS

Like all other sports, the Billiards also has its own terms. There are a lot of terms that are used in Billiards. These terms are as follows:

Billiards - This is the name of the game. It has some differences with other similar games. It has a bigger table than Snooker and the colour of the balls are also different.

Distraction - This is a term that prevents the non-striker to do anything that can distract the striker.

Double - The term `Double` is used when the striker enters a ball into the pocket after striking one or more cushions.

Draw shot - is a shot where the players apply draw to the cue ball that is stroked.

Duration - This is the term that indicates about how long the play is going to last. The play can last in an agreed length of time or until one player or a side reaches an agreed number of points. In Billiard, a game is known as a Frame.

Follow - This is an opposite shot of the Draw Shot. This is a stroking technique where the player is allowed to make the cue ball "follow" in the same general direction as the object ball after it strikes an object ball. Players apply this shot by striking the cue ball above center.

Free ball - Here, if a player plays a foul shot and snookered his opponent then his opponent can nominate any coloured ball as red or as the ball `on`. If he pots the nominated ball as a red, he scores 1 and then after that he can nominate a colour in the normal way.

Frozen ball - When a ball rests against another ball or a cushion, it is referred to be `Frozen`.

Game - In Billiards, a game is made up of a number of frames that is decided by the organisers of the tournament. The World championship final usually is made up to 35 frames.

Half-ball shot - The Half-ball shot is a contact where half the cue-ball covers half the object-ball at the moment of impact.

Hazard - The term `Hazard` means a pot, an in off or the combination of both.

Head of table - This is a short rail where the manufacturer`s nameplate is marked. This opposes the foot of table that is unmarked by the manufacturer`s nameplate.

Head string - This is a line that runs from the second diamond on the side rails through the head spot. The officials call the area between the head string and the head of the table as "within the head string" or as a 'balk'.

Hold - This term usually turn over English. This is normally applied to a cue ball that tends to hold the cue ball back from the course that the ball normally would take. It is driven in a certain direction.

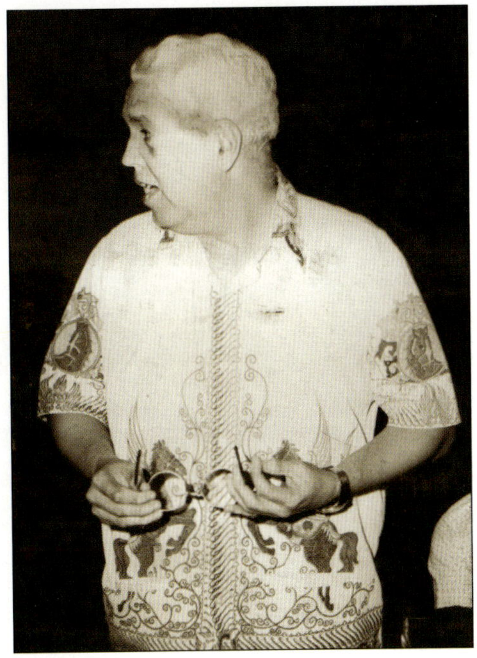

Inning - This term means a turn of a player at the table. This is the duration that a player stays at the table from the time he officially makes the first shot. The `Inning` lasts until the player ends his turn either by missing, fouling or scoring the maximum number of balls allowed or by concluding the game.

In-off - The `In-off` is a scoring shot where the cue-ball enters a pocket after contacting an object-ball. Traditionally, it is called as a losing Hazard.

Kiss Canon - If the cue ball touches the two object balls lightly and softly, a cannon or carom is achieved.

Lighting - In order to make the Billiard tables well lighted, some special lighting equipments are normally used.

Line-up - This term is used to refer to a pocket Billiards game. This is also used to indicate about a method of spotting balls in game of line-up.

Live Ball - The `Live Ball` is a ball that is being played under the rules. The cue ball is also called as `Live Ball` when it is in live action. It is opposite to a dead ball.

Long in-off - This term is used to refer an in-off shot that is played into a top pocket when the cue-ball is in hand. This is called as a long loser as well.

Loser - If any striker manages to pocket

his own ball after touching it with any of the object balls then it is called as `Loser`. Here, points are scored in favour of the striker. If the loser is off the red ball, 3 points are scored and it will be 2 points if the loser is off the white ball.

Miss - if a player fails to strike any object on the table, then it is called as a `Miss`.

Natural angle - This is an angle that the cue ball may take after it strikes an object-ball at a medium pace and it does not receive any spin, side, screw, or stun.

Nurse - The term `Nurse` refers to a technique of the game. This technique allows the player to keep balls in position in order to score consecutively.

Object Ball - This is a ball that is aimed by the player with his own ball. It is one of the 15 balls that are of red or other six colours. The cue ball is always intended to hit the `Object ball`.

Officials - In any tournament of any sport, there are some referees who control the game. In Billiards also, there is a referee to control the game and he is the sole judge of fair play as well. Sometimes, he is assisted by the marker, who keeps the score.

On the black - If in any stage of the game, there are less than 7 points between the players and only the black coloured ball is left on the table, the game is referred to be `On the Black`. In this case, if the black is potted or if any player commits a foul by missing the black or going in-off, the game ends.

Plant - This is such a position where the player plays the first object-ball on to the second object-bal in such a way that he is going to make the second ball enter the pocket.

Pocket - There are six open-mouthed pouches in the Billiards table where the object balls are stroked. Each of these pouches is called the `Pocket`. These openings are located in each corner of the table and one in each side cushion, halfway between the end cushions.

Pot - `Pot` is the main scoring shot of the game. Here, the player sends an object-ball into a pocket with the help of the cue-ball. This shot is traditionally referred as a winning hazard.

Potting - playing a `Pot` successfully is called `Potting`. Here, the player`s cue-ball hits anyone of the object-balls and the object ball goes into any of the pockets.

Push stroke - This term refers a foul shot. The officials refer a shot as `Push Stroke` when the player keeps the cue in contact with the cue ball after the ball begins to move forward or it strikes an object ball.

Pyramid - This is the triangular placement of the object balls in Billiard games. Here, the balls are racked in a triangle on the foot spot to start the game. This placement is called so as it is similar to the structure of the Egyptian Pyramids.

Rail nurse - This term is used to indicate about a technique. In this technique, the player is allowed to `nurse` the balls along the rail so that he can keep them in position and score consecutively.

Red ball - This is the name of a carom game in which it is required that the red ball is the first object on all shots during the game. It also refers the object ball that is used in carom games, snooker, etc.

Referee - `Referee` is the official person who controls the game totally. He has a lot of activities in the game like giving rulings, resetting the balls, calling the scores, etc.

Rests - Sometimes the players enjoy the facility to use a `Rest` in order to support the cue for a shot.

Reverse - In the English Billiards, the players apply back spin to the cue ball so that when it hits a cushion or another ball, it tends to stop and rebound.

Rotation - This is the name of a pocket game where the player has to drive the cue ball against the object balls in numerical order. This also refers the sequence of play where two or more players are involved. This is called as "rotation of play".

Run - If any player scores or counts consecutively in one inning, this is called as `Run`.

Run Through - This term refers a stroke that keeps the cue ball moving after hitting an object ball. The term can also be referred to the result of such a stroke.

Safe Position - is such a situation where a scoring stroke looks almost impossible.

Safety Shot - If the player plays a shot with no intention of scoring, but to prevent his opponent from scoring.

Scoreboard - Like all the other sports, in Billiards also the `Scoreboard` means a board where the score is recorded and that shows units, tens and hundreds.

Scoring - `Scoring` means the occurrence when the striker scores points in order to win hazards, losing hazards, and cannons. All points accumulated in a shot are counted.

Screw - The term refers the art with which the reverse spin is applied. This is a back-spin that is put on to a cue ball and make it come back after hitting the object ball.

Set - This term refers such a position where two object balls are touching in such a way that the second ball will surely be potted no matter how the player strikes the first object-ball.

Set-up - This is the name of a very easy shot in Billiard.

Shot - This term is usually applied to the roll of the cue ball as it approaches to the second object ball in carom games. A ball starts spinning if it comes off the last cushion at a sharp angle.

Shot to nothing - This is a shot where a player attempts to pot a ball in such a way that he is trying to leave himself in a position to continue his break if successful. He also tries to leave the cue-ball in a bad position so that his opponent becomes unsuccessful.

Snooker - This term refers a position where the cue ball cannot hit an object-ball directly as there remains an intervening ball.

Spotting - When the referee replaces the balls on the table as a requirement of the game, the replacement called as `Spotting`.

Starting play - This is a process where a coin is tossed by the referee in the air to decide who will play first. When the game begins, the starter plays the "D" at any red ball.

GENERAL RULES OF BILLIARDS

There are different types of games that are being played in the game of Billiard such as the 8-ball game, 9-ball game, 14.1 continuous, one pocket game, wheelchair competition etc. Though all of them have some different rules and regulations, there are some General Rules of Billiards that have been followed in all the games of Billiards. These rules are as follows:

1. Tables, Balls, Equipments: All the games of Billiards are designed for the tables, balls and the equipments that meet the international standards.

2. Racking The Balls: A triangle must be used when the balls are being racked on the table. The apex ball should be spotted on the foot spot. The referee should line up all the balls behind the apex ball and press them together so that all the balls have contact with each other.

3. Striking Cue Ball: The player is required to strike the cue ball only with the cue tip in order to make a legal shot. If he fails to meet this requirement, he will commit a foul.

4. Calling Shots: In the games where call-shots are used, a player can shoot any ball according to his choice, but he must indicate the called ball and called pocket before he shoots. He does not need to indicate in details such as kisses, caroms, combinations, or cushions.

5. Failure To Pocket A Ball: When a player fails to pocket a ball on a legal shot, the referee can announce the player`s inning as over. After that his opponent gets his turn at the table.

6. Lag For Break: This rule is implemented in order to determine the player who will start the game. It is mandatory for each player to use balls of equal size and weight. Usually the balls are shot simultaneously to the foot cushion and back to the head end of the table with the balls in hand behind the head string. One player stays to the left and the other player to the right of the head spot. The player, whose ball remains

closest to the innermost edge of the head cushion, wins the lag and gets the chance to start the game. The lagged ball must contact the foot cushion at least once. The player may loss the lag automatically if "The ball that he shot crosses into the opponent`s half of the table"; "The ball fails to contact the foot cushion"; "The ball drops into a pocket"; "The ball jumps off the table"; "The ball touches the long cushion"; "The ball rests within the corner pocket and pass the nose of the head cushion" and if "The ball contacts the foot rail more than once". In any case where both the players have violated the automatic-loss lag rules and/or the referee is unable to determine which player`s ball is closer, then the lag is stated as a tie and the players play it again.

7. Opening Break Shot: The referee determines the opening break shot by implementing either lag or lot rule. The player who wins the lag or lot enjoy the facility to choose whether he will perform the opening break shot or assign it to his opponent.

8. Cue Ball On Opening Break: The player takes the opening break shot with cue ball in hand behind the head string. The referee positions the object balls according to specific game rules. Once the player strikes the cue ball by the cue tip on the opening break, the game is considered to have commenced.

9. Deflecting The Cue Ball On The Game`s Opening Break: If any player stops or deflects the cue ball after it has crossed the head string and is prior to hit the racked balls on the break shot, he will commit a foul and loss his turn. Then, his opponent will have the option to receive the cue ball in hand behind the head string or pass it back to the offending player. In this case, the referee must give a warning that states that a second violation of this rule during the match will result in the loss of the match.

10. Cue Ball In Hand Behind The Head String: If in any game, the opening break is administered or a player`s scratching is penalized by giving the incoming player the chance to have the cue ball in hand behind the head string, then this rule is implemented. Here, the incoming player can place the cue ball anywhere behind the head string. The player who is shooting can shoot at any object ball till the ball is on or below the head string. He cannot shoot at any ball that is based above the head string. He can shoot such balls after he shoots the cue ball below the head string and then hit a rail that causes the cue ball to come back above the head string and hit the object ball. The base is the point of the ball touching the table. This base determines whether it is above or below the head string. In case of the incoming player unintentionally placing the cue ball on or below the head string, the referee or the opposing player should inform the shooting player about the improper positioning of the cue ball before he makes shot and the shooting player will have to reposition the cue ball. If the opposing player fails to inform the shooting player before the shot is made, the referee will consider the shot as legal. It will be considered as a foul if a player positions and shoots the cue ball completely and clearly outside the kitchen. Until the player strikes the cue ball with his cue tip, the cue ball remains in hand (not in play). When the cue ball remains in hand, the player can adjust it by his hand or cue, etc. But, once the cue ball is in play, the player may not impede it in any way and if he does so, it will be a foul.

11. Pocketed Balls: A ball will be considered as pocketed if it drops off the bed of the table into the pocket and remains there as a result of a legal shot. If a ball rebounds from a pocket back onto the table bed, it will not be considered as a pocketed ball.

12. Position Of Balls: The player judges the position of a ball by the base or center where it rests.

13. Foot On Floor: This rule is very much mandatory for the player to keep at least one foot in contact with the floor at the moment he contacts the cue ball with the cue tip. If he does not do so, he will commit a foul.

14. Shooting With Balls In Motion: The referee will consider it as a foul if a player shoots while the cue ball or any object ball is in motion.

15. Completion Of Stroke: When all the balls on the table become motionless after a stroke, the stroke is completed and counted.

16. Head String Defined: The head string does not include the area behind it. That means if an object ball is dead center on the head string, it is playable. However, in some specific games, it is required that a player must shoot at a ball past the head string. Similarly, when the cue ball is in hand behind the head string, it cannot be placed directly on the head string. It should always be behind the head string.

Famous Indian Billiards Players

Who Created History !

India has been home to a horde of prodigious Billiards players who have enthralled the audience with their artistry and genius. This bunch of world-beaters has brought the nation to its feet by winning a plethora of crowns in the international stage.

Wilson Jones' victory in the World Amateur Billiards Championship in 1964 gave India its first world champion in any sport. Michael Ferreira was more than able to fill the void created by Jones's departure and went on to amass four world billiards titles. He demanded fair treatment for Indian Biliards players who have won laurels for the country.

Geet Sethi is undoubtedly one of the most famous Indian billiard players. In his glorious career, Sethi has won an astounding eight world billiards titles and is widely regarded as one of the best the game has ever seen.

The latest addition to a long list of talented Indian billiards players is the prodigious Pankaj Advani. Advani has shot into limelight by becoming the first player to win both the points format and the time format titles in the World Billiards Championship in 2005. His feat will surely inspire young Indian billiard players to make a mark at the world stage.

Sir Wilson Jones and Mr. Hameed

Wilson Jones congratulating to Michael Ferreira

Wilson Jones and Geet Sethi

WILSON JONES

Achievements: Won the National Billiards Championship 12 times; won the World Billiards Championship twice (1958 and 1964); Arjuna Award in 1962; Padma Shri in 1965; Dronacharya Award in 1996.

The fact that Wilson Lionel Garton Jones was the first Indian world champion at any sport speaks volumes about the quality of the man. During an illustrious career, Jones won the World Billiards Championship twice and reigned supreme in the national stage, winning the National Billiards Championship a whopping 12 times.

Born at Pune in Maharashtra on May 2 1922, Wilson Jones studied at the local Bishop High School and St. Vincent's High School before joining the War Service in 1939. Jones shot to limelight in 1950 when he won his first National title defeating T. A. Selvaraj in the final. From 1950 to 1966, Jones remained Amateur Billiards Champion of India for 12 years.

Wilson Jones' first endeavour in the World Billiards Championship did not make much of an impact as he finished last. Undaunted, he persisted with grit and determination and soon carved a niche for himself in the international stage. Finally, in 1958, came his biggest moment when he became the first Indian to win the coveted World Amateur Billiards Championship held at Great Eastern Hotel in Calcutta. Jones won the crown again in 1964 in New Zealand.

Post-retirement, Jones acquired a formidable reputation as a billiards coach, passing on an invaluable experience of eight World Championship appearances. That many of his wards like Subhash Agarwal and Ashok Shandilya went on to become professional world champions bears testimony to his coaching prowess.

In honour of Wilson Jones' contribution to the three-ball game, the nation conferred him with the Arjuna Award in 1962, Padma Shri in 1965 and the Dronacharya Award in 1996. His demise in 2003 has left a void in the cue sports arena.

MICHAEL FERREIRA

Achievements: Won the World Billiards Championship four times; in December, 1978, created history by becoming the first amateur to make a 1000 point break in billiards

Michael Ferreira, nicknamed "The Bombay Tiger," was born in Mumbai on October 1, 1938. Ferreira, four times world Billiards champion, proved to be an able successor to the prodigious Wilson Jones.

Ferreira made his debut in the Nationals in 1960 and in 1964 made a sensational appearance in the World Amateur Champion Championship in New Zealand where he lost in the semi-finals by a whisker. Ferreira won his maiden World Amateur Billiards

Championship in 1977 and followed that triumph with the World Open Billiards Championship title at Christchurch, New Zealand, completing a unique double.

Gradually Ferreira gained in stature and produced records galore on his way to another two world billiards titles. In December 1978, he created history by becoming the first amateur to cross the 1000 point barrier by making a new world record break of 1149 in the national championships. His achievements during the seventies and eighties gave a fillip to the three-ball game in India and spurred youngsters like Geet Sethi to shine in the international arena.

True to his fiery spirit, Michael Ferreira was vociferous in demanding equal treatment for all the sports in India. His rebellious trait came to the fore in 1981 when he refused to accept the Padma Shri award conferred on him after winning the world title for the second time. He opined that his accomplishments in billiards were in no way inferior to that of Sunil Gavaskar's in cricket who was bestowed with the more prestigious Padma Bhushan.

GEET SETHI

Achievements: Winner of eight world titles - five World Professional and three IBSF World Billiards Championships; featured in the Guinness Book of World Records for being the first amateur in the world to compile the maximum 147 break in Snooker; made a break of 1276 in the 1992 World Professional Billiards Championship,

a World Record; Padma Shri (1986); Arjuna Award (1986); Rajiv Gandhi Khel Ratna Award (1992-93)

In a remarkable career spanning 30 years and counting, Billiards maestro Geet Sethi has become synonymous with the three-ball game in India. Born in Delhi on April 17, 1961, Sethi's precocious talent blossomed when he shifted to Ahmedabad at a young age.

Geet Sethi startled billiards aficionados when he defeated the mercurial Michael Ferreira to win the National senior title in 1982. Carrying on the good work, he won the IBSF World Billiards Championship in 1985 by defeating Bob Marshall in a marathon 8-hour long final. He went on to win an amazing eight world titles - five World Professional and three IBSF World Billiards Championships.

Besides winning crowns aplenty, Geet Sethi has achieved many a record-breaking feats. He featured in the Guinness Book of World Records for being the first amateur in the world to compile the maximum 147 break in Snooker. Moreover, Geet Sethi constructed a break of 1276 in the 1992 World Professional Billiards Championship, which is the World Record under the three pot rule and was the highest break made in the last five decades.

Geet Sethi was Michael Ferreira's heir-apparent and his classic encounters with archrival Mike Russell were the stuff legends are made of. In a tribute to his achievements, the nation has conferred on him some of its most prestigious awards -- Padma Shri (1986), Arjuna Award (1986) and Rajiv Gandhi Khel Ratna Award (1992-93).

PANKAJ ADVANI

Advani made his international competitive debut at the Asian Billiards Championship 2002, held at Bangalore, in which he finished as a finalist. After an amateur World Snooker Champion title win in 2003, he won the IBSF World Billiards Championship in 2005 at Qawra, Malta, where he became the first to achieve a "grand double" by winning both the time and point formats, a feat he repeated at the 2008 event in Bangalore. He is the only Indian to have won the amateur world title in both snooker and billiards.

He is also the youngest person to have won all these world titles in English billiards, for a record 8 times. Advani also remains the only person to have won all five national, regional, and world billiards tournaments in a single season, a feat he achieved by winning the Indian Junior National Championship and Senior National Championship, the Asian Billiards Championship, and both the World Billiards Championship (point format) and World Billiards Championship (time format).

Advani won the WPBSA billiards title, at Leeds in 2009, against the defending champion Mike Russell; Advani won 2030–1253, after gaining an 800-plus lead at his opening break. He became the first person in the world to win the trio of the WPBSA World Billiards Champion pro title (which he has held twice, in 2009 & 2012), and the IBSF World Billiards Champion amateur title, as well as the IBSM World Snooker Champion amateur title.

In April 2012, Advani won the Asian Billiards Championship in Goa, India to become the first player to win 5 Asian Billiards Champion titles. This takes his total tally of international majors to 17 - 8 Worlds, 5 Asian Billiards, 2 Asian Games Golds, 1 Australian Open and 1 Asian Team. It was announced in May that Advani had accepted the Indian wildcard place on the main snooker tour for the 2012/2013 season.

In October 2012, in Leeds, England, Advani won his seventh (counting professional and amateur) World Billiards Champion title, eighth world title overall, beating defending and nine-time WPBSA World Billiards Champion Mike Russell again, in the timed division final (Advani did not make it to the points division final). He was awarded Padma Shri, India's fourth highest civilian honour in 2009 and Rajiv Gandhi Khel Ratna, India's highest sporting honour, 2005-06 apart from other awards.

The 2013/2014 season saw the introduction of a ranking event in Advani's home country of India for the first time which he qualified for by beating Matthew Selt 4–0. At the tournament in New Delhi Advani defeated Marcus Campbell 4–1 and Mark Allen 4–2. His match with Allen finished at 11pm local time, with Advani back in last 16 action at 10am the next morning to play Stuart Bingham. The match went to a deciding frame and when Bingham broke down on a break of 30, Advani stepped in to compose a match winning 86. Advani played compatriot Aditya Mehta in the quarter-finals in an iconic match in Indian snooker as the winner would be the country's first ranking event semi-finalist. The match was heavily focused on safety and it was Mehta who advanced with a 4–3 win. His best run in a ranking event during the rest of the season was at the World Open, where he narrowly beat Xiao Guodong 5–4 to set up a last 32 meeting with Ding Junhui. Advani had a lead of 4–2 in the best of nine frame match and was 35 points to 0 ahead in the seventh frame to be on the cusp of a shock result against the player who had already won four ranking events this season. However, Ding made a break of 52 to win the frame, compiled a 136 to draw level and won the deciding frame in one visit to defeat Advani. Advani's successful season saw him finish inside the top 64 in the world rankings for the first time as he was placed 56th.

In 2014 / 2015 season, Advani didn't enter any tournaments until September 2014, when he announced that he was relinquishing his snooker tour card in order to concentrate on his billiards career and spend more time with his family. He received an invite to participate in the wildcard round of the 2015 Indian Open, but lost 4–3 to Rhys Clark.

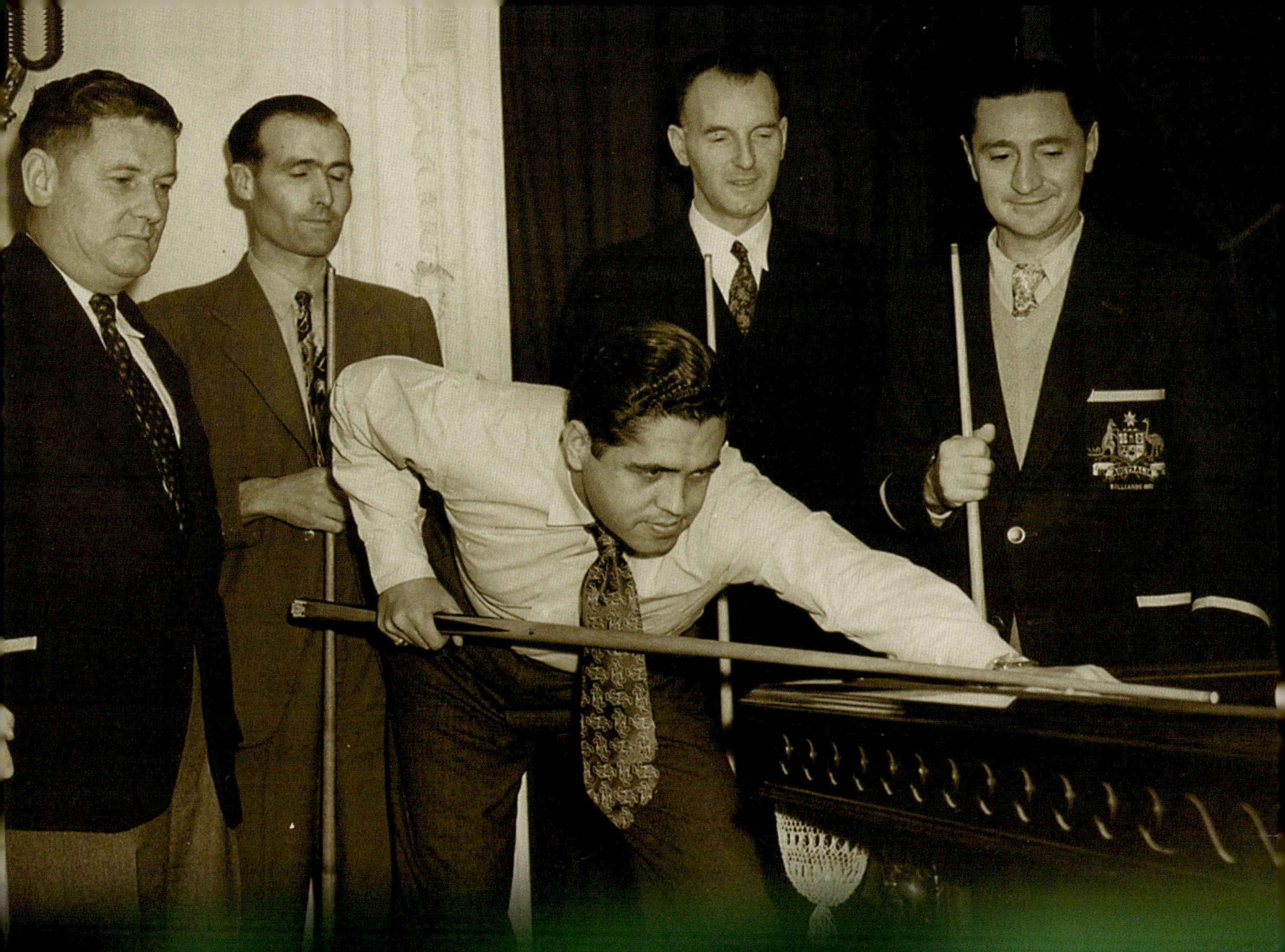

Time & Tide in the Life of WILSON JONES

It is early September and torrential rains are still splashing Mumbai. I made my way to Worli Sea- face to approach "Sportsfield', the abode of former World Billiards Champion Wilson Jones. Sports luminaries like Ajit Wadekar and Sunil Gavaskar, adorned the sprawling nine-storey building near the sea, where only sports men reside. Tucked away in a corner on the third floor lives the Billiard's Icon.

Going to sports field is not new for me. In fact, it is a pilgrimage. My visit to Wilson Jones was always a must in my itinerary. But this visit was different. I knew that I will not be having my customary cup of tea with my favourite sportsman; liberally sprinkled Billiards folk tales. My heart was heavy as I darted from the monsoon fury, my camera and a draft of Rs. 51000/- given to the maestro by Managing Director, Mr. Ravindra Kumar Gupta. I rang the bell and Mrs. Peggy Jones opened the door, who gave me a forlorn look. She had difficulty in recognizing me at first glance. I don't blame her, as visitors wanted to have a look at the ailing Wilson Jones are constantly harassing her. After exchanging pleasantries, I made my way to the patriarch of Billiards fraternity in this country.

The man was fast asleep. He has been giving a well-deserved rest to his legs tired

of playing Billiards over the years. "He is sleeping a lot these days", chipped in Mrs. Jones. I looked at the face of the old man, who was primarily responsible for changing face of Billiards in this country. I stood near him a little longer than necessary praying that he will open his eyes. Few seconds looked like eternity as he seems to be dreaming about the relentless struggle he had put on to attain the supremacy in his youth. When Michael and Fay Ferreira went to pay their respect to him, he could not recognize and started looking into oblivion. The Fay in her inimitable style said "Wilson do you remember the mustard and ham sandwitch we had in a New Zealand Pub". He started grinning. That was that. I stood in silence beside him for fraction of second, clicked a picture or two and quietly walked.

" There is no visible improvement in his health. He is like a child in my arms", said Mrs. Jones with her eyes being moist. She further went on to say," He is having his normal quota of food without any fuss and rancor, like he used to do all his life. Yesterday he could not wink at his favourite granddaughter, and instead looked at the turbulent sea waves across his room". I started looking at the various memorabilia strewn in his living room. I looked with nostalgia about his accomplishment.

There was no sign of taxi outside sports field. I crossed the road and started walking on pavement near the sea. The rain had stopped. The lovers came out in droves. They were embraced in stoic silence. The hawkers started yelling. The children were gleefully trying to protect themselves from rising time and tide. I stood up and started looking at the flat of the great man. With utmost reluctance. I whispered a 'Good-bye' to the man who shaped the destiny of Billiards in his country.

YASHBIR SHARMA

A Tribute to Wilson Jones

by Michael Ferreira

from One Great Man to Another

With the passing away of Wilson Jones, a golden era in Indian sports comes to an end. These words might seem presumptuous in so far as they apparently intrude into an area outside the limits of billiards, the game that gave Wilson his reputation. But when you consider how he put India on the map in a game which was the white man's exclusive preserve, the manner in which he instilled pride in Indian sportspersons and the inspiration he provide to a whole generation of players who went on to become world beaters at a time when money did not drive the mare, his contribution cannot be viewed only from the narrow prism of the three ball game. His deeds furthered the cause of Indian sports as a whole to an extent that was remarkable.

Wilson finally achieved his dream at the 1964 World Championship held in quaintly-named Pukekohe, a little market town just 30 miles from Auckland, when he finished unbeaten in a star-studded field. My finishing third on debut so pleased him that it set him down a path that was unfortunate, from the Indian stand point the thought of retiring.

Billiards to an incurable romantic like me is the well-spring of life. It is art, science, coordination of mind and body, grace, character and discipline all rolled into a wonderfully textured amalgam. For as long as we were subjects of the British Crown, trying to master its subtle skills to match the English or Australians was, by all accounts, an impossible dream. I daresay that this colonial hangup extended to other sports as well. We did have entrants to the World Billiards Championships right from the 1930s, but I suspect those were merely to make up the numbers.

The grim determination and burning desire of a certain Wilson Lionel Garteon-Jones from Pune changed all that. Fascinated by the game from his early teens when he secretly watched his uncle and Indian hockey player Ossie Massey from the window of the local saloon, the youngster was finally let into the room on attaining the age of 18. He took to the game like a duck to water and was soon better than anyone else in the region. His winning the Evening News of India Snooker Championship in Mumbai, a particularly noteworthy feat for someone from the boondocks without any previous exposure to speak of, caught the eye of R K Vissanji, a business magnate who was keen about the game.

'Vadabhai', as Vissanji was affectionately known, promptly offered the gentle six-footer a job in Mumbai. The rest, as they say, is history.

His road to the top was long and hard, and was characterized by a relentless drive for perfection. I maintain that all great persons in any walk of life have an amazing resistance to fatigue. Wilson once told me that he never missed a practice session for 20 years, and that included Saturdays, Sundays and Holidays. I thoughts I had pretty satisfactory work ethic, but his statement flabbergasted me. His contemporary Chandra Hirjee, with whom he had many a battle royal, was arguably the more gifted, but was streets behind Wilson in application, determination and dedication. These qualities really spelt the difference between Wilson and the rest of the pack. His finest moment was undoubtedly his pivotal match against defending champions Leslie Driffield in the 1958 world championship in the Great Eastern Hotel, Calcutta. Trailing by over 600 points in the final session against one of the fierest competitors in the world, Wilson had the crowd in raptures as he went for broke, flashing his cue at everything. When the final ball shrilled he was ahead by a mere 136 points, the greatest Houdini act ever seen in the game at that time. I feel a pang of infinite regret, which I am sure is shared by all Indians, that there was no TV record the moment when India's first world champion was crowned.

But Wilson knew that to cement his place in history, it was necessary to win the title again and away from home turf. He failed in his title defense in Edinburgh in 1960 and again in Perth in 1962 when he raised quite a few eyebrows by comfortably beating hot favorite Bob Marshall in his own backyard in the league phase. However, the nuggety little Aussie stormed back in the knockout to set up an India vs. Australia final. It was cut and thrust for most of the eight hour match, till one fiery session saw Marshall streak to his third world title with a record session average of 128.4.

Wilson finally achieved his dream at the 1964 World Championship held in quaintly-named Pukekohe, a little market town just 30 miles from Auckland, when he finished unbeaten in a star-studded field. My finishing third on debut so pleased him that it set him down a path that was unfortunate, from the Indian stand point the thought of retiring. He had been toying with the idea for some time, much to the consternation of his admirers, but now decided that it was the right time to hang up his cue. "The game in India is in good hands" he was kind enough to say, a compliment that I shall always cherish. He finally returned in 1967 after winning the last of his 17 national titles at the comparatively young age of 45. I maintain that he was good enough to cap another world title or two, but alas, it was not to be.

Obviously history will have its own perspective on Wilson Jones the player. On Wilson Jones the man, I can supply fond personal footnotes. He was one of the most chivalrous competitors I have ever played against. He was always concerned about my well-being as was shared special relationship over since I had timidly asked him for his autograph as 15 year old. "Sit down Michael" he once softly advised me in between the strokes of a massive break against me. He saw that in my youthful inexperience I was unnecessarily consuming nervous energy by fretting about being kept off the table.

His courtesy and thoughtfulness were a byword. He never failed to write to my mother in that lovely copperplate handwriting of his whenever I did well and always sent a prompt 'thank you' note when she congratulated him on his performances. Forced to drop out of school because of circumstances, he nevertheless acquired polish that was quite astonishing. Wilson could speak extempore in virtually any subject, a quality that had even his mother-in-law in constant state of wonder. The secret of course is that he spoke straight from the heart with no hint of artifice of posturing. And simplicity, attributes that, as much as his play, won him a legion of fans. He was my boyhood hero and my greatest inspiration. It is now time to bid him farewell. When my time comes, if history judges me even half as kindly, I will consider my life to have been well spent.

MICHAEL FERREIRA

GEET SETHI

Makes History in Maiden Appearance

Geet Sethi is the World amateur billiard champion. At last, Bob Marshall looked his age when Geet was triumphantly piling breaks after breaks. Geet made a stunning 293 in his 50th visit, made in 14.08 minutes which probably incommoded him. The crowd saw Marshall abbing away and missing some sitter red pots. Consistency, concentration and tenacity were the hallmark of Geet's success. The nation salute the new world title holder who won 3809-2453.

At the end of first session, Marshall's fate was virtually scaled when Geet coasted to an unassailable lead. The giant score board in Durbar hall of Taj Palace road read 2930-1763 with 46 in hand, in Geet's favour. He continued the good work when the overnight tally off 235 reached 345. On this score Geet played an attempted cannon of the white but he saw the red slightly dithering away.

The cheer had hardly died down when he came with an another run of 293 points. A unique feature of this break was that Geet was able to pin the object ball in position for top table play. Such was his mastery that the white refused to move. The white ball was in trance and lying there in deep slumber. The break ended when Geet tried a none-too-difficult red in-off in the top pocket. Twice the marker made a mistake by calling his score less than he actually made. Marshall, relaxing in his chair said," That is the way I can win. "The crowd was seen in raptures.

Geet made a follow through cannon then rolled the red in top pocket and found to his horror that the ball got stuck in pocket No 4. Marshall had a white in-off on a platter but missed it and the sign of nerves became more pronounced. Geet made runs of 348, 293 and 115 in the first session, while Marshall failed to register even a

lone three figure mark. His highest in that was only 93 on his 50th visit. He made that break immediately after Geet had compiled a 293.

On resumption in the final session both the players were seen missing some easy shots. They could not make even a hundred. Geet Sethi broke the hoodoo after he amassed 132 on the 74th visit.

He had further two double century runs of 232 and 257 in the fag-end of the last session. Marshall exhibited some brilliant cushion and two cushion cannons.

When Geet was on 257, Marshall twice waved the white handkerchief to signal his survival in a jovial manner. He scored only one break of 147 on his 86th visit.

Geet put aside all conjectures whether the four times champion Bob Marshall who won the titles in 1936, 1951 and 1962 would set an all time record or the reigning champion from India Michael Ferreira, would emulate the Aussie titan's feat. Geet thus proved the main thorn in the aspirations of Bob Marshall, Michael Ferreira and Subhash Agarwal.

When I asked Brian Bennet, the chairman of the International Federation of Billiard and Snooker, about Geet Sethi, he said. "His all-round play is not so good but when it comes to top of the table he is quite deadly. He is by far the most magnificent player I have seen in that area."

On Bob Marshall, he said:" That is most fantastic achievement playing in an international tournament of this nature at the age of 75. Nobody including Bob had any idea about what was in store for him in Delhi. We thought he'll able to keep the ball upto three or four places. He is a fantastic player."

When Bob Marshall retire from the game, Geet was still in hi cradle. Geet had won the national title in 1981 and 1985. Geet won the world title in his maiden appearance. This is the sixth time that the Arthur Walker Trophy has come to India. Wilson Jones won it 1958 and 1964 and Michael did it in 1977, 1981 and 1983. The trophy is now in the safe hands of Geet Sethi.

After the final, the players demonstrated some trick shots. When Bob displayed a kiss cannon in the centre pocket. There was a ripple a laughter from the crowd.

President Zail Singh gave away the prizes at a glittering ceremony.

Professional	Turned Professional in the year 1989
Highest Sports Qualification	9 times World Billiards Champion (Five Pro-Billiards, Three Amateur Billiards & One Team Snooker) First Amateur in world & only Indian to have 147 Maximum in Snooker
Highest Break	Billiards - 1276 Snooker - 147
Record	**Billiards:** Created a world record of 1276 points break in the 1992 World Professional Billiards Championship, and holded for 15 years i.e. upto 5th October, 2007, when Peter Gilchrist of Singapore broke by making 1346. Geet also holds an unofficial break of 1617 in 70 minutes (while practicing). **Snooker:** The First amateur in World & only Indian to have 147 maximum in Snooker Championship. He recorded this break on 21st February,1988. **These records are also entered in Guinness Book of World Records too.**

Tournament Records

2010
IBSF World Billiards Championship (Time Format) - Bronze Medalist

2010
IBSF World Billiards Championship (Point Format) - Bronze Medalist

2009
76th Indian National Billiards Championship - Runner-Up

2009
G.Raman Nair Annual Billiards Championship 2009 - Winner

2008
5th PYC-ATC Snooker Challenge (Team Event) - Runner Up (Team: Strachan Champs)

2008
75th Indian National Billiards Championship - Runner-Up

2008
IBSF World Snooker (Masters) Championship: Wels (Austria) - Runner-up

2008
IBSF World Billiards Championship (Point Format): Bangalore (India) - Runner-Up

2008
World Pro Billiards Championship :: Leeds (UK) - Runner-up

2008
English Billiards Open Series @ Prestatyn - Winner

2007
Indoor Asian Games English Billiards - Silver Medal

2007
Kharagpur South Institute Invitational Billiards Championship - Winner

2007
Kharagpur South Institute Invitational Snooker Championship - Winner

2007
MIG Club All India Invitational Snooker Championship - Runner up

2007
Irish Open Billiards Champion

2007
73rd Indian National Billiards Champion

2006
Doha Asian Games (Billiards Doubles) - Bronze Medal (with Ashok Shandilya)

2006
USA Sr. Team Snooker Championship - Winner (along with Devendra Joshi & BVS Moorthy)

2006
World Professional Billiards Champion

2005
IBSF World Billiards Championship - Runner up

2003
IBSF World Billiards Championship - Runner up

2002
Asian Games Billiards Singles Bronze Medalist

2002
Asian Games Billiards Doubles Silver Medalist

2002
IBSF World Billiards Championship - Runner up

2001
IBSF World Billiards Champion

1998
World Professional Billiards Champion

1998
Asian Games Billiards Doubles Gold Medalist (with Ashok Shandilya)

1997
Indian National Billiards Champion

1996
World Professional Billiards - Runner up

1995
World Professional Billiards Champion

1993
World Professional Billiards Champion

1992
World Professional Billiards Champion

1988
Indian National Billiards Champion

1988
Indian National Snooker Champion

1987
IBSF World Billiards Champion

1987
Indian National Billiards Champion

1987
Indian National Snooker Champion

1986
Asian Billiards Champion

1986
Indian National Billiards Champion

1986
Indian National Snooker Champion

1985
Indian National Billiards Champion

1985
Indian National Snooker Champion

1985
IBSF World Billiards Champion

1984
International Points Snooker Champion 1984

1982
Indian National Billiards Champion

The two Aussies

Walter Lindrum and Don Bradman were contemporaries in 1930s. Bradman, who is known as the greatest cricketer, showed inclination towards tennis, billiards and cricket. In the end, there was toss up between tennis

and cricket. Tennis was loser as Bradman went on to score phenomenal runs in cricket in general and for Australia in Particular. But Walter Lindrum had no such diversions. For him billiards was be all and end of all life.

Walter Lindrum and Don Bradman were contemporaries in 1930s. Bradman, who is known as the greatest cricketer, showed inclination towards tennis, billiards and cricket. In the end, there was toss up between tennis and cricket. Tennis was loser as Bradman went on to score phenomenal runs in cricket in general and for Australia in Particular. But Walter Lindrum had no such diversions. For him billiards was be all and end of all life.

Don Bradman never received any public coaching and used his backyard to hone his skills. He would throw a golf ball at one of the walls and on rebound used to play with a wicket. He never used to hit on the mid-off since there lay a pond. Perhaps this was the only flaw in this stroke filled batsman.

Stories on Don Bradman can fill volumes but I am going to write only a few. In a country match when he was plumb leg before, the bowler vociferously appealed for LBW, but was promptly negated by the umpire. After the over, the sullen bowler enquired from the umpire "why you gave him not out". The umpire told him tersely, "You stupid fool, the public has comes to see Don Bradman bat and not to see your heroics with the ball!"

During his 1948 tour in England, Bradman was confronted with an unusual problem. He used to receive a staggering mail of around 600 letters per day. A letter showing Bradman paid a tribute to English postal authorities.

In a country match, a young bowler was bowling to Bradman and score read like this, 4, 6, 4, 6, 4, 6. Bradman scored thirty runs in that over. The captain come across and patted the bowler and said "well bowled". The bowler aghast on hearing the sarcastic comment of his captain, who further said, "You kept Bradman guessing whether to hit four or a six!"

Like Bradman, who slammed centuries galore, Lindrum too went on to amass unbelievable and mammoth breaks for his country. Once his pregnant wife was knocked down by a moving bus and was in a precarious condition in hospital. At that time, Lindrum was in the midst of a game and was leading by over 3000 points. Soon after getting the news of his wife's accident, his lead started dwindling. After the day's play, he went to see his hospitalized wife. She asked him to amass a break of 2000 for her sake. Lindrum, so spurred, went on to play the next day and compiled a break of 2002 on the trot. However, the match was abandoned on account of his wife's tragic demise. At that time, Lindrum was leading 21431-19308 against Clark McConachy of Newzealand.

In those days, Billiards matches were played for almost a week and nursery cannons were in vogue resulting in such mind boggling scores. This stupendous break according to Lindrum was one of the finest which he made in his career. It was made under sheer and emotional turmoil and traumatic pressure. When his wife departed he concentrated more on billiards which was now his only love. He started playing with amazing zeal and mission.

In 1932 he made the clock almost stop when he compiled a runaway break 1000 in 39 minutes. The break terminated at 1, 116 which took 43 minutes.

Another instance of Lindrum's perfection in billiards can easily be summarized in the following story. He gave an exhibition in Billiards against King George VI at Buckingham Palace. He regaled and mesmerized the crowd by his crafty play and won accolades from the King. The King went to greet him and said, "How is the table behaving". Lindrum paused for a while and said, "It is a unique table but there is some defect just near the center pocket". The King was aghast as most of the billiards accessories came from England and to cap it all it was the Royal Table. The table fitter was summoned and was asked to rip off the cloth, which revealed the presence of a small piece of human hair between the cloth and the slate! Whenever he played a center pocket in – off, the object ball used to drift a bit. Who can say that in sports perfection is not granted to mortal !

Both the Aussies were class apart in their respective fields. Perhaps we might never see the likes of Bradman and Lindrum in our life time.

YASHBIR SHARMA

TIME WAS ON FERREIRA'S SIDE

Michael Ferreira is the World Amateur Billiard champion! Nursing a torn pectoral muscle he arrived in New Delhi with not so high hopes. However, the wounded tiger ran amuck with an incredible performance in the Mohan Meakin world amateur Billiard championship at Hotel Maurya Sheraton .

The epic Ferreira-Dagley clash will linger in the memory of those fortunate ones watching one of the greatest finals in the annals of the history of this green baize game. Forty minutes to go and it was anybody's game. At this stage the supreme billiards title could have gone either to England or India.

coming. It should be his endeavour to see that it remains here when the battle resumes at Malta in 1983.

On the eve of the final match, Dagley was indisposed causing considerable concern in the English camp. I went to his suite around mid-night at Lodhi Hotel to enquire about his health. His fore-head was burning but Dagley was cool, calm and unruffled. His optimism was truly remarkable when he said, I'll be there to play, and I'll play my might. Such trifling matters do not bother me at all!"

The next morning Dagley left his illness in his bed and played cracking good billiards. His lead crossed the 500 mark and I started wondering who was indisposed. It looked as if Ferreira was having Dagley fever! At last Ferreira woke up from his trance to start his magnificent fight-back, converting the deficit to a lead of nearly 1,000 points.

A simple red loser terminated Dagley's break of 296 to give the Indian ace a new lease of life. He erupted like a volcano from a seemingly barren position to display an amazing purple patch of strokes to come out with a life-saving break of 244 in 19.41 minutes.

Michael Ferreira was only 20 minutes and 300 points away from the world crown when Dagley started his last desperate attempt, a race against time. He crossed the hundred mark but the clock was running in favour of Ferreira.

The England champion lost his cool on 182 and well over a thousand spectators gave a standing ovation to the world champion Michael Ferreira. Dagley's last visit on the table produced 9 points in as many seconds leaving Ferreira 96 in front.

By lifting the world crown, Ferreira has emulated the feat of his famous predecessor, winning the coveted title twice-the first time was in 1977, at Melbourne. He must have been immensely pleased with this home-

After the finals, Ferreira said, "the break of 244 was the turning point in my favour, made just at the right moment. I am going to cherish this break for the rest of my life. It should also silence those critics who talk about my so- called suspect temperament."

As Wilson Jones often used to say, "the best player in the world is someone with Mike's brilliant play and the nerves of Norman."

However, Jones was never in doubt about the eventual outcome of this championship. He told me in Bombay almost a month before the tournament that Mike was going to be the next world champion. He further added, Only Norman is capable of stretching Mike and Subhash can tickle him!

As a mark of respect to 13 out of the 14 participants, I decided not to disclose this statement, during the tournament.

Subhash Agarwal started his campaign in a whirwind fashion, only to fizzle out in the end against the might of Ferreira and Dagley. In his opening match against S.W. Boteju, Agarwal chalked out a break of 218 in only 9.55 minutes, the first hundred coming in a shade over four minutes. It is a phenomenal rate of scoring under the present three- pot rule.

The very next day he was in devastating mood registering two world records-1,596 in two-hour session and an aggregate of 3,010 in a match. The man who was subject to this Emro, our distinguished guest from Egypt.

Before the start of this championship I had a very interesting interview with E.A.A. Amro.

WR: What is your highest break?

Emro: Ninety (90).

WR: In Snooker?

Emro: No. In billiards, my highest break is ninety!

WR: How come you are here to play in a world championship?

Emro: Because very few people play billiards in my country. That is how I am here !

Emro's highest break in the championship turned out to only 51!

Subhash Agarwal magical form vanished against Dagley and Ferreira. Before the championship, Ferreira was all praise for Aggarwal and said.

"Subhash is a dangerous billiard player, capable of trouncing the mightiest on his day. His greatest asset is that he is a hungry man. He is the player to watch.

George Ganim from Australia, Jeo Grech (Malta), Stan Brooke (co-chairman, international Federation of Billiards) and chairman Brian Bennet all came out with one common statement: "Subhash will be world champion one day."

The world crown does not grow on trees. Agarwal has to sweat it out before starting the Journey for Malta.

The surprise packet of this tournament was Latif Amir Bux from Pakistan. In his first match against Michael Ferreira, he failed to produce his best form but gave enough indication of the shape of things to come. He convincingly defeated Joe Grech and third seed Bob on his way to the last-four stage. In all, he made a sensational debut in the world championship. With this feel of international experience, he should be a force to reckon with in future.

Joe Grech of Malta sparkled only in the end but had the satisfaction of scoring, the first 400-break of the championship. A smiling Grech said, "I showed Michael and Dagley how to make a break of 400!"

Ferreira got the message and three days later made breaks of 527, 532 and 630 against Subhash Agarwal. The last was a world record under the three-pot rule.

Joe Grech collected money for his well wishers in Malta as his association refused to finance the trip.

After the tournament most billiard lovers kept wondering why Norman Dagley had not accelerated in the final stages against Ferreira. He maintained his now famous relaxed speed when he was supposed to run for his life.

When I enquired the reason from Dagely, his answer was short and crisp: "I never look at the clock at score. To me, billiards is a game and I play accordingly. I do not change my pace even at the cost of losing my place in the sun!"

Not that Dagely is all that casual. For instance, on November 20, the players and delegates went to see the Taj Mahal at Agra. Only Dagley and Ferreira decided to stay back in the semi-finals. The other two semi-finalists Bob and Agarwal dashed to Agra, undertaking a journey of over 500 kilometers.

Both these 'Agraites' lost in their semi-final matches. When I asked Dagley why he was not going to see the Taj, he coolly replied, "I have come to play billiards".

For the Delhi Billiard Snooker Association the opportunity to organize this premier world event was a dream come true. It all started in 1978 at Calcutta, in a meeting of the Billiards and Snooker Federation of India at the Bengal Rowing Club.

India was allotted the 1981 World Championship but there were no takers from several States. I was representing the D.B.S.A. at that meeting and raised my hand to express my willingness to organize this event. The Association at that time was only two-years old. Despite this, the D.B.S.A. come out of the cradle to organize one of the finest billiard shows in the country.

YASHBIR SHARMA

Michael Ferreira

A Versatile Genius

Wilson Jones took the country to the Himalayan heights by being the first Indian to win an individual World Billiards Title in the year 1958. He repeated the feat in the year 1964. Wilson retired even as he had enough gas in the tank. The question was, who's next? Michael Ferreira answered the call in no uncertain manner by emulating his role- model who was no other than Wilson Jones.

Wilson Jones took the country to the Himalayan heights by being the first Indian to win an individual World Billiard Title in the year 1958. He repeated the feat in the year 1964. Wilson retired even as he had enough gas in the tank. The question was, who's next? Michael Ferreira answered the call in no uncertain manner by emulating his role- model who was no other than Wilson Jones.

Wilson Jones and Michael Ferreira have come to Banglore many numbers of times and have demonstrated their skills time after time. Wilson, in the most unambiguous terms proclaimed Michael to be his successor and true enough the later succeeded his guru in sheer hardwork, Michael enjoyed collecting a few tips from the maestro and made full use of them. With gracious consent of his beloved wife, Fay, he took another wife in the shape of Billiards. Wedded, as he was to the game and drawing inspiration from Fay, he went about the business with zeal and fervour bordering on the obsession. He went one step further than Jones in winning the World Title thrice in the year 1977, 1981, and 1983. This by itself constitutes a record of high credentials.

Michael firmly believed in the saying, "he who aimeth at the stars shoot much higher than he that means a tree". With an insatiable thirst to reach new milestones, Michael kept punching at records, as only record books would speak. His achievements are briefly set out hereunder:

- Four times World champion- three amateur titles and one World Open. Seven times National Champion. World record holder who is mentioned in the Guinness Book of World Records.
- Recipient of the Arjuna and Shiv Chatrapati awards. Also honored with the Padma Bhushan by the Government for outstanding services to the nation.
- Sportsman of the Year in 1970, 1977 and 1983. Gentleman of the year 1984.
- Awarded the International Fair Play Award by the International Olympic Committee in 1983.

Like any other champion, he has retired from first-class Billiards, while still in a good shape. The Billiard-fever has not deserted him and he has kept his closeness to the game in other capacities. He is today, the Senior Coach recognized by the BSFI. He is a wonderful after-dinner speaker; his pen moves and fills pages with language, sublime to the extreme; a competent compeer, and an astute critic bringing into full play his Billiards-background and expertise. He

Throw a lucky man into the sea and he will comes out with a fish in his mouth. The English proverb fits Michael Ferreira like a shot with a slight difference that luck plays a very little role in his life. He keeps luck in his hip pocket for rainy days. He has come up to this level by sheer dint of labour. As a lawyer, player, administrator, speaker, Television commentator, Journalist and coach, his credentials are immaculate. I distinctly remember M.L. Kotru, the then editor of statesman told me in the early ninetees that Michael Ferreira's commentary on Snooker is a startling revelation. He does every thing to perfection. He has a gift of the gab.

I remember with gratitude the role played by Michael Ferreira in the year 2001, enabling me and my Managing Director to witness the World Professional Championship at Crucible Theatre. Hotels and tickets for the event were chock-a-block full way back in advance. Michael adviced me to board the flight to London "we will squeeze in. Come along". He and Geet Sethi very graciously managed a room in the hotel but the crowning glory came when Michael was braving the rains to give us complimentary passes. This is a touch of humility in an otherwise stern looking man. He is wonderful human being. Shades of Wilson Jones. But many people are not aware of this characteristic in him. He is true Libra to the hilt.

EDITOR

World Records

- 1149 break (five-pot rule) and 962 unfinished (tow-pot rule) duly acknowledged in the Guinness Book of World Records.
- An Unfinished 498 in half an hour game aginst Geet Sethi in 1986.
- Two hour session average : 243.63.
- Four hour match average : 157.95.
- Two breaks over 900 in a four hour match.
- Three breaks over 600 in a four hour match.
- 16 centuries in a four hour match.
- In addition he has five other world records under the three pot rule.

is one person who can hold his own in any company and stands head and shoulders over others. Not all are given to this all-round gift. Yet another portfolio has come his way. He is today the President of M.S.B.A. He fully deserves the signal honour. I have full faith that he will acquit himself creditably in the new chapter going by his track record and his insight into the game and its demands.

I recall his classic words, "At the risk of sounding melodramatic, or even foolish, considering the response, I am likely to get, I hereby place my passion, my skills, my experience, my contact and my knowledge of men and matters unreservedly at the disposal of the country.

Given the mandate, I, For one, would catch him at his words and commend to the country to capture him and accept the challenge. He could perhaps be a fine Ambassador of sports and goodwill at the national level with liberty to go around the globe with a message of goodwill through sports. He has the stuff in him; he is a finished-product; he has the capacity

Haji Jaffar

and surely he will deliver the goods in a glorious manner. Michael is cut for it – a diamond that can shine and radiate the shine wherever he goes. I am sure, I have a sound proposition to offer. Let us hope, the idea click ere-long.

HAJI JAFFAR

The tragedy of being Satish Mohan

Satish Mohan was an enigma and he remained one throughout his life. His life was mountain and valley, full of vicissitude, turmoil and uncertainty. The road which he led was full of pitfall and swindles, at times it was as smooth as the journey of Rolls Royce. In fact he was the Rolls Royce of Indian cue sports.

The winter was about to set in Delhi, when a tall, lanky young man with a cue in his hand descended from the stairs in Delite Billiards room. He looked young with a bronzed face. He quietly sat in a corner patiently waiting for his turn to play. He unfolded his single piece cue when I asked him, "how about a betting game with me?" He refused the bait at once and sat on his seat & said that he does not play for money. I reluctantly decided to play seeing his predicament. I opened the frame and his eyes lit up when he saw red hanging in the pocket. He was at his nimblest and most lusty with panther like gait. He polished the table plucking balls like picking up pebbles. The atmosphere reached a wild crescendo when he sunk the last black. There was deafening roar from the enthusiasts who had gathered in large numbers as the news spread that a magician is at large. I was as good as spectator as the rest, and muttered, "I could have done the same thing to you had I got a chance." My answer was feeble and voice was choked in surprise. As Ajit Singh, the owner of Delite Billiard Room was arranging for refreshment for him, he was gone in a breeze. Ajit Singh asked in bewilderment- who was he? Satish Mohan –I mumbled while flickering the pages of Indian Express where his photograph had appeared.

He rattled and mesmerised everyone by winning the national Billiard Title with gusto, several years in a row. The most aggrieved person was Michael Ferreira, who had taken the cue from Wilson Jones after his retirement. His play in snooker was also very effective. When on song he used to get accolades and awe from the crowd.

In 1973 Billiards and Snooker Federation of India had organized amateur World Billiard Championship in Bombay, where world's top cueist assembled in the Badminton Hall of CCI. According to the connoisseur of the game, Satish Mohan was expected to lift the World Cup, which included a galaxy of players like Michael Ferreira, Mohd. Lafir and Phil Tarrant. As expected Satish Mohan won the first five games with consummate artistry. I distinctively remember that it was Saturday evening when I was sipping whisky in Bar Room of CCI, when a husky voice came from behind "A double large for me". I was taken aback and looked back to found Satish Mohan standing there with a frown on his face. He gulped his drink within few seconds and asked for a refill. He had couple of more lethal dose of whisky. When I tried to intervene, I was quietly brushed aside.

The next day he had his vital match with Mohd. Lafir, who was also in great form. Lafir chalked out a mammoth break of 859. Satish Mohan after his tirade with drinks was not at his best and succumbed in the match. That was the beginning of a frightful end.

In an another match Aussie star Phil Tarrant was leading by almost 400 points against Satish Mohan with barely half an hour to go. He looked at his watch and started playing with break neck speed. The Badminton Hall of CCI was packed like sardines and gave standing ovation to the maestro. He finished his break to forge ahead of Phil Tarrant and signaled for a glass of water. The inimitable Wilson Jones personally handed over the glass of water to him. The crowd again burst out in applause and the noise once again reverberated with joy.

In 1978 he went to Australia to participate in the World Championship where he once again started hitting the bottle. He was hospitalized and deported to India.

I was staying at YMCA for the Calcutta Nationals, when there was a constant hammering on the door in the morning. I opened the door with misty eyes and found a lanky man with beard but with unmistakable stamp of Satish Mohan. Before I could say anything he said, "I have given up whisky and come to Saturday Club for celebrations!" When I arrived, I was given a toast of Vodka with orange juice! When I enquired about the goof up he replied nonchalantly – I have given up whisky. That was Satish Mohan for you.

In Saturday Club when Michael Ferreira was writing history by making an astonishing break at 1149, he tumbled upon the wooden stairs and fell down. I rushed him to the hospital where he was discharged after first aid.

Several years later he fell from the bus and died on the spot. It was simply a case of dissonance of tempers and conquest.

The tribute is being penned by M. Chenniappan the Chairman of the famous Nilgiri Dairyfarm, former President of K.S.B.A. and a friend, Philosopher and Guide to

T.A. SELVARAJ

the Old Willy Fox

T.A. Selvaraj with other contestants in an International meet

Among the unsung heroes in Billiards, T.A. Selvaraj tops the rung. Selvaraj, a man of exceptional talent, was one of the finest players the country has ever produced.

K.B Parikh with T.A. Selvaraj

HIS RECORD NATIONAL CHAMPIONSHIP TITLE

	Winner	Runner-Up
SNOOKER:	1946	
	1949	
		1950
	1951	
	1955	
BILLIARDS:	1949	
		1950
		1951

Note: He won the 1949 the Snooker Crown without conceding even a single frame – a record of sorts.

In one of the Nationals, he reeled off six frames in a row after trailing by five fames.

Selvaraj hailed from a relatively poor family with limited means. He earned his bread by working as a driver in a European Company. But it did not hamper his love for the Billiards a wee bit. He used to go to beck's Billiard Saloon on Brigade Road, at Sharp 1 p.m., and resume his duty at 2.30 p.m. on the trot, only to come back at 6.30 p.m. to restart his flirtation with his first love. He excelled mainly in Billiards but he was equally adept in Snooker. He also excelled in skittles, which is a very interesting game but is totally disapproved these days. It was considered to be an honour among players to play with him. Drinking and then his work. But he was very punctual in his work. He was held in a high degree of respect by his employers.

There was one Ball & Bush Bar and Billiards on Brigade Road where I learnt playing. It was a daily ritual for me to go there and play. But the main purpose was to see the great man in action. I became very friendly with him.

In the early forties, just a few rupees were required to travel from Bangalore to Madras. There were a number of good players participating in the South India Billiards and Snooker Tournament and prominent among them were Jimmy James and Leslie Wilson from Bangalore, C.J. Coel from Madras and V.R. Frier from Madurai. Friends use to take care of Selvaraj when he was there. He made a habit of winning the tournament in Madras.

When he conquered all the peaks in the vicinity, it was suggested to him to cross over to Calcutta for playing in the All India Billiards & Snooker Championship. He expressed his inability to go there as it involved a lot of expense. The trip was estimated to cost Rs. 200/- which was a huge amount in those days, but for sheer love of the game and to back the exponent of the game, I decided to donate the estimated sum. He went to Calcutta and returned to Bangalore alongwith the 1946 Snooker title. I continued to help him financially and he, in return, never disappointed me as he always obtained excellent results. Later on my friend Mr. B.C. Ananthasayanam joined me in my crusade to help Selvaraj. He was mainly instrumental in encouraging me to start a Billiards and Snooker Tournament in our own State in 1944. The success prompted us to conduct many exhibition matches in which outstanding foreign players participated to give Selvaraj a run for money. Later we formed our own association which got affiliated to All India Billiards Association.

Selvaraj was 'Tiger' on the table and a 'Saint' off it. A true sportsman with strict principles. The success and glory did not move into his head. After retirement from Hindustan Aeronautics Ltd. and from the game, he continued to coach youngsters. He was given a purse of Rs. 48000/- after his retirement from the game he loved so much. He died in almost the same circumstances as another champion Satish Mohan, who fell down from the moving bus in Ahemdabad on September 12, 1981. As usual, Selvaraj was pedaling on his cycle towards the Association at Miller Tank Road. He was nearer to his destination but alas he could not reach there and fell down from his cycle and breathed his last. Karnataka State was robbed of the services of a great sportsman. However, the Tiger of Karnataka was finally laid to rest with the office bearers of the association acting a pallbearers, paying their regards to a great sportsman.

YASHBIR SHARMA

Down the Memory Lane

By M.S. Haji Jaffer

A famous address in Bangalore, 4, Museum Road, which belongs to Haji Zaffar is really a museum ! Antiques consisting of chandeliers, rare crockery and Victorian furniture are filled up to the brim of his drawing room. I was treated to Darjeeling tea brewed to perfection in a porcelain cup with imported biscuits to boot.

His passion is racing. He was the judge of Mysore Race Club. His drawing room is littered with rare photographs of horses in all hue and cries. Haji Zaffar, an advocate by profession, powerful orator and lover of the green baize game, built arduously the edifice of Karnataka Snookers and Billiards Association. He loves South Indian cuisine and is always ready to motor down to Mavalli Tiffin Restaurant known as M.T.R., at the slightest pretext.

The author went in a nostalgic mood to recount the B.A.C.C.I. meeting in Kolkata. It is replete with billiards history.

- Editor

Not till 1958 did I visit Calcutta. That year took me there for a meeting of the Billiards & Control Council of India. The venue was the Great Eastern Hotel.

The minutes of the previous meeting confirmed, the matter taken up for consideration was how far the rotation of the National Championships to the different affiliated States in the country feasible ?

My Association was firmly of the opinion that a rotation of the National Games was the need of the hour which found favour with Wilson Jones representing Bombay, lending stout support; A.N. Sinha from Bihar joined us in our campaign. At this point of time, was it enough to tilt the balance on our side with Bengal having the majority of votes? I had carried with me a newspaper cutting concerning the statement of Jaipal Singh, M.P. recommending that the Nehru Trophy at Delhi should move to other parts of the Sub-continent. On pure logic; this had a point on our side. I also had a press statement of the late Leslie F. Wilson in his famous "Straight from the Shoulder" column proclaiming a case for us. This apart, I made a fervent appeal to the members present, about fifteen in all, to rally around us and concede rotation.

Before presenting the point at the meeting, I made a courtesy call to the late M.M. Begg, the President of the B.A.C.C.I who, I was told, was ailing. That was the first time I met Mr. Begg. I, at once, was impressed by his personality and the force of his voice. It did not take time for me to know and understand his interest and passion for the game in which he was a champion in his days. At his residence, I met his personal physician, who opined that his health was not conducive to his attending the meeting on the 20th of January, 1958. With a twinkle in his eye, which I still remember, he dodged the physician's opinion and assured me that he would be there notwithstanding the advice. And true enough, he was there at the meeting.

I could read the care and concern in his eyes about the moot point which engaged the attention of the members present. As I said earlier, I had solid support from Wilson Jones and A.N. Sinha. That was not enough to deliver the goods. Deliberations were on when the Physician arrived at the meeting with a clear message that he should excuse himself from the meeting in the interest of his health. There also arrived his wife and daughter to persuade him to leave the meeting and go home. The late M.M. Begg was made of a very firm stuff and he brushed aside all the suggestions to go home observing that a very important point was on the anvil and that nothing could pull him out till the matter was resolved.

A full-dressed debate ensued and finally it was suggested that the resolution even if passed had to go to the General Body for a confirmation. At this stage I read out the pertinent point that in the rules there was nothing to suggest that only Calcutta be the centre. My submission inter-alia was that it was an accident of geography that Calcutta conducted the Nationals but the rules did not prohibit the Championship moving to other Centres. At this point, Mr. M.M. Begg in a firm voice commended that it was time for the members to grant rotation if only it was on a trial basis. This observation clinched the issue and a resolution granting rotation was passed with a proviso that Calcutta would conduct the games every alternate year. Mr. Begg warned the States that they had to take sufficient care and protection lest Calcutta could take over again. You could see in the Chairman, the Champion, the giant, a deep sense of statesmanship as only he could reveal. The meeting was over, he requested his wife and daughter to leave for home promising to reach them ere-long. Mr. Begg instead of leaving for his home requested A.N. Sinha, Wilson Jones and myself to join him on dinner at Maxims. There at dinner also, he spoke of nothing but billiards and cautioned us to handle the new assignment with care. There was the elder statesman talking to his juniors who had – nothing but love and affection for his total involvement in the game.

Yet another person that caught my imagination was the late B.K. Roy, father of P.N. Roy, my erst-while colleague. B.K. Roy was a Director of the Great Eastern Hotel, the first 5 – Star Hotel in the country. B.K. Roy in his large munificence placed the Billiard Room at the disposal of the King of Indoor Games year after year seeking no monetary return but a promise for promotion and popularity of the game. As my friend Yashbir Sharma in the magazine Cue Sports put it "Every triumph in the country had the stamp of B.K. Roy". There was in very fact of B.K. Roy, a majestic love of the game so difficult to get these days.

The day after the meeting, T.A. Selvaraj, 'the Tiger' and I were leaving Calcutta in the train bound for Bangalore. As we were set to board the train, who comes to bid good-bye was B.K. Roy, his hands were full, one carrying a box of cakes and the other of patties, quantitatively enough and more for our entire journey. One final word from the stalwart which is ringing in my ears" you have won the day but not to lose the benefits". The golden words can be written in letters of gold. Here again was yet another tall person who cannot be forgotten by billiard-loving fraternity. Such were the Stalwarts.

BOB MARSHALL

A Great Billiards Player

Three Generations of World Champions in Billiards

Bob Marshall (playing), Michael Ferreira & Geet Sethi.

Robert James Percival Marshall, OAM, (born in Kalgoorlie on 10 April 1910; died in Perth on 23 February 2004) was a notable Australian amateur player of English billiards, who won the World Amateur Billiards Championship in 1936, 1938, 1951 and 1962 and was runner-up three times, as well as a national snooker champion.

Marshall was born in the same town as another legend of the game, Walter Lindrum. Throughout his career he was compared favourably with Lindrum who, in 1954, himself declared that Marshall was one of the greatest amateur players he had ever seen. Ten years later, the contemporary English snooker professional Fred Davis said of Marshall, "Most noticeable about his style is his compactness, so like Walter Lindrum, and the shortness of his back-swing, hardly more than a couple of inches."

Marshall dominated amateur billiards before and after the war with a career that spanned six decades, broken by retirements in 1963 and 1970 followed by come-backs.

Marshall's first job was as a hairdresser, and he later opened a successful dry-cleaning outlet. He became the World Amateur Champion for the first time in 1936, and took the title again in 1938. During World War II, he spent four years in the Royal Australian Air Force. In 1951 he again won the World Amateur Championship, and in 1952 was runner-up. In 1953 while playing his regular rival Tom Cleary in the final of the Australian Championship he compiled a break of 702; the then-highest ever made by an amateur in a championship match. This record remained unbeaten until 1984 when Subhash Agrawal compiled a 716 break. He took another World 2nd place in 1954.

In 1962 Marshall was invited to India to compete in the national billiards and snooker titles. He won both.

He entered politics in 1965 when he won the seat of Maylands in the state election for the Liberal party. In 1969 he made a comeback for a series of exhibition matches against New Zealand professional Clark McConachy and regained his Australian title the same year, defending it successfully in 1970 before retiring once again.

In 1985 he won the Australian title at the age of 76. This success encouraged him to travel to New Delhi, India for an attempt at his fifth world title where he won all matches except the final which was taken by rising Indian champion Geet Sethi. The following year he won the Australian title again, his 21st, and retired shortly afterwards, 50 years after his first Australian title win.

His best break was 1,056 which he made in practice in 49 minutes. In the 1953 Australian championships he made a break of 702 in 37 minutes. He twice recorded seven breaks of 100 or more in a two-hour session and in the 1938 World Championship final in Melbourne, made a break of 335 in just over 15 minutes. He used top-of-the-table techniques for his break-building, and all of his records were made under the "two-pot rule". Other records by Marshall which still stand under the two-pot limitation include: the highest aggregate in two hours play (1,876), four hours (3,391), and a two-hour session average of 118.7.

SNOOKER

As a snooker player, he contested four Australian amateur finals, and was Australian National Champion in 1956. His best break was 139.

AWARDS AND HONORS

In 1963 he was named Western Australian Sportsman of the Year, and in 1980 was awarded the Order of Australia (OAM). He was inducted into the Western Australian Hall of Champions in 1985.

Since his death at the age of 93, the memorial Bob Marshall Medal is awarded each year by the Australian Billiards & Snooker Council. His biography My Life and Times was written with Cyril Ayris and Ross Haig.

Like FATHER... Like SON...

Syed Habib was born on 25th December, 1941 on a Billiards table. His mother Saeeda Habib started getting labour pains around mid-night. Madras at that time was flooded due to torrential rains and there was no hospital in the vicinity. His father used to dabble in Billiards table and its accessories. The tables were strewn all over the place and Saeeda Habib was placed on the slates, writhing in pain. Thus Syed Habib came into this world and his infatuation towards Cue Sports was inevitable. He had a feel of the table seconds after he was born.

He was the most perfect genial giant and was embodiment of sportsman spirit. He helped many a budding cueists generously gifting the Billiards accessories and giving genuine advice.

He was perennially India's No. 2 three times consecutively in early eighties and once losing in the decider. His long potting was so tremendous and electric. At times his opponent relaxed after guiding his Cue ball behind the baulk line. All of a sudden his tranquility use to get disturbed as Syed Habib used to invariably pot the ball with a thud. That was enough to upset his opponents rhythm. And the rest was usually history.

He crossed India's shores to represent his country in Canada, Singapore, Kuala lumpur and Karachi.

He personally taught the rudiments of the game to his son Rafat Habib, particularly to wriggle at of dicey situations.

Rafat Habib partnered Yasin Merchant by winning the elusive team Gold medal at Busan 2002, Asian Games.

He passed his legacy to his son as the rightfull heir. His was mighly pleased when his son got the title at 9 ball pool championship in Kolkata.

A unique record was established in year 1992 when Syed Habib became India No. 4 and his son attained the No. 5 spot.

In the quarter finals he lost to the legendary Ronnie O'Sullivan. He was beaten fair and square but not disgraced. He had the distinction of hitting the Snooker maximum twice in practice and 135 in match play. He lost in the semi-finals in RKG Snooker South Zone Championship recently at Chennai leg.

A boy walked in Billiards room of YMCA Calcutta to watch the proceedings from a corner. He was an avid table tennis player and was equally proficient in his studies. He had no idea that he was about to hook to the lure of Billiards leaving his passion for table tennis in the lurch. He learnt the basics from the markers and compiled his first century break after few months. He had no idea that this event will change the destiny of his life. That break spurred him to play greater role in Billiards of his State where there is always a Bengal famine of sportsmen.

He continued his successful run till one day he got a wild card entry in world Amateur Billiards Championship as India was hosting the event in Banglore. He was mightly pleased and thrilled, at the same time in awe to be in such august company.

He started his campaign in carefree and whirlwind manners while climbing the ladder of success and glory. He started the final against compatriot Ashok Shandilya in rather dismal note trailing in three out of four sessions. He pulled up all his energy at his command to make grand recovery against gusty Ashok Shandilya. He lifted the Arthur Walker Trophy in the midst of tumultuous applause by the knowledgeable crowd of Banglore.

Back home he was given a rousing welcome by the press, public, officials and friends. He became an overnight celebrity. His son Sourav was a little child but was mesmerised at the adulation and accolades his illustrious father got. He promised to himself to emulate his father one day. Manoj did not rest on his laurels and went on to claim the doubles Billiards Title in Wigan, U.K. in 1995 pairing with Ian Williamson of England.

He got into training mode having completing his course for six months under legendary Steve Davis. Recently he got the Khel Guru award by Ms. Mamata Banerjee. He was a first class mechanical engineer and revolutionized the scientific method of coaching youngsters.

His son Sourav started playing at the same venue YMCA in the year 1997.

He started in right earnest under the disciplined, stern and watchful eyes of his father. He always tells him the capacity to smile and laugh even in adversity. He further told him that if you lose a game leaves that on the table and starts afresh. Sourav takes the advice of his coach and father to the hilt. You will notice that Sourav, has dazzling smile and a pleasing personality. You can rarely find him in a pensive mood.

The year 2014 was a fabulous year for him having won his first national Billiards title and maiden Asian Billiards Championship. He went on to win the silver medal in World Championship in Glasgow and a bronze medal in World Billiard Championship in Leeds. He is equally adept in snooker but has failed to win any major titles. It is a happy augury that he is beginning to blossom.

His mother and sister were also state level players. Together they make a colourful portrait in the field of Billiards and Snooker. Today he is trying to replicate his father and the reputation Manoj has so assiduously built.

Sheel Chandra was an ardent Bridge and Billiards player. He was one of the richest man and had a palatial house in Lutyens Delhi. After his earlier forays in Billiards he struck to Bridge. Tarun Chandra learnt the rudiments of Billiards from Sheel Chandra and struck a purple patch very early in his career.

Sheel Chandra was an ardent Bridge and Billiards player. He was one of the richest man and had a palatial house in Lutyens Delhi. After his earlier forays in Billiards he struck to Bridge. Tarun Chandra learnt the rudiments of Billiards from Sheel Chandra and struck a purple patch very early in his career.

Ram Kishan Dalmia's son Bunny Dalmia used to study in Delhi's prestigious Modern School. He along with Tarun made life miserable for members of Chelmsford Club by switching from dependents and members table at will. They made rapid progress in cue sports by hitting century breaks in front of a captivating audience.

Tarun played for his state and won the state title in Billiards cracking a run of 143

against Subhash Sood. It was considered a big break considering Delhi was in infancy. But it was in snooker where he made his mark at Calcutta national in 1979, when he completely tarnished the reputation of redoubtable O.B. Agarwal, crushing him with 4-0 verdict. (But he soon went into oblivion due to his business commitments. He wanted to instill everything whatever he lacked in his career).

Film star Feroz Khan was camping in Delhi's Taj Man Singh scouting for film distributor for his film Qurbani. There were no takers! It was a mighty surprise as it becomes a super duper hit, subsequently. Feroz Khan during his sojourn in Delhi came to Chelmsford Club and met Tarun and Bunny. There was one thing common between them - snooker. Together they played hundreds of games of high quality snooker. The place was cramped in those days as people flocked to see the dapper and terribly handsome film star from Bollywood. The marker David had a torrid time in keeping pace with the rampaging snooker stars. After the days play was over Feroz used to tip him liberally for his efforts. The result was predictable in favour of Delhi duo. As their friendship grew, Feroz invited them to stay and play in his sprawling form house in Bangalore. According to Tarun, Feroz was very kind hearted, wonderful sportsman and a perfect gentleman. We need such benevolent and generous people to come forward for the cause of cue sports.

Manan Chandra was hailed as a child prodigy and started hitting the lime light very early in his life. His initial job apparently was to pot the balls right from the word go. He cared to hoots for safety play and percentage snooker. It was in ample evidence in 1999 Delhi national where he threw safety to winds and won both the tiles inspite of his impatience, flamboyancy and impetuosity.

I distinctively remember during 1997 Calcutta senior national, Tarun who was sitting in the stands with me used to direct in a voice which was louder than whisper whenever his son used to commit folly and faltered in the finals.

After his, meteoric rise Manan storm abetted a bit. He had developed a slight problem in his eye sight which was corrected by wearing contact lens. He found solace and comfort in pool as the table was shorter to claim an amazing seven national titles and represented his country abroad. He is by far the most prolific player in 8 and 9 ball pools. Now pool tournaments have since dried and he is least interested in pursuing Billiards. By the process of elimination only Snooker remains.

Though he won his Junior title in 1997 but had to wait for 9 years to graduate to the senior title in 2006 beating Pankaj Advani. He again won it in 2013 having got better of Brijesh Damani. His break building came to the fore when he amassed a break of 146, which prompted him to play in U.K. professional championships where he played with fair degree of success. He won the six red, championship at Karachi in 2008.

He married woman snooker star Anuja from Mumbai to make it a truly snooker family. This is the unique story of Kal, Aaj Aur Kal! We eagerly wait for further extension of this family in cue sport.

They also made us Proud in the realms of Cue Sports

(BILLIARDS)

Chandra Hirjee Jewraj

Chandra Hirjee was a flamboyant and vastly gifted player who ruled the imagination of his admirers on and off the table. He paid, heavy price of being contemporary to Wilson Jones, who ruled Billiards for more than a decade. In the year 1946-47 he was the undisputed king of Billiards but his tenure became shaky when Jones in a magnificent spurt made him play second fiddle to him. He regained his composure when he started cat and mouse game winning in 1956, losing 1957 and again regained the title in 1958. Though his forte was Billiards but was dangerous player in Snooker as well, bring runners-up to Wilson Jones and Mohd Lafir on more than one occasion. In all he national title four times and perennially runners-up in Snooker. He was always clad in traditional dress of dhoti and kurta, when asked to wear shirt pant and tie, was an anathema to him. He spurned the offer instead Michael Ferreira crossed the Indian shores. Bengal always kept their sporting hero wrapped in cotton wool. He was proud to be one who refuses to don the western culture.

Subhash Agarwal

Subhash Agarwal who learnt fundamentals and rudiments of game from Wilson Jones, missed the world title by whisker on a couple of occasions. In the year 1978 when Michael Ferreira was creating history with a mammoth break off 1149, Subhash was waiting in the wings of full 70 minutes for his turn. He replied with a double hundred in this own inimitable style. He was least daunted, which was a big psychological battle in the initial forays of his career.

He decimated all his rivals with amazing dexterity but fumbled at the crunch moment. According to this writer he was the fastest player of Billiards and his top table play was a revelation. In the end turned out to be a simple case of so near yet so far.

Tony Monteiro

He was under study to great Shyam Shroff, who won a staggering 7 national titles. Tony Monteiro always had an insurmountable odds to overcome Wilson Jones, Arvind Savur and Shyam shroff. He managed to come out unscathed twice to win the National Snooker titles. He represented his country several times in the World Championship unsuccessfully. He could never get his due which he so richly deserved. He was perhaps one of those players who were born to blush unseen.

Alok Kumar

The seasoned Right Handed Cueist was born on 05th october'1968 in mandi Govind Garh in Punjab. His highest Sports Qualification is IBSF World Billiards # 2 – 2013, IBSF World Snooker # 3 – 2006 Asian Snooker Champion - 2004

Asian Billiards Champion – 2011 Asian Games Pool Bronze – 2010.

His highest break in Billiards is 398 & in Snooker 142. He won 2014 Asian Billiards Championship - Silver Medalist, - 2013 World Billiards Championship (Timed Format) - Bronze Medalist, 2013 Asian Team Snooker Championship - Gold Medalist, - 2013 Asian Billiards Championship - Silver Medalist, - 2011 Asian Billiards Championship – Winner, - 2011 Asian Billiards Championship – Winner

Anuja Thakur

Anuja Thakur is an Indian amateur player of Snooker and English Billiards.

She won the WLBSA Ladies World Billiards Championship title in April 2005, and reached the semi-final at the 2006 IBSF World Snooker Championship in Amman, Jordan, where she was eliminated by Jaique Ip 4–2.

Thakur is a native of Mumbai, Maharashtra. She has won several state and national championships in both Snooker and Billiards. Her sister, Meenal Thakur, is also a player in both disciplines. Anuja is married to Manan Chandra, another Indian amateur Billiards player.

Rupesh Shah

Born in 1974, Rupesh in his younger days, Rupesh Shah admired the way cue sports legend Geet Sethi asserted his domination at the world level. His remarkable consistency appealed Shah and he dreamt of emulating Sethi's exploits. Inspired by his astonishing nine world titles, Shah, who learned the tricks of the trade under Sethi's able guidance in Ahmedabad made his master proud by being nominated for the prestigious Arjuna Award.

The veteran bagged his second World Championship crown by registering a comprehensive 6-2 victory over Australia's Matthew Bolton. Earlier, in the tournament held in Leeds, he defeated defending champion Mike Russell and Peter Gilchrist. "I was nervous before the announcement but at the same time confident of getting the prestigious award this time as I had won

the World Championship title again and I felt that I deserved to win the award," said Shah.

Fondly known as "Rupla" in the circuit, he backed up his World Championship crown with the Asian Billiards title win 6-4 over compatriot Alok Kumar in Indore earlier in the same year. "I have worked really hard on my game in the last five years and been focused right throughout. It feels really great when all the hard work you put in rebound with successful results."

Brijesh Damani

Brijesh Damani born on (22 November 1982) at Kolkata, West Bengal is India's professional Snooker player. He won the 2008 Indian National Snooker Championship. He also won silver medal in 2010 Asian Games in China.

The BSFI has nominated his name for Arjuna Awards for his contribution to the Cue Sports in 2014.

Devendra Joshi

He shot into prominence when he reached Billiards national finals as early as 1991. He had to wait for seven years to claim national title, but this time in Snooker. He registered an empathetic win 2001 in National Billiards title. He was shuttling

between Billiards and Snooker which was perhaps proved to be his undoing. His biggest triumph came into 2003 Asian Billiards Championship to arrive on the world scene. In 2007 he won 8 ball pool championships to claim the tag of a perfect all-rounder.

Revanna Umadevi Nagaraj

She was born on 11th February 1965 in Karnataka, is an Indian professional player of Billiards. She is a World Women's Billiard champion in2012 and a three time Indian national Billiards champion. She had defeated World No 13 Eva Palmius in during the London 2012 Championship to become the World Champion.

SNOOKER

Section - 2

THE ORIGIN OF SNOOKER

The game of snooker is a cue sport which emerged in its modern form in the late 19th century, with roots going back to the 16th century form of English Billiards. Billiards was popular among the British Armed Forces stationed in India. As billiards was only a two player game, new games such as life pool and pyramid pool were developed in order to accommodate more players. Eventually, these two games were combined to form snooker.

Did John Roberts (left) meet with Chamberlain in 1885, or was it perhaps Fred Shorter (right)

HISTORY OF THE GAME

THE BEGINNING

In the 19th century, the Billiards became quite popular among the British Armed Forces stationed in India. Billiards was a two-man game in its original form, which was played with 3 balls, of which two were cue balls, one for each player. This led to the formation of multi-player versions. New versions included life pool and pyramid pool. Life pool involved several coloured balls used as both cue balls and object balls. In pyramid pool, there were 15 red balls and a white cue ball, and each player received one point per red ball potted. Along with the new games being developed, the table was taking steps toward its current state.

Black pool was the next version created. Black pool was similar to pyramid pool, except that the black ball from life pool was added to the game and could be potted for more points. In 1875, at the officers' mess in Jabalpur in the Central Provinces, Colonel Sir Neville Francis Fitzgerald Chamberlain suggested adding the other coloured balls to the new version. The game was beginning to resemble snooker in its current form, though the blue and brown balls were added in later years.

The name snooker comes from a comment Chamberlain made about a player who missed a shot. He called him "a real snooker", referring to his lack of experience, "snooker" being a slang term for a first year cadet. The first official set of rules for snooker were drafted in 1882 at Ootacamund in Madras Province. When British Billiards Champion John Roberts travelled to India in 1885, he met Chamberlain and decided to introduce snooker to England when he returned home.

THE EARLY YEARS

The first official competition, the English Amateur Championships, took place in 1916. In 1927, Joe Davis helped to establish the first Professional World Championship of snooker. Joe Davis won and took home the prize of £6.10. At that time, the standard of play was not very high considering that the highest break of that tournament was just 60. By the 1930s, Snooker was becoming one of the most popular cue sports.

Joe Davis continued to dominate the era, winning every World Championship until his retirement in 1946. Between 1952 and 1957, a dispute had arisen among the games' governing body, the Control Council, and the Billiards Association. As a result, only two people participated in the official World Championship, although an unofficial one was organized. At the time, the winner of the unofficial tournament was generally

A typical military mess in the 1870's

The clubhouse at Ootacamund

considered the best player in the world. During this time frame Horace Lindrum won the official World Championship. Due to a decline in popularity, there were no world championships between 1958 and 1963.

RISE IN POPULARITY

In 1969, the BBC launched the Pot Black tournament at the BBC Studios in Birmingham, which proved to be very successful in helping put snooker back into public view. The BBC began broadcasting in colour and were looking for programmes that could exploit this new technology. The programme first aired on 23 July 1969, on BBC2. Pot Black was a British series of (non-ranking) snooker tournaments televised by BBC which played a large part in the popularisation of the modern game. In 1972, a twenty-three year old Alex 'Hurricane' Higgins clinched the first of his

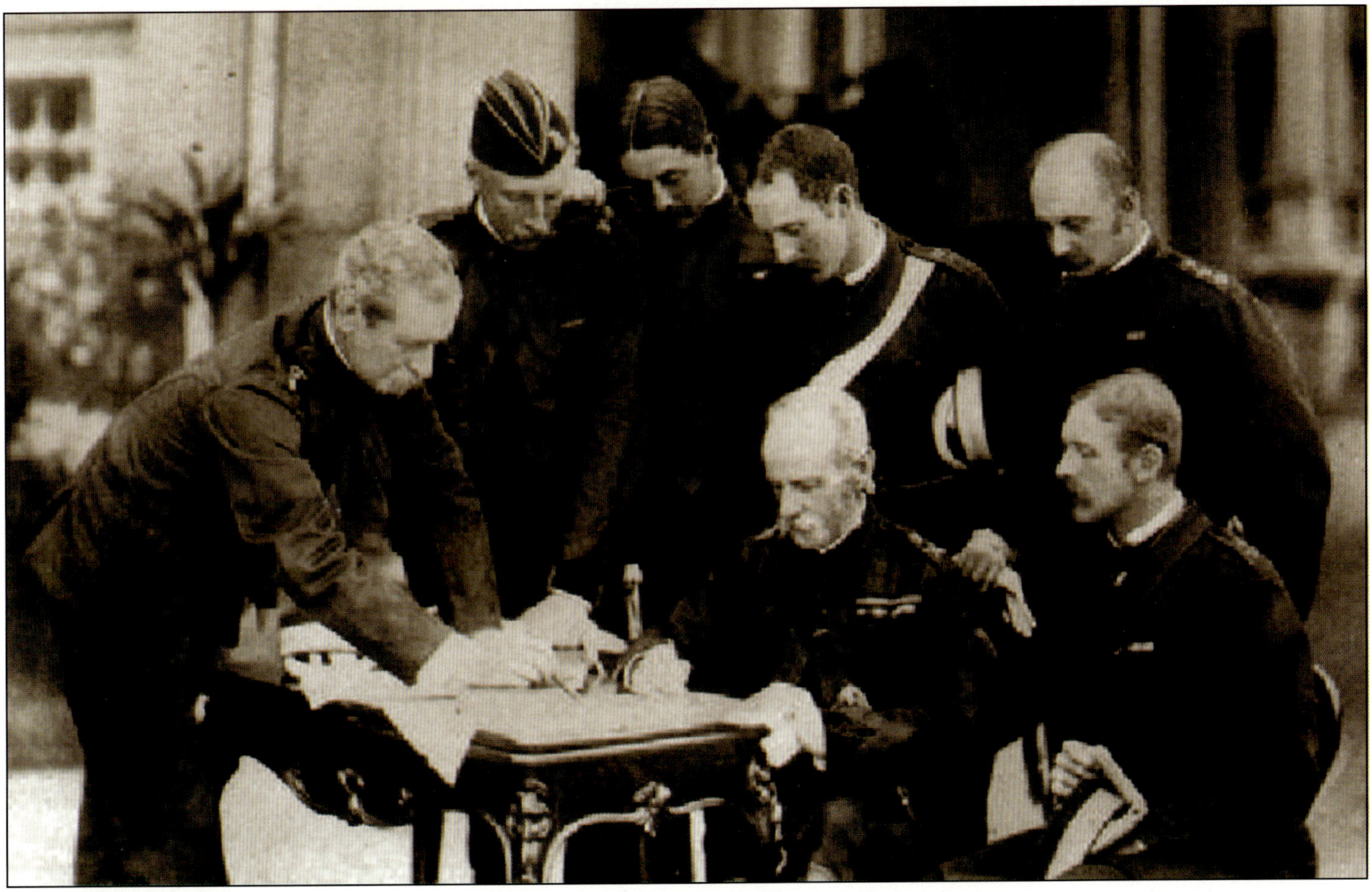

Lord Roberts & Staff at Ooty in 1883: L-R (Standing) Col. Stewart; Maj-Gen Godfrey Clark Adjutant-General; Lt. Neville Chamberlain ADC; Cat. Ian Hamilton ADC; Col. du Caine RA. (Seated) Sir Fred Roberts; Lt.-Col. George Pretyman, Millitary Secretary.

Mark William

two World Titles and through a mixture of bravado, charisma and an ability to make headlines helped to popularise the sport in the new age of colour television. The event continued until 1986, returned in 1990, but was discontinued after the 1993 event.

Pot Black was revived in the form of several one-off tournaments throughout the 1990s and up to 2007. Pot Black helped transform snooker from a minority sport with just a handful of professionals into one of the most popular sports in the United Kingdom. Mark Williams holds the events' highest break record of 119. The World Championship was first televised in 1973. World Rankings were introduced in 1976, and, in 1977, the World Championship was held in the Crucible Theatre in Sheffield, where it has been ever since. Daily television coverage of the World Championship began in 1978.

The 1980s capitalised on the sport's already growing popularity.

Steve Davis dominated for much of the decade thanks to a smooth technique, all-round game, dedication, and the PR savvy of his ambitious manager Barry Hearn.

Maverick left-hander Jimmy White came along as a people's champion very much in the mould of his good friend and idol Alex Higgins.

The number of tournaments on the calendar was to increase further as from the 1984/1985 snooker season ITV started to televise three new ranking events, the International, Classic and British Open.

In the 1985 World Snooker Championship Final, heavy favourite and 8-0 early leader Steve Davis lost after a comeback by the Northern Ireland player Dennis Taylor. The 35th and deciding frame lasted for 68 minutes, Taylor sinking the final black at 12.20 a.m with a UK record audience of 18.5 million TV viewers watching. Though the record viewing figure was never topped, the 1986 World Snooker Championship Final between Steve Davis and Bradford underdog Joe Johnson, in which Johnson surprisingly won 18-12, also drew a strong audience figure of 16 million. In the build-up to the 1986 World Championship, the novelty anthem "Snooker Loopy", recorded by Chas and Dave featuring the Matchroom Mob (Barry Hearn,Steve Davis, Dennis Taylor, Willie Thorne, Terry Griffiths and Tony Meo), hit number 6 in the UK Singles chart.

Steve Davis

The domestic success of snooker continued to remain strong into the late 1980s. During this time, with the help of Barry Hearn, tournaments were starting to expand globally into Europe, Asia and North America. The 1988 Canadian Masters was the first ranking event to be staged outside the UK.

In December 1988, the invitational Matchplay (featuring the worlds top 12 players) was the first ever professional tournament to have a £100,000 winner's prize. In the late 1980s, Steve Davis' dominance was starting to be challenged by future World Champion Stephen Hendry.

By the end of the decade, there were more than 200 playing professionals on the circuit, a figure which increased to more than 400 professionals during the 1990s.

STANDARDS RISE, POPULARITY SLIDES

A new generation of players came to the fore in the 1990s, most notably Stephen Hendry who went on to dominate for much of the decade. Hendry eclipsed many of Steve Davis' records including most World Championships, most ranking titles and most (BBC) major titles. Hendry's type of attacking, breakbuilding game which often clinched frames in one visit ushered in a new era of player. In 1993, at the age of 17, Ronnie O'Sullivan became the youngest ever winner of a ranking event by beating Hendry himself at the 1993 UK Snooker Championship Final.

Though the standard of snooker continued to rapidly increase, the immense popularity that Snooker enjoyed started to wane. ITV stopped screening ranking events after the 1993 British Open and during this period, much attributed to the economic recession, prize money totals started to stagnate or decrease for events outside the World Championship. Snooker also suffered from the recovery of football's reputation after the 1990 World Cup and especially after the foundation of the Premier League in 1992.

From the mid-1990s onwards, Snooker still enjoyed decent exposure thanks to BBC continuing to televise the major events and the continuation of tobacco sponsorship. Due to the increasing restrictions or eventual ban on tobacco advertising in sport, Benson and Hedges last sponsored the invitational Masters in 2003 and Embassy's long-standing association with the World Championship concluded after the 2005 tournament.

With cutbacks necessary (due to loss of tobacco funding) and less events, the main tour roster was reduced to 96 professionals for the start of the 2005/2006 season.

Afterwards, the number of events on the circuit started to dwindle. However, since the loss of tobacco sponsorship, the online gaming and gambling industry has stepped in to sponsor numerous events on the calendar. The WPBSA chairman Sir Rodney Walker was ousted in a vote of no confidence in December 2009, which cleared the path for the longtime sports promoter Barry Hearn to attempt to revitalise the sport.

An Introduction of SNOOKER

RULES OF THE GAME

It derives from billiards and other similar games, and is played on a full-sized billiards table with six pockets. The 22 balls comprise 15 reds, six colours and the white cue ball. The reds are placed on the table in a triangular frame so that the base of the frame is parallel with and nearest to the top cushion and the apex is as near to the pink ball as possible without touching it. The black ball goes on the billiards spot (red spot in billiards), pink on the pyramid spot, blue on the centre spot, brown on the middle spot on the baulk line, green on the left-hand corner of the D, and yellow on the right-hand corner.

The white cue ball is used alternately by both players and can be placed anywhere in the D for the opening stroke of the game; from that point onwards it is played from where it comes to rest. A game is known as a frame after the frame used to position the red balls. Points are scored in two distinct ways: by potting balls into the table's six pockets, and by penalties. Each player must initially strike a red ball. When a player succeeds in potting a red (value one point) he must then play at a colour. Colours have the following values: black, 7; pink, 6; blue, 5; brown, 4; green, 3; yellow, 2. If the nominated colour is potted it is replaced on its own spot before another red is attempted, and so on, alternating reds and colours until all the reds have been potted. The colours are then taken in ascending numerical value—yellow first, black last, until only the cue ball is on the table. The compilation of a sequence of pots is called a break. A player forfeits his place at the table only when he has failed to pot a ball or has committed a foul in doing so. Failure to strike a red when that is the object ball has a penalty of four points (the minimum for any foul stroke) but the penalty points incurred increase to five, six, or seven if, instead of a red, the cue ball makes initial contact with blue, pink, or black. An "in-off" carries a four-point penalty, or more if the ball which the cue ball initially struck before falling into a pocket is of a higher value. Following an in-off, the other player (the recipient of the penalty points) may place the cue ball

anywhere in the D. Failure to hit a nominated colour also has a four-point penalty, or more if the ball involved is of higher value. Thus, if pink is nominated but black is struck the penalty is 7, the maximum.

The majority of points are obtained by potting; some from the penalties mentioned. Penalties often result from carefully laid snookers. A snooker occurs when the balls are so placed that a player cannot strike the ball he is due to play without first hitting a cushion (the cushioned edge of the table) or making the cue ball swerve. Snookers often occur through skilful safety shots.

Other fouls are: a push shot (simultaneous contact between cue tip, cue ball, and object ball); forcing a ball off the table; playing a shot with both feet off the floor; striking or touching a ball other than with the tip of the cue; causing the cue ball to jump over any other ball; playing with the balls wrongly spotted.

A vital rule concerns the free ball (which may often be decisive in a frame. If a player is snookered on the reds after a foul shot by his opponent he may nominate any coloured ball as a red. This is known as a free ball. If it is potted it counts one and a colour can then be nominated in the usual way. If no red remains, a free ball is valued at the same number of points as the lowest value colour remaining and the colours are then taken in sequence.

If a player makes a foul stroke which leaves his opponent in an awkward position the opponent is entitled to ask that he play again. This rule, like the free ball rule, is intended to prevent a player from gaining any advantage from a foul stroke.

In 1885, John Roberts, the greatest billiards player of his era and a notable entrepreneur, met Chamberlain in Bangalore, India, and brought the game back to England. The John Roberts Billiard Supply Company commercialized the game with sales of snooker sets. Professional players disapproved of it, but amateurs took to it and the Amateur English Championship was inaugurated in 1916. The Billiards Association had been formed in 1885 and they recognized snooker's first set of rules in 1900.

The first professional championship was held in 1927 through the initiative of Joe Davis, the best player of his time. Davis won and held the championship until he retired

from world championship play in 1946. His great influence and skill established the game and displayed its possibilities. After Joe Davis, the champions in the late 1940s and 1950s were Fred Davis (Joe's younger brother), Walter Donaldson, John Pulman and an Australian, Horace Lindrum, who was the brother of Walter Lindrum. The World Professional Championship was held until 1952 when the professional players and the governing body, the Billiards Association and Control Club, had a disagreement. This concerned a match between Horace Lindrum and Clark McConachy of New Zealand which was given world championship status. The professionals did not recognize this and seceded to organize their own championship—called the Professional Match-play Championship. This expired in 1957 but was revived in 1964. In 1969 it became a knock-out event—as it is now.

In 1969 John Spencer became world champion (he was champion again in 1971 and 1977). From 1969 the world championship was held annually, and all finals since 1977 have been staged at the Crucible Theatre, Sheffield. In the 1980s the leading player was Steve Davis (world champion six times). The other leading players included Cliff Thorburn, Alex Higgins, Dennis Taylor, Stephen Hendry, and Jimmy White. In the early 1990s the outstanding players were Hendry, White, John Parrott, Steve Davis and, towards the end of the decade and into the new millennium, world titles were won by Ken Doherty, John Higgins, Mark Williams, and Ronnie O'Sullivan.

For women, billiards and snooker have been games of minority interest, but from the 1970s there was growing enthusiasm for snooker. The Women's Billiards Association, later the Billiards and Snooker Association, was founded in 1931. It ran the Women's Amateur Billiards Championship from 1931 and the Women's Amateur Snooker Championship from 1933.

Apart from Britain, the main countries where snooker is played to a good standard are Canada, Australia, New Zealand, India, Pakistan, Sri Lanka, Malta, and Malaysia.

Important tournaments, apart from the World Championships, are the Rothmans Grand Prix (formerly the Professional Players Tournament) begun in 1982, the Mercantile Credit Classic (formerly sponsored by Lada and Wilson's Brewery) and begun in 1980, the United Kingdom (UK) Open, first held in 1977, the British Open, first held in 1980, the European Open (1989), the Asian Open (1989), the Benson and Hedges Masters (1975), the Benson and Hedges Irish Masters (1978), the World Cup (1979), the Scottish Masters (1981), and the World Matchplay Championship (1988).

Amateur World Championships were first held in India in 1963 and became an annual competition from 1984. These are run by the International Billiards and Snooker Federation (IBSF) which became the non-professional game's governing body in 1985. The first World Championship for women was staged in 1976 in conjunction with the men's event. The UK Women's Open Championships were first held in 1986.

Art & Facts of Green Baize History

1870

First recognised World Billiards Championship Played. The final, is between William Cook and John Roberts, Cook wins.

1870

Later in the same year John Roberts Junior restores family pride by defeating Cook for the title.

1870

Joseph Bennett beat Roberts Junior for his first win.

Over the next few years cues begin to appear containing either badges or engravings that refer to these early champions, the Roberts cues appear along with a cue with a cherry splice with a great thick butt and the name Joseph Bennett inscribed on the front face.

1875

Snooker as a separate game, is invented by Sir Neville Chamberlain. The game is derived from several recreational and gambling games including Life Pool, Black Pool and Pyramids. In 52 years Joe Davis will reinvent this after dinner passtime and become world champion. Early references to the game of Snooker are recognisable as they call it Snookers Pool.

1889

Charles Dawson from Huddersfield wins his first World billiards Championship.

1890

W J Peall makes his break of 3,304 constructed largely of potting the red from the spot. The Peall cue is born following the publicity surrounding this break.

1894

John Roberts Junior makes his largest ever break, (spot barred) the break is 1,392.

1899

Charles Dawson makes his largest ever break of 823. Did I mention that he was from Huddersfield?.

FACTS WITH FUN

1. Billiards evolved from a lawn game similar to croquet played sometime during the 15th century in Northern Europe (probably in France).

2. The term "poolroom" now means a place where billiards is played, but in the 19th century a poolroom was a betting parlor for horse racing. Billiard tables were installed so patrons could pass the time between races. The game of billiards and the poolroom became connected in the public's mind. Today, the two terms are used interchangeably.

3. Pool is one of the safest sports in the world.

4. Pro player and trick shot specialist Paul Gerni is nicknamed the "Ambassador" and speaks six languages.

5. The dome on Monticello, Thomas Jefferson's home, conceals a billiard room. In Jefferson's day, billiards was illegal in Virginia.

6. The term "scratch", as applied to a pocketing of the cue ball, was derived from the penalty assessed for such a foul. In pool's early days, the score was often kept on a chalkboard. When a player pocketed the cue ball, his opponent "scratched" a point off the shooter's score.

1901

Joe Davis is born in Chesterfield.

1901

H W Stevenson wins his first world Billiards Championship defeating Charles Dawson who did not feel too well in this year.

1901

Edward Diggle makes his highest personal break of 791.

1901

Cox and Yemen put out a cue with the name of H W Stevenson on the badge, this cue is available in an original two piece version.

1906

Inman makes his 300 off the red break and inspires the facsimile Inman cue.

1907

William Cook makes the largest ever official record break at Billiards, 42,746 mainly using the rocker or Anchor cannon. The Cook facsimile cue is born and carries representation of this break on the badge.

1907

Tom Reece makes his mammoth break of 499,135 using the Anchor stroke, this break is denied official recognition as neither press nor public are present throughout. Oddly there must have been both a referee and a marker but this seems not to have been enough to sanctify the achievement? However the Reece cue is created that does indeed recognise and immortalise this huge break that lead to the outlawing of this kind of scoring method.

1909

Melbourne Inman wins his first World Billiards Championship after the previous year having been declared champion due to political and contractual wranglings.

1911

George Gray visits the United Kingdom and signs a contract with E. J. Riley Ltd. While here he makes a top break of 2,196 this break is made up of in off's into the centre pocket. This break is remembered on the George Gray facsimile cue made by Riley and carries the break figure also. George Gray also writes an instruction book in this year.

1912

H W Stevenson makes a break of 1,016,

7. There are 15 colored balls in billiards, 7 "solid", 7 "striped" and the black 8-ball.

8. According to research conducted a few years back, billiards champions have the highest average age of any sport, 35.6 years.

9. Tom Cruise did his own trick billiard shots for the 1986 film, The Color of Money, except for one in which he had to jump two balls to sink another. Director Martin Scorsese said he wanted to let Cruise learn the shot, but it would have taken two extra days of practice, which would have held up production and cost thousands of dollars. The shot was instead performed by professional billiards player Mike Sigel.

10. Billiards was the first sport to have a world championship (1873).

11. Throughout history, billiards has bridged the gap between the aristocracy and the masses. Both gentlemen and street toughs played.

12. In 1586, the castle of Mary, Queen of Scots, was invaded and captured. The Invaders made a note of forbidding her the use of her billiard table. They then killed her, and used the covering of the table to cover her body.

this break is made up of all round scoring methods. A cue exists that commemorates this break.

1916

Tom Reece makes an all round break of 901, this break is referred to on later Reece cues by Burroughes and Watts along with the 499,135 break that he made in 1907.

1920

Willie Smith wins his first World Championship title, Billiards of course.

1921

Tom Newman wins his first World Championship title, unfortunately Willie Smith pulled out for reasons of his own so these two great players and the public were denied a clash between them.

1921

Tom Newman makes a break of 1,274, Burroughes and Watts are quick to put out a cue which commemorates this achievement.

1924

Billiards How to Play & Win - Melbourne Inman makes a break of 950. He also writes his little instruction book, Billiards How to Play & Win in this year.

1924

Tom Newman makes the largest ever break with Ivory Billiard Balls, the feat is recorded on many of the Newman champion and facsimile cues. Mr Newman writes a number of books in this year and must be very busy. Willie Smith also pits pen to paper with match winning Billiards by Mills and Boon.

1925

Ivory balls no longer used in the championship from this year.

13. In 1765 A.D., the first billiard room was built in England. Played there was One-Pocket, which was a table with one pocket and four balls.

14. The first coin-operated billiard table was patented in 1903. The cost of a game on the first pay-for-play table: one penny.

15. Before the invention of celluloid and other new-age plastics, billiard balls were made out of ivory. The elephants can thank their present existence on the invention of plastics. Because billiard balls had to be cut from the dead center of a tusk, the average tusk yielded only 3 to 4 balls.

16. Captain Mingaud, the inventor of the leather cue tip, was imprisoned for political reasons during the French Revolution. With the help of a fellow prisoner, he was able to have a billiard table installed in his cell. It was during his incarceration that be became obsessed with the game, that he devised and perfected his invention. His obsession became so intense, that at the end of his prison term, he actually asked for a longer sentence so that he could complete his study of the game.

17. The world's largest billiard hall was built during billiards' "Golden Age". "The Recreation", a mammoth seven-story

1927

First World Snooker Championship is held, Joe Davis wins and does so for 20 years holding the crown 14 times in all.

1927

Joe Davis makes a break using the pendulum stroke of 2,501 at Billiards of course. This break is made by keeping the balls close to the jaws of a corner pocket and scoring long runs of cannons while controlling the balls with close skill. The break is recorded on many Joe Davis cues by either E J Riley or Peradon Ltd, often the Billiard break is recorded alongside his latest Snooker break.

1927

Willie Smith makes a break of 2,030, which does not include nursery cannons. This break appears on the Willie Smith record cue by Burroughes and Watts and the later cues by Peradon with a front splice M/s and H/S versions appear.

1928

Joe Davis wins his first World Billiards Championship title.

1928

Walter Lindrum makes a break of 3.262 Predictably a cue is released marking this achievement.

1928

Joe Davis makes a break of 2,052.

1928

Tom Newman makes a break of 1,827. As far as I know no cue exists to commemorate this break.

1928

Walter Lindrum makes a break of 4,137. As Walter needed money to return to Australia this break appears on many cues and he publishes his book on Billiards.

health spa, was a bustling Detroit business in the 1920's. It featured 103 tables, 88 bowling lanes, 20 barber chairs, three manicuring stands, 14 cigar stands, a lunch counter on each floor, a restaurant that could seat 300, and an exhibition room with theater seating, that could accommodate 250 spectators.

18. Charles Goodyear – the inventor of vulcanized rubber, which revolutionized billiard cushions and countless other industries – died a virtual pauper. His company failed, he was imprisoned for debt, and he profited little from his breakthrough invention.

19. The Hustler was based on a novel by Walter Tevis. The novel, however, was based on a short story he had earlier submitted to Playboy. Before "The Hustler" was released, the "Philco TV Theater" aired an episode called "Goodbye, Johnny", which bore an uncanny resemblance to the Playboy short story. In it, Cliff Robertson portrayed the cocky young hustler, making Robertson – not Newman – the original "Fast Eddie" Felson.

20. Marquetry – the art of making pictures or designs with thin slices of wood, shell or other materials – has long enhanced the beauty of tables and cues. The art form is hardly a recent development. It has been practiced in Egypt and the Orient for more than 3,000 years.

21. Many handicapped people have played the game of pool, but the story of "Handless George" Sutton is truly one of inspiration. Born in 1870, Sutton lost both hands in a sawmill accident at the tender age of eight. Despite his handicap (and long before the days of advanced prosthetics), he studied medicine and graduated from the University of Milwaukee. During his college years, he took up the game of billiards. He became so proficient, he set an 18.2 Balkline world record with a run of 799, in 1921. He took his playing skills on the road, touring the country and amazing audiences for nearly 35 years. He left an everlasting legacy – the resolve of the human spirit – upon his death, in 1938.

1933

Walter Lindrum wins his first World Billiards Championship title.

1993

Walter Lindrum plays his last match in great Britain and takes the Billiards Championship title home to Australia.

1933

Joe Davis challenges Walter Lindrum for the title, narrowly loses and then takes months to save up the money to come home by touring and giving exhibitions.

1947

Walter Donaldson wins his first World Snooker Championship, this is the first final not to feature Joe Davis as he retired undefeated the previous year.

1947

Fred Davis wins his first World Snooker Championship and gets revenge over the so-called Lone Scot in the final.

1951

Clark McConachy edits the history books by beating John Barrie and takes his rightful place at the top of the professional tree.

1952

Horace Lindrum wins the unofficial World Snooker Championship final against Clark McConachy as all the home grown players decline to enter due to a dispute with the ruling body. Fortunately his name still appears on the cup originally purcahsed by Joe Davis and still competed for today.

1955

Joe Davis makes first competitive recognised 147 break.

1965

John Pullman wins the first of his World Snooker titles against Fred Davis.

22. W.C. Fields, despite his slapstick persona, was an accomplished pool player.

23. Wille Hoppe was truly a legendary player. Yet, his most famous match strangely had more to do with a penknife, than his unequaled wizardry of the game. In 1925, he met Robert Cannefax, the Three-Cushion champion. After several games, Cannefax, who preferred a fast cloth, asked to move the match to a different table. Hoppe, who was leading, said the cloth was just fine, and refused to allow a change. An incensed Cannefax drew a penknife and savagely cut the cloth down the center of the table. Hoppe was immediately awarded the match, and Cannefax was suspended from competition for a year. Ironically, Cannefax never played another match. He toured vaudeville for several years, and then died of meningitis in 1928.

24. Throughout most of the 1800's, the chalk used on the new leather cue tips was carbonate of lime, better known as blackboard chalk.

25. Most chalk used today is comprised of fine abrasives and does not contain a speck of chalk.

26. The Church has long been a part of billiard history. From its earliest days, the game was often denounced as a sinful, dangerous, morally corrupt activity. In 15th century France,

billiards play was forbidden, by the Church, as well as the King. In early American history, actual laws were passed (thanks to religious influences), outlawing the game in many parts of the land.

27. Until almost 1920, American billiards was dominated by the carom games. Pool was a dead, or dying sport. When the first championship of pool tournament was held in 1878, the winner, and the event itself, all but went unnoticed.

28. The first 18.2 Balkline Championship was held in Paris, in 1913. It will probably be the only world championship in history ever decided by the courts. After six days of play, three contestants were tied for the first place. When a tie-breaking playoff was suggested, Maurice Vignaux, the French champion and notorious whiner when things weren't going his way, scoffed at the suggestion. He insisted the title should be awarded based on the highest overall average (which he, of course, had at the time). Vignaux refused to continue, and the matter wound up in the French courts. (Which, of course, awarded Vignaux, their countryman, the title, after a delay of more than two months).

29. No one knows exactly who, when or where the first billiard table was built. The earliest documented record of a billiard table was made in 1470. In an inventory of the possessions of King Louis XI of France, his table was said to have contained the following: a bed of stone, a cloth covering, and a hole in the middle of the playing field, into which balls could be driven.

30. Harvey Hendrickson probably made as much money as anyone with his "limited" skills at the billiard table. He actually toured the country and amazed audiences. Not with his ability to run racks or pocket balls, but with his freakishly unique ability to pick up and hold 15 billiard balls at once using one hand.

31. What is billiard cloth made of? Amazingly, the main component of billiard cloth has remained unchanged for over 400 years. Wool was used in the 1500's, and remains the fabric of choice today. It has, of course, undergone some perfecting (and some wool/nylon blends are also produced).

32. The word "cue" is derived from the French queue, meaning tail. Before the cue stick was designed, billiards was played with a mace. The mace consisted of a curved wooden (or metal) head used to push the ball forward, attached to a narrow handle. Since the bulkiness of the mace head made shots along the rail difficult, it was often turned around and the "tail" end was used. Players eventually realized this method was far more effective, and the cue as a separate instrument grew out of the mace's tail.

33. There were few, if any, women's tournaments in the early 1890's. Whatever titles there were, were local, and usually self-proclaimed. Until, of course, Frances Anderson came along. The Indiana native merely proclaimed herself Champion of the World, and offered $5,000 to any woman who could beat her at pocket billiards. Anderson toured the country, playing both men and women. Legend has it, she went undefeated for 25 years against her female competitors. She was paid handsomely for her

appearances throughout the 1920's, taking on challengers and giving exhibitions, in both America and Europe. She followed this up with a well-publicized announcement that shocked the pool-playing world. Her real name was Orie (from Kansas), not Frances – and she was actually a he.

34. Behind the eight-ball – A dangerous position from which it is unlikely one can escape. From a version of the game of pool. The balls are numbered and must be potted in order. The game is forfeited if a player's cue ball hits the (black) eight-ball first. A "behind the eight-ball" position leaves a player in imminent danger of losing.

35. In the course of play, one day a visiting military cadet remarked that first-year cadets at this particular academy were known as "snookers". When the cadet missed a particularly east pot, a remark was made "Why, you're a regular snooker"!

36. Tables originally had flat vertical walls for rails and their only function was to keep the balls from falling off. They resembled riverbanks and even used to be called "banks". Players discovered that balls could bounce off the rails and began deliberately aiming at them. Thus a "bank shot" is one in which a ball is made to rebound from a cushion as part of the shot.

37. At times, including during the Civil War, billiard results received wider coverage than war news. Players were so renowned that cigarette cards were issued featuring them.

History Of World Snooker Championship

and

The Crucible Theatre, Sheffield

The first championship was held in 1927 and Joe Davis helped to organise the event. Matches were held at various venues, and the final took place at Camkin's Hall, Birmingham. Joe Davis won the event, beating Tom Dennis 20–11. His prize money was £6.10s. The highest break of the tournament was 60 by Albert Cope.

The first championship was held in 1927 and Joe Davis helped to organise the event. Matches were held at various venues, and the final took place at Camkin's Hall, Birmingham. Joe Davis won the event, beating Tom Dennis 20–11. His prize money was £6.10s. The highest break of the tournament was 60 by Albert Cope.

In subsequent years, finals were held at various venues. Joe Davis won every year until 1940. Despite an upsurge in interest in snooker there were only two entrants for the 1931 professional championship. The event was staged in the back room of a Nottingham pub, owned by Tom Dennis. The fact that he was playing on his own table didn't help as Joe Davis ran out a 25–21 winner for his fifth consecutive victory.

In 1940, Joe Davis just beat his younger brother Fred 37–36. No tournaments were organised during the remaining years of World War II and it only resumed in 1946 when Joe Davis won again for the 15th time, a record that still stands. Joe Davis never contested the World Championship again, though he continued to play professional snooker.

Walter Donaldson won in 1947, but it was Fred Davis who dominated the next few years, winning it three times in 1948, 1949 and 1951.

Fred Davis

John Pulman

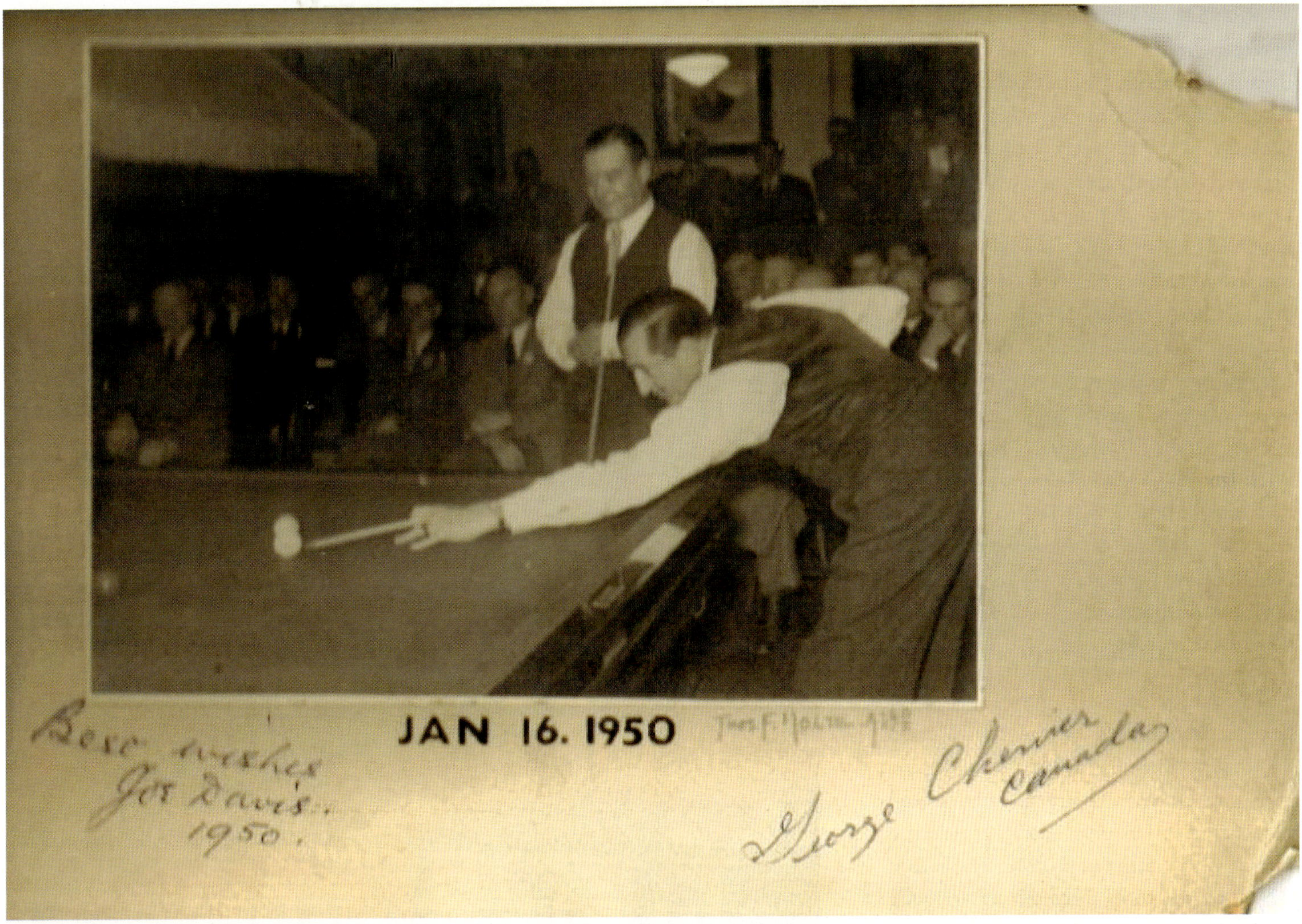
JAN 16. 1950
Best wishes
Joe Davis
1950.
George Chenier
Canada

In 1952, as a result of a disagreement between some of the players and the Billiards Association and Control Council (BACC), two tournaments were held. The Professional Matchplay Championship, organised by the players and widely viewed as the "real" world championship, continued until 1957. The BACC event only lasted one more year. Meanwhile the 'official' World Championship did attract only two entrants, Horace Lindrum from Australia beating New Zealand's Clark McConachy – and Lindrum's name is inscribed on the familiar trophy. However, his victory is often ignored due to the dispute, and Cliff Thorburn is usually referred to as the first overseas player to win the world title, while Neil Robertson was generally referred to as the first Australian-born world champion when he won in 2010.

Snooker then went into a period of decline, and no tournament was held between 1958 and 1963. In 1964, with the approval of the BACC, Rex Williams revived the championship on a challenge basis, a format which lasted until 1968. This meant that matches took place on an irregular basis, sometimes more than once a year. John Pulman completely dominated during this period, overcoming all challengers in a total of seven matches.

Following the formation of the World Professional Billiards and Snooker Association which took over regulation of the professional game from the BACC, the championship has been staged as a knockout tournament since 1969 on an annual basis, with all the seeded players coming in at the same round. That year it was won by John Spencer, but it was Ray Reardon who was to dominate over the coming years, winning six times between 1970 and 1978.

1976 was the first year the championships were sponsored by the cigarette brand Embassy. The following year, the event moved to the Crucible Theatre in Sheffield and the BBC started providing major television coverage. The Crucible seats fewer than a thousand people with the front row of seats only a few feet from the players. This was about the time snooker started attracting very large television audiences and for many fans it is synonymous with snooker. The most successful players at the Crucible are Steve Davis, who won six times in the 1980s, and Stephen Hendry, who won seven times in the 1990s. Recently, the tournament has been more open, with six different players winning in the 2000s. In the 1985 final, Dennis Taylor beat Steve Davis 18–17 on the final ball of the final frame, in one of the most closely contested matches of all time. It finished at 00:19 but was superseded as the latest finish first by the 2006 final (00:52 BST), then the 2007 final (00:55 BST). However, with an audience of 18.5 million, it remains the most watched programme in the history of BBC2, as well as the record post-midnight audience for any channel in the United Kingdom.

1985 World Championship Final

WORLD SNOOKER CHAMPIONSHIP 2015 - PRIZE MONEY

Winner	: £ 300,000	Last 16	: £ 20,000	Stage 1 high break	: £ 1000
Runner Up	: £ 125,000	Last 32	: £ 12,000	Stage 2 high break	: £ 10,000
Semi - Finalist	: £ 60,000	Last 48	: £ 9,000	Total	: £ 1,364,000
Quarter Finalist	: £ 30,050	Last 64	: £ 6,000		

Ravindra Kumar Gupta (RKG)

Yashbir Sharma

Legislation in 2003 placed restrictions on tobacco advertising, including sponsorship of sporting events. Embassy received special dispensation to continue snooker sponsorship until 2005. In 2006 888.com took over the sponsorship of the event, and they signed a five-year deal, but pulled out after just three years. On 15 April 2009, the World Snooker website announced that Betfred.com would be the new sponsor of the World Championship for the next four years. The event was sponsored by Betfair in 2013, and by Dafabet in 2014. In March 2015, it was announced that Betfred would sponsor the World Championships for the next three years.

On 27 April 2009, it was confirmed that the World Championships would stay at the Crucible for at least another five years (until 2014). On 30 April 2010 it was announced that this agreement had been extended to 2015.

On 23 April 2014, World Snooker chairman Barry Hearn announced a number of changes that would come into effect for the 2015 championship. All living world champions would be extended an opportunity to play in the qualifying rounds. The top 16 seeds would still qualify automatically for the first round at the Crucible, but all non-seeded players would have to start in the first of three qualifying rounds. The overall championship would increase from 128 to 144 players, with the additional places made available to former world champions and players from emerging countries.

On 18 January 2015, it was confirmed that a new deal had been signed by Sheffield City Council and World Snooker, that means the Crucible will continue to host the World Championships until at least 2017. Barry Hearn has stated on a number of occasions that he wishes for the tournament to remain at the Crucible forever, providing it continues to draw large numbers of visitors and revenue to the city of Sheffield.

World Snooker Championship
ROLL OF HONOUR

Year	Winner	Runner-up	Final score	Season
1927	Joe Davis	Tom Dennis	20–11	n/a
1928	Joe Davis	Fred Lawrence	16–13	n/a
1929	Joe Davis	Tom Dennis	19–14	n/a
1930	Joe Davis	Tom Dennis	25–12	n/a
1931	Joe Davis	Tom Dennis	25–21	n/a
1932	Joe Davis	Clark McConachy	30–19	n/a
1933	Joe Davis	Willie Smith	25–18	n/a
1934	Joe Davis	Tom Newman	25–23	n/a
1935	Joe Davis	Willie Smith	25–20	n/a
1936	Joe Davis	Horace Lindrum	34–27	n/a
1937	Joe Davis	Horace Lindrum	32–29	n/a
1938	Joe Davis	Sidney Smith	37–24	n/a
1939	Joe Davis	Sidney Smith	43–30	n/a
1940	Joe Davis	Fred Davis	37–36	n/a
1941–1945 no tournament held				

1946	Joe Davis	Horace Lindrum	78–67	n/a
1947	Walter Donaldson	Fred Davis	82–63	n/a
1948	Fred Davis	Walter Donaldson	84–61	n/a
1949	Fred Davis	Walter Donaldson	80–65	n/a
1950	Walter Donaldson	Fred Davis	51–46	n/a
1951	Fred Davis	Walter Donaldson	58–39	n/a
1952	Horace Lindrum[1]	Clark McConachy	94–49	n/a

Challenge Matches				
1964	John Pulman	Fred Davis	19–16	n/a
1964	John Pulman	Rex Williams	40–33	n/a
1965	John Pulman	Fred Davis	37–36	n/a
1965	John Pulman	Rex Williams	25–22 (matches)	n/a
1965	John Pulman	Fred Van Rensburg	39–12	n/a
1966	John Pulman	Fred Davis	5–2 (matches)	n/a
1968	John Pulman	Eddie Charlton	39–34	n/a

Joe Davis

Ray Reardon

John Spencer

Knockout tournaments				
1969	John Spencer	Gary Owen	37–24	n/a
1970	Ray Reardon	John Pulman	37–33	n/a
1971	John Spencer	Warren Simpson	37–29	n/a
1972	Alex Higgins	John Spencer	37–32	n/a
1973	Ray Reardon	Eddie Charlton	38–32	n/a
1974	Ray Reardon	Graham Miles	22–12	1973/74
1975	Ray Reardon	Eddie Charlton	31–30	1974/75
1976	Ray Reardon	Alex Higgins	27–16	1975/76

The Crucible						
1977	John Spencer	£ 6,000	Cliff Thorburn	£ 2,000	25–12	1976/77
1978	Ray Reardon	£ 7,500	Perrie Mans	£ 3,500	25–18	1977/78
1979	Terry Griffiths	£ 10,000	Dennis Taylor	£ 5,000	24–16	1978/79
1980	Cliff Thorburn	£ 15,000	Alex Higgins	£ 8,000	18–16	1979/80
1981	Steve Davis	£ 20,000	Doug Mountjoy	£ 10,000	18–12	1980/81
1982	Alex Higgins	£ 25,000	Ray Reardon	£ 12,500	18–15	1981/82
1983	Steve Davis	£ 30,000	Cliff Thorburn	£ 15,000	18–6	1982/83
1984	Steve Davis	£ 44,000	Jimmy White	£ 22,000	18–16	1983/84
1985	Dennis Taylor	£ 60,000	Steve Davis	£ 35,000	18–17	1984/85
1986	Joe Johnson	£ 70,000	Steve Davis	£ 42,000	18–12	1985/86
1987	Steve Davis	£ 80,000	Joe Johnson	£ 48,000	18–14	1986/87
1988	Steve Davis	£ 95,000	Terry Griffiths	£ 57,000	18–11	1987/88
1989	Steve Davis	£ 105,000	John Parrott	£ 63,000	18–3	1988/89
1990	Stephen Hendry	£ 120,000	Jimmy White	£ 72,000	18–12	1989/90
1991	John Parrott	£ 135,000	Jimmy White	£ 80,000	18–11	1990/91
1992	Stephen Hendry	£ 150,000	Jimmy White	£ 90,000	18–14	1991/92
1993	Stephen Hendry	£ 175,000	Jimmy White	£ 105,000	18–5	1992/93
1994	Stephen Hendry	£ 180,000	Jimmy White	£ 110,000	18–17	1993/94
1995	Stephen Hendry	£ 190,000	Nigel Bond	£ 115,000	18–9	1994/95
1996	Stephen Hendry	£ 200,000	Peter Ebdon	£ 120,000	18–12	1995/96
1997	Ken Doherty	£ 210,000	Stephen Hendry	£ 126,000	18–12	1996/97
1998	John Higgins	£ 220,000	Ken Doherty	£ 132,000	18–12	1997/98
1999	Stephen Hendry	£ 230,000	Mark Williams	£ 135,000	18–11	1998/99
2000	Mark Williams	£ 240,000	Matthew Stevens	£ 140,000	18–16	1999/00
2001	Ronnie O'Sullivan	£ 250,000	John Higgins	£ 147,000	18–14	2000/01
2002	Peter Ebdon	£ 260,000	Stephen Hendry	£ 152,000	18–17	2001/02

2003	Mark Williams	£ 270,000	Ken Doherty	£ 158,000	18–16	2002/03
2004	Ronnie O'Sullivan	£ 250,000	Graeme Dott	£ 125,000	18–8	2003/04
2005	Shaun Murphy	£ 250,000	Matthew Stevens	£ 125,000	18–16	2004/05
2006	Graeme Dott	£ 200,000	Peter Ebdon	£ 100,000	18–14	2005/06
2007	John Higgins	£ 220,000	Mark Selby	£ 110,000	18–13	2006/07
2008	Ronnie O'Sullivan	£ 250,000	Ali Carter	£ 125,000	18–8	2007/08
2009	John Higgins	£ 250,000	Shaun Murphy	£ 125,000	18–9	2008/09
2010	Neil Robertson	£ 250,000	Graeme Dott	£ 125,000	18–13	2009/10
2011	John Higgins	£ 250,000	Judd Trump	£ 125,000	18–15	2010/11
2012	Ronnie O'Sullivan	£ 250,000	Ali Carter	£ 125,000	18–11	2011/12
2013	Ronnie O'Sullivan	£ 250,000	Barry Hawkins	£ 125,000	18–12	2012/13
2014	Mark Selby	£ 300,000	Ronnie O'Sullivan	£ 125,000	18–14	2013/14
2015	Stuart Bingham	£ 300,000	Shaun Murphy	£ 125,000	18–15	2014/15
2016	Mark Selby	£ 330,000	Ding Junhui	£ 137,500	18–14	2015/16
2017	Mark Selby	£ 375,000	John Higgins	£ 160,000	18–15	2016/17
2018	Mark Williams	£ 425,000	John Higgins	£ 180,000	18–16	2017/18
2019						
2020						
2021						
2022						

Group photo of players at Crucible - World Snooker Championship 2018

RKG at Crucible

The main arena of Crucible Theatre.

A Tribute To

Alex Higgins

Snooker's Most Outrageously Talented Player

During the fifties and sixties Snooker suffered a lengthy decline in its fortunes, primarily due to the lack of positive marketing and promotion but also because of the lack of new players for viewers to watch. There was little or no snooker coverage in the national press and the national game was seemingly more interested in developing amateur stars, rather than the six active professional players at this time.

Things began to change in the late sixties as a number of corporate bodies began to consider the sport as a useful media tool to reach their target audience. Although press coverage remained non-existent, John Player (a tobacco company) began to sponsor individual professional players in exhibition matches, in an attempt to reach the large market which snooker, social and working mens clubs represented.

Around this time in 1968, a new snooker player was beginning to emerge from the amateur ranks. His name was Alex Higgins and he would become one of the most famous sportsman in Britain and arguably the most famous snooker player of all time.

Soon after the 1968 World Championships Higgins became the youngest ever winner of the Northern Ireland Amateur title at the age of 18 and followed this up by almost single-handedly winning the British Team Championships for Belfast YMCA.

Following Reardon's 37 - 33 victory over Pullman in the 1970 World Championships, and Spencer's win against Warren Simpson in 1971, Alex moved from Ireland to Lancashire, England in an attempt to break into mainstream British snooker. He was the talk of the county as no-one had previously seen a player seemingly so reckless, but who seldom seemed to miss. Off 14 start, he played Spencer in numerous challenge matches for £200 a match, winning the first 23-18.

The 1972 World title began in its new format in March 1971, where Higgins drawn to play Ron Gross at a snooker club in Ealing. Higgins was never in danger and won easily 16-5. Gross was a three times English amateur champion in the 1960,s but never looked like beating Alex.

A break in the World Championships saw Alex play Jack Rea for the Irish title. Higgins beat him 28-12 to become Irish champion, but was then drawn to play him again, this time in the World Championships, with Higgins winning 19-11. Into the quarter finals, Higgins then played John Pullman and defeated him 31-23 to move into the semi finals against Rex Williams. This match was extremely close throughout, with Williams 12-6 up, then 26-25 behind, before the match leveled at 30 frames apiece. The last frame was a little scrappy due to the extreme pressure of the occasion, but Higgins potted the final green to book his place in the final against John Spencer.

Spencer was the pre-match favourite but Higgins was in superb form and playing with huge confidence. Early in the final session Higgins clinched the title 37-32 and became the game's youngest ever snooker world champion. No-one would envisage a ten year gap before Higgins was crowned world champion again. Following his title victory Higgins quickly became the highest profile player in the sport, enhanced when a Thames TV documentary about him took 25th place in the television ratings for that week.

The build up to the 1973 title again centered around Alex but there was to be no repeat victory. After beating Fred Davis 16-14 in the quarter finals, Higgins lost 23-9 to Eddie Charlton in the semi's. Reardon meanwhile was defeating Spencer in the other semi-final and after numerous twists and turns defeated Charlton 38-32 in the final.

Alex meanwhile was making the news wherever he went. Broken commitments, damaged hotel rooms and excessive drinking stories seemed to follow him daily. The 1974 championships saw him beat Bennett 15-4 in the second round but lose to Fred Davis 15-14 in the quarter finals. Reardon however was making steady progress on his way to the winning his second consecutive title 22-12 against Graham Miles.

The 1975 championship saw Alex beat David Taylor 15-2 in the second round and then Rex Williams 19-12 in the quarter finals. In the semi final Higgins drew Ray Reardon and the match was evenly poised at 10-10 before Reardon won 9 of the next 13 to win 19-14. Reardon went on to beat Charlton 31-30 to win the title for the third consecutive year.

1976 saw the first Embassy sponsored snooker world championships, with Higgins reaching the final after wins over Thorburn 15-14 in the second round, Spencer 15-14 in the quarter finals and Charlton 20-18 in the semi finals. The final did not go well for Alex with Reardon playing a steady if unspectacular game on his way to winning, with a session to spare 27-16 . In numerous frames Alex conceded frames with reds still on the table.

Following the first Embassy sponsored championships, Reardon won the Pontins Professional, whilst newcomer Doug Mountjoy won the Pontins Open for the second time in three years and also the Welsh Amateur. Higgins beat Reardon to win the Canadian Club Masters, which was subsequently shown by Yorkshire television. Charlton beat Reardon to win the World Professional Matchplay championship, a result which created confusion as to who was now the official world snooker champion.

The 1977 championships were moved from the venue in Wythe Shaw which held the '76' final and relocated to the Crucible Theatre in Sheffield. This decision immediately proved to be hugely successful with 20,000 spectators watching over the fortnight of the competition.

Alex lost a pulsating first round match with Doug Mountjoy 13-12. From 10-12 down Higgins won the next two to level at 12-12. After leading for most of the frame a missed pink allowed Doug in to recover to make it a black ball shoot out. After two or three shots apiece, Mountjoy potted the black to win. Meanwhile Spencer was making steady progress, defeating Virgo 13-9, Reardon 13-6 and Pulman 18-16 to meet Cliff Thorburn in the final. Thorburn in his first final played very well, but Spencer's experience stood him in good stead as he recorded a 25-21 victory.

Following the 1977 championships, Higgins won the Pontins Professional from 864 entries and the Canadian Open after beating Reardon and Spencer in the last two rounds. The BBC had committed to televising the final of the Benson and Hedges Masters, (which Higgins won 7-5 against Thorburn), Pot Black and the final of the UK championships. BBC's decision to cover daily sessions of the 1978 Embassy championships however, gave snooker wide spread media coverage, raising profile and awareness of the game to a new level. This was the single most influential decision made in the history of snooker.

Broadcasting live matches was still deemed to be extremely risky, as a boring frame could eat away valuable airtime. This was overcome with the two-table coverage and selected moments form matches being shown on the television. No-one could possibly anticipate the television success story of the 1978 championships. On the first Monday there was an audience of five million for the recorded highlights. On the Wednesday, six million people tuned in and by the end of the championship fortnight over seven million people were regularly watching sessions.

In the first round their were two last frame losers. Unfortunately for the viewers, Alex lost 13-12 to Patsy Fagan from 12-10 in front. The 23rd frame was won on a tie-break the 24th on a black ball finish and the decider on the last pink. The other last frame loser was Willie Thorne, defeated 13-12 by Charlton from 12-9 in front. The tension was unbearable, the coverage impeccable. Televised viewers loved it.

Fred Davis and Perrie Mans progressed to one semi-final, whilst the other was between Eddie Charlton and Ray Reardon. Mans came through 18-16 against Davis,

"Evening of Life"

while Reardon beat Charlton 18-14. The final was split at 10 all, before Reardon built up an 18-14 lead at the end of the fourth session. Mans recovered to 18-17 before Reardon responded with seven frames out of eight to win his sixth and last world crown 25-18.

Unfortunately, this championship saw the great Joe Davis taken ill whilst watching his brother Fred in the semi-finals. Complaining of back pains Joe was taken from the arena to his hotel and the following day to the hospital. An operation saw him through the crisis, but he never fully recovered and died six weeks later. A true sporting gentleman and one of the primary reasons for snooker's growth and success, Joe's death was a tragic loss to the game.

Alex's form in 1979 was somewhat sporadic. Doug Mountjoy defeated him in the UK championship's at Preston and Perrie Mans beat him 8-4 to take the Benson and Hedges Masters at Wembley, without making a 50 break in the entire competition. Reardon beat him 11-9 to take the Daily Mirror Champion of Champions, but Alex responded by winning the Tolly Cobold Classic and the first prize of £750 in an open tournament at the Castle Club.

The build up to the 1979 World Championships saw a number of new players introduced into the tournament. One of them was Steve Davis. Slowly but surely the status quo was changing, with the older established players finding things harder as fierce competition raised the overall standard. Another new entrant was Welshman Terry Griffiths, playing in his first world championships. For him to go on and win the title was a remarkable achievement for someone with very little experience of long matches condensed into a fortnight's play. After beating Perrie Mans in the first round he was then drawn to play Alex in round two.

Higgins lost the first frame after a 61 clearance from Terry, but then made consecutive centuries of 105 and 112 and looked all set for a third until he broke down unexpectedly on 45 in the fourth frame. Griffiths cleared with 63 to win on the black and leveled at 2-2. Higgins then won the next four to finish at 6-2. The next session Griffiths won the last three to level at 8-8, before the next six frames were shared with the match level at 11-11. The following session saw all the frames shared before Griffiths clinched the decider with a break of 107. Many argued that this was one of the best matches ever seen at the Crucible Theatre.

Griffith's then defeated Charlton in a titanic struggle in the semi-final, a match that was in stark contrast to the quarter final with Alex. Long bouts of safety play and tactics saw the final session last over five hours, but Griffith's stayed focused and emerged triumphant 19-17. In the other semi-final Dennis Taylor beat John Virgo 19-12 to book his place in the final for the first time after suffering the disappointment of two losing semi-finals.

The final was the best of 47 frames, spread over three days as opposed to the 35 frames over two days format, which would take place in 1980. After leveling at 15-15, Griffith's then moved into a 17-16 lead before winning the next seven frames on his way to the title and a winning margin of 24-16.

No individual is bigger than the game, but every now and then along comes a special player whose name becomes synonymous with their chosen sport.

TOURNAMENT WINS

SNOOKER WINS

Ranking wins

- World Championship - 1982

Other wins

- World Championship - 1972
- Irish Professional Snooker Championships - 1972, 1978, 1979, 1983, 1989
- Men of the Midlands - 1972, 1973
- Watney Open - 1974
- Canadian Open - 1975, 1977
- Canadian Club Masters - 1976
- Benson & Hedges Irish Championship - 1977
- Benson & Hedges Masters - 1978, 1981
- Tolly Cobbold Classic - 1979, 1980
- British Gold Cup - 1980
- Padmore / Super Crystalate International - 1980
- Coral UK Championship - 1983
- Benson & Hedges Irish Masters - 1989

Team wins

- World Doubles Championship - 1984 (with Jimmy White)
- World Cup - 1985, 1986, 1987 with All Ireland team

Pro-Am Wins

- Pontin's Spring Open

Amateur wins

- All Ireland Amateur Champion - 1968
- Northern Ireland Amateur Champion - 1968

Pool

- Mosconi Cup - 1995 with team Europe

EMBASSY
WORLD SNOOKER
CHAMPIONSHIP

Over two thousand people in the Crucible gave a tumultuous applause to vent and simulate their pent up emotions to herald the new World Snooker Champion, 2002 – Ronnie O'Sullivan defeating John Higgins of Ireland. Embedded with tension and turmoil throughout his career, he had threatened to quit the game, finally played with timorous attitude against him. He was a verdant young man blessed with an enviable talent to explode in the Crucible. His problem was that he was too talented. The genius sometimes goes astray. His personal life was full of rancor, misery and sorrow. He overcame that impediment to lift the world cup. The real Sultan of Snooker has arrived.

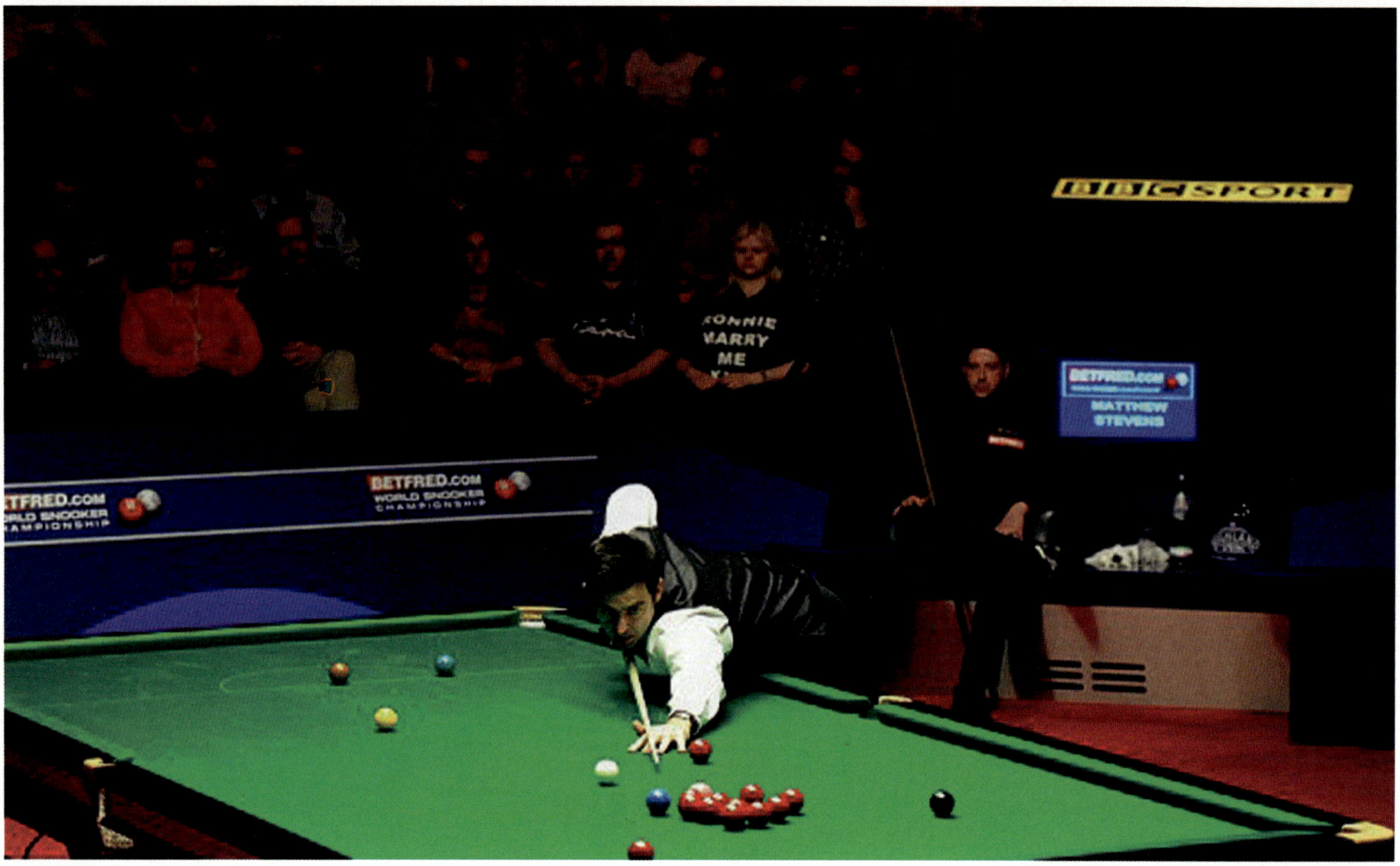

He started his now famous onslaught to trounce the first round Andy Hicks, who did not know what had hit him. It is a rare occurrence that O'Sullivan could not muster a century run in the entire match. He is a people's champion and thrives on entertaining them. The crowd gave him standing ovation though O'Sullivan kept on shrugging his head as he was not satisfied with his performance. He touched sublime form against Dave Harold. He was in a punishing mood, especially in the end, making splendid runs of 114 and 116. he earlier made a hundred and over fifteen fifties. He virtually toyed with his opponent reducing him to the status of a spectator in the end.

He crossed another hurdle with consummate artistry against Peter Ebdon who earlier had vent his feelings against Stephen Lee, the outburst which millions of people saw on the television. Crucible is synonymous with exemplary behavior. But this time he was banging his head against a wall. It looked as if he is drained of his energy. O'Sullivan completed the massacre with a verdict of 13-6. His ominous form makes him tournament favorite.

Joe Swail earned sobriquet of 'come-back-kid' after he cut short the ambition of Mark Williams. He had a history of such astonishing come backs and when Mark Williams was leading 8-3, he was not

prepared to sit on his laurels. Playing a water tight game against his famed adversary, Swail inched and clawed his way to a famous victory by 13-12 which embellished breaks of 101 and 140 which turned out to be the highest break of the tournament.

No player in the world can held a candle before the redoubtable Stephen Hendry. The entire nineties belong to him. He fired an unbelievable 534 centuries in his illustrious career. Lifted the world crown seven times, even one with a hairline fracture in his right hand. He became a legend in his life time. This snooker icon is considered by many and experts as the greatest the game has ever produced. He defied his age, from and bookies in the earlier two rounds. He met Matthew Stevens but suffered a humiliating and sad loss of 13-5. He scored a lone century in the match, otherwise, outplayed in all departments of the game. He lacked finnese of the yore. It looked as if the young age of thirty two is getting up with him ! Is he already a veteran at this age? Is it the end of road for him? Yes. It is highly improbable that he will capture his old glory. But everybody knows that in sports it is better not to make predictions, especially in snooker. We may hear more of Stephen Hendry.

Matthew Stevens who lost his father two months ago, is able to wither this personal tragedy. His semi-finals clash with John Higgins produced champagne snooker. It is by far the best match I have ever seen in my life. It was full of intrigue, suspense and bloody suspense. Higgins shot into an early lead only to seen Matthew galloping almost a neck behind him. They were locked in and 8-8 verdict after which the pendulum kept on swinging each way. When Matthew compiled 133 he had his hundredth tournament century.

Two frames remained etched in my mind for a long time to come. They came in the session which had lot of bearing on the out come of their grueling struggle. Matthew rolled it in a cluster and Higgins tried to wriggle out of it. Then soon it became a crisp and touch situation. This controlled madness went on for fifteen minutes during which the crowd was on tenterhooks with their lips sealed. In the end, Matthew saw a very thin light at the end of the dark tunnel and potted the red and subsequent ball.

After that I witnessed the frame of the century which lasted for fifty two minutes and forty seconds. When it looked to be a curtain for a player, he wriggled out of it to spring into new leads of life the next second. Players dying and reborn was the order of the frame. It was top class exhibition playing a snooker and counter snooker. The Crucible crowd were extremely generous in applauding through hand clapping notwithstanding the Oohs and aahs. It was like in a game of soccer when in ten penalties none crossed the goal line or imagine a Sachin Tendulkar not opening his account after facing fifty balls. Their only predicament was that one had to lose. Matthew Stevens was the unfortunate player when he bowed to the inevitable. Higgins won the marathon encounter 17-15.

Ronnie O'Sullivan conquered another peak to get past Joe Swail in the semi-final encounter. He could not contain his rampaging opponent. O'Sullivan wanted to conquer one glory which rested with Joe Swail, his compilation of 140, the tournaments highest run. Ronnie went on to compile and possibly touched 140 when he potted the pink from the spot via one cushion on to find his cue ball traveling an inch too far. O'Sullivan was on 133 and he rolled the black via one cushion in the top pocket with the aid of long rest. To the onlookers it seemed that the ball was merrily sailing towards the top pocket, Swail's pulse was going past the barrier but the jaws came to his rescue. The ball wobbled in the pocket. The relief was writ large on Swail's face. O'Sullivan completed the massacre 17-10.

The moment gladiators entered the arena, the whole Crucible went berserk. The cries of 'come on John' and 'come on O'Sullivan' started in the theatre. I mentioned elsewhere in the magazine about the antic of the so called soothsayer. He was shouting vociferously that Ronnie will make it 6-2. The lead, he could never recover. The next twenty four frames were shared by the two players. It provides in an ample measure what bad session can do for you.

Higgins flirted with the three wins in the final session. But Higgins, to his credit, produced a resilient performance and kept up the pressure when O'Sullivan made the rare mistake. But the Scot will rue a crucial red missed in the 30th frame after notching a break of sixty. O'Sullivan jumped to a 17-13 lead, and the die was cast. O'Sullivan signed, sealed and delivered the coup de grace with a refreshing run of eighty to win a great final. It is Crucible's history that the champion does not put a signature again on the trophy barring Ray Reardon, Steve Davis and Stephen Hendry. When O'Sullivan lifted the trophy which eluded his mentor Jimmy White. His victory was more sweet considering his personal problems which he was facing. He now contemplates taking the trophy in prison to show it to his father.

YASHBIR SHARMA

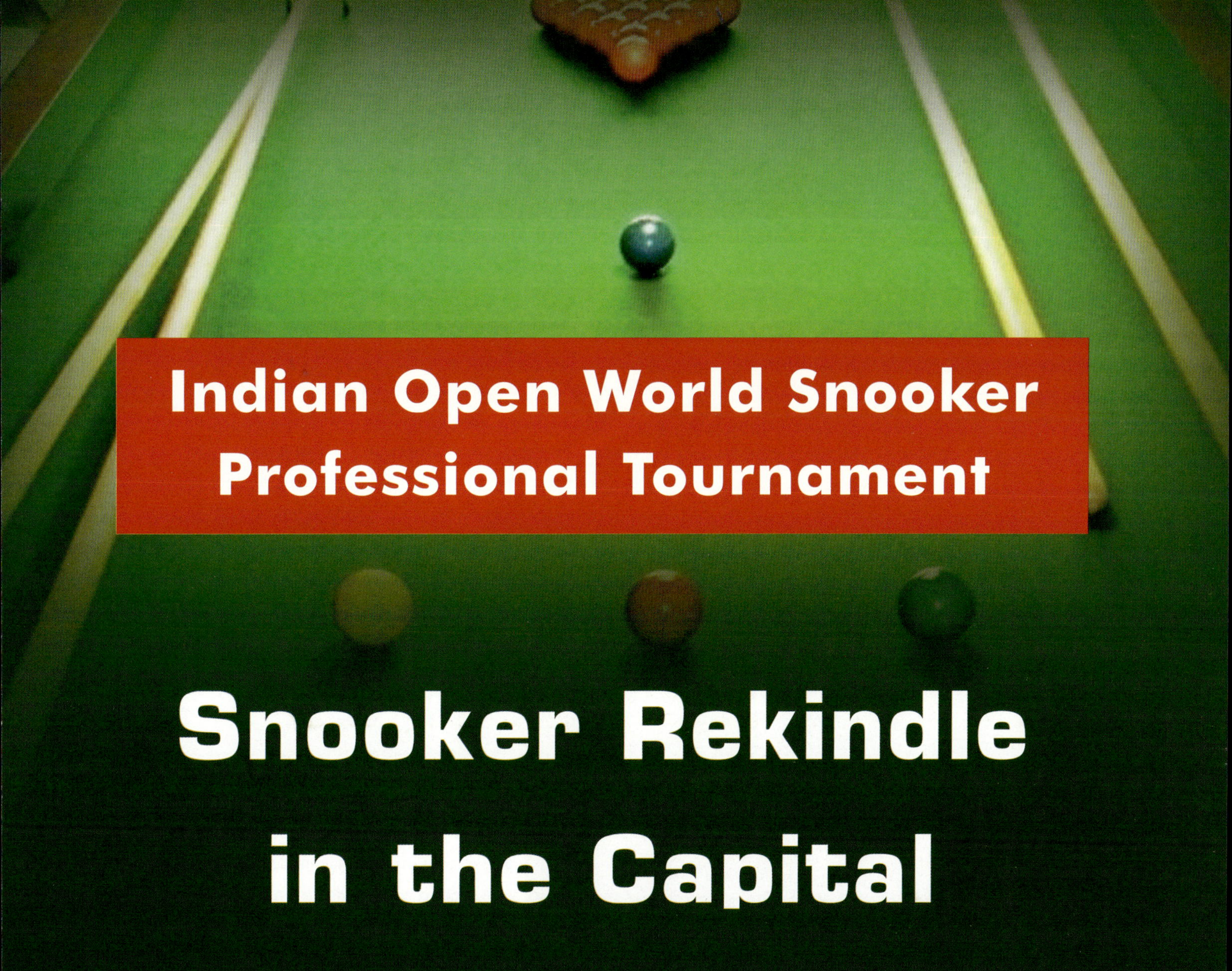

Indian Open World Snooker Professional Tournament

Snooker Rekindle in the Capital

It was for the first time a professional ranking tournament was organized at Le Meridien Hotel from 14-18 October 2013. It was done on a gigantic scale with every detail has been chalked out meticulously. It was organized at the behest of Capt. Mohan on behalf of Billiards & Snooker Federation of India. It was a thumping success particularly the press coverage which was out of the world almost at par with cricket. The spectators response had been a phenomenal with almost every outing was packed to capacity. The prize money was staggering £ 300,000 which if translated in to Indian rupees comes out to Rs. 30 millions. With so much at stake two Indian stars Pankaj Advani and Aditya Mehta were ready to take the plunge.

All the Indian wild card entrant were wiped out with only who escaped the onslaught with single exception of Dharminder Lilly that too entered the second round with a walkover, only temporarily. He was defeated soundly by Mark Selby 4-0.

Aditya Mehta started the proceeding on a sound note accounting for Peter Ebdon in the decider. The format, best of seven was too short to stage a recovery. Another Indian Challenge, the pride and joy of Indian cue sport, Pankaj Advani, trounced Marcus Campbell 4-1 to enter the 2nd round.

Aditya Mehta came into his own when he accounted for Hammad Miah with a brilliant display. He won 4-1 with refreshing win. Pankaj Advani had to sweat it out with 4-2 verdict against Mark Allen. Stuart Bingham won with identical margin against T. Thirapongpaiboon.

Ding Junhui was lucky to survive in the championship winning his first match with the skin of his teeth 4-3 against Barry Pinches. He struggled to get past Mark Joyce, that too 4-3. Pankaj Advani gets

past Mark Allen 4-2 but his baptism by fire came against the might of Stuart Bingham when in an absolute thriller Pankaj showed the exit door to his celebrated opponent 4-3. While Aditya Mehta also staged a coup against highly rated Mark Williams 4-2. The success of these two cueists augurs well for the future of Indian Snooker.

The expected clash which the snooker lover and press were eagerly waiting for. The fair which the Indian duo dished out was electric and mind boggling. It was perhaps one of the longest matches played in this format. No one made big breaks but the play was of a very high standard. Aditya won the Quarterfinal in the midst of terrific excitement to win 72-20, 0-70, 82-68, 43-58, 24-65, 66-45 and 72-00.

A beaming Aditya said after his great scalp “A couple of years ago, no-one would have imagined that an Indian player could win a ranking title, but now only two matches away.” He further said , “ If I do win, I hope it will be a great thing for Indian sports. I want to be the first Indian to win a ranking title and be sitting here tomorrow night with the trophy.”

Ding came into his own after earlier narrow escape to face the might of John Higgins. Ding was playing like a robot to outclass John Higgins by 4 frames to 2 to herald his announcement in the semi-final. He won with an identical margin against Neil Robertson to set the final clash with Aditya Mehta who played a great against Stephen Maguire defeating him 4-3.

Ding Junhui was all the guns blazing against Aditya Mehta in the finals. The Mumbai star did not do anything wrong yet found himself occupying the chair throughout the match. Ding had an amazing sequence of breaks of 52, 87, 107, 93 and 116 to seal an emphatic victory and lifted the trophy.

YASHBIR SHARMA

Indian Open World Snooker Professional Tournament

THE MUMBAI BONANZA

After the fairytale saga, India Open Snooker scene shifted to Grand Hyatt Hotel - Mumbai. The BSFI did a splendid job in conducting the tournament which was beyond the reach of snooker aficionado. There was tremendous excitement all over India with snooker fence flocked to see the gladiators in action.

The BSFI pulled up all their resources at their command, leaving no stone unturned to make this a grand success. The response of the public was that of euphoria and excitement.

Captain Mohan the President and Secretary Bala Subramaniam camped in Mumbai for its superlative success. After that a Indian Open is going to be held in Hyderabad, which will open the floodgates of snooker. With Captain Mohan at helm, a dazzling show is in store for snooker fans.

Indian wild card entrant Neeraj Kumar, Sumit Talwar, Brijesh Damani, Faizal Khan made early exit without giving a semblance of a fight. Pankaj Advani, quarter finalist in Delhi Open bowed out of the competition after putting up stiff resistance against R. Clark. Dharmindra Lilly met with similar fate losing in the decider against Lyu Haotian. The defending champion Ding Junhui, who was summarily beaten by J.U. Nook in the last sixty four. Ding takes time in settling down as was witnessed in Delhi when he won his first three matches in the decider and went on win the title at ease. Ding during the Delhi outing showed no emotion with a poker and stern face.

India's lone hope Aditya Mehta in a heroic fight succumbed to Mark King winning 4-3. But in the next round King had to bite the dust when he lost 2-4 against Ricky Walden who reach the finals only to lose against Michael White. Another reason for crowd's tepid response was due to the fact that no Indian Player was left, there was a fodder of thoughts amongst Indian audience.

In the 2000 World Professional Championship at Crucible Theatre, Matthew Stephen was beaten by John Higgins, which was full of intrigue and suspense, which lasted 32 frames of high quality snooker. Stephen lost the match, but now he is a shadow of his former self. He lost the match 2-4 against Jerrod Green. The passage of time how time changes. John Higgins beat Jamie Burnett 4-2 and enjoyed the identical score against Jamie Cope. Higgins comes out a cropper against Mark Davis, was blanked 4-0. The Champion of yester year was a silent spectator throughout the match.

Mark Williams rapid strides against Eden Sharav 4-2, then accounted for Peter Ebdon 4-3 in the decider and enjoyed great luck and pluck against D.Trump. He serenely went past Robert Milkins 4-1 but had the mortification to lose to the championship winner 4-2. Thus Mark Williams' epic march to glory ended in Indian Open.

On the other hand Michael White had to struggle to keep his flag high against Cao Yupeng 4-3 beat Matthew Selt 4-2, Li Hang with an identical score and Chris Wakelin 4-2.

The final was almost a repeat of 2013 Finals in which Michael raced to 5-0 verdict against Ricky Walden he compiled breaks of 81, 77, 58, and in the last frame chalked out a splendid run of 85, to lift the trophy.

YASHBIR SHARMA

JOHN SPENCER

Snooker champion at the forefront of the game's new-found popularity

The snooker player John Spencer, who won the world title at his first attempt in 1969 - then took it again 18 months later, and repeated the feat in 1977, the first year the championship was staged at Sheffield's Crucible Theatre - has died of stomach cancer aged 70.

Born in Radcliffe, Lancashire, he attended Stand grammar school. When he was 14, his father, who had lost an arm in the first world war and used a clothes brush as a makeshift bridge for his cue, introduced his son to a full-sized table. Previously he had played only on an upturned 4ft x 2ft bagatelle table, with pairs of nails defining the pockets and tightly drawn tape for cushions. Spencer made his first century break when he was 15, but remained a strictly local hero as the game was in the doldrums. Called up for national service at 18, he did not hit a ball for 11 years until an old friend recruited him for a £5-a-head challenge match for Longsight billiard hall against that in Salford.

Having anchored Longsight to victory, it struck Spencer that if these were the best amateurs in Lancashire, he had been underrating himself. He reached the final of the English amateur championship at his first attempt in 1964, losing to Ray Reardon, who later won six world titles. Having taken the English amateur champion title in 1966, Spencer returned to Lancashire as runner-up from the world amateur championship in Karachi that year on the point of retirement after a row over expenses.

In those days there was no tournament circuit, and he had no thought of a professional career. Players survived through charity exhibitions in clubs and, out of the blue, the National Spastic Society offered him £14 an engagement, plus a small commission on what he could raise through auctions and raffles. Pontin's, Blackpool, offered him £20 a week for a summer season - and his professional career was born.

When John Player decided to sponsor a revived world championship, Spencer borrowed £100 from his bank manager and won the first prize of £1,780, then a fortune in snooker terms. Beaten by Reardon in the April 1970 semi-final, he recaptured the title in Sydney that November, making three centuries in four frames in the final. Although hot favourite to retain the title, he lost the 1972 final to Alex Higgins, whose emergence was to be an important factor in the game's commercial success.

Three times Spencer won Pot Black, the BBC2 one-frame tournament that exploited the advent of colour television to bring the game to a substantial new public. At a time when snooker, after a long spell of obscurity, needed new heroes, he was at the forefront of that small cast. Although he won the inaugural Benson and Hedges Masters in 1975, his form deteriorated as the 1970s wore on. His cue was an unprepossessing 15oz Excalibur, held together by a nail in its butt and bought for eight shillings from the Radcliffe billiard hall, the Grott. It was broken into four pieces when he crashed after falling asleep at the wheel of his car in 1974, an incident in which he was lucky not to have died.

Incredibly, the cue was pinned together by a cue doctor, but it never felt quite the same. Eventually, two months before the 1977 championship, Spencer changed to a Canadian two-piece, and regained the title, not in his old, assertive style, but with a percentage game underpinned by concentration, tenacity, tactical acumen and experience. In 1979, in the Holsten International at Slough, he became the first player ever to make a 147 maximum in competition, albeit an event denied television exposure because Thames TV, anxious to avoid overtime payments, had awarded the crew a meal break.

Spencer's career and life were shattered on May 9 1985 when he woke up with double vision, quickly diagnosed as myasthenia gravis, the disease which, in his case, had caused a deterioration of his eye muscles. Steroids fought the problem with intermittent success but the long-term side effects were hellish.

He worked as a BBC Television summariser and was, from 1990 to 1996, chairman of the World Professional Billiards and Snooker Association. His tenure, he was to admit, included several periods in which his condition and medication produced deep depressions, ungovernable spasms of aggression, an obsession with suicide and, finally, inoperable stomach cancer. It was all a dreadful contrast to his sunny, good-natured younger self, a great lover of practical jokes, golf and gambling on horses.

A year ago, Spencer declined further treatment: "Even if I only have another 12 months left to live, at least I'll die happy. I realised that I could have another 10 years, but be miserable with the treatment, or take my chances without it. I'm determined to stay around a bit longer, but I've had a good innings. I've been round the world too many times to remember and met some fabulous people."

He remained, as he had been for 20 years, a dedicated fundraiser for the Myasthenia Gravis Association, even undertaking a sponsored parachute jump last year, and completed his autobiography, Out of the Blue, Into the Black. He is survived by his wife Margot, with whom he remained on the friendliest of terms after their separation, and Jean Shepherd, his partner of 15 years.

THE SNOOKER WIZARD OF THE CENTURY

For Stephen Hendry, Snooker life began at a very tender age. He was barely fourteen years of age when he had his maiden triumph in the under 16 British Championship. Since then he has not looked back and bagged innumerable titles, which even he can't recollect or remember. There are five all time great players in the history of this game, starting with Joe Davis and followed by Ray Reardon, Steve Davis and Stephen Hendry. Out of these four, Joe Davis was perhaps unique in more than one ways. In those days, heavy crystallite balls were in use and a break of 32 or 40 was considered great. The players used to play a game or two of Snooker, in the interval of a Billiards match, just to break the monotony.

Joe Davis then went on to become a professional Snooker player of repute, so much so that Billiards was erased from his mind. Before the advent of the last three of his successors. He was arguably the most decorated player in Snooker having won the World titles as many as 15 times. Then came Ray Reardon, who claimed six world titles, and his play was very refreshing. There was a healthy rivalry between Reardon and John Spencer, who dazzled for a while and then went into obscurity.

Before Spencer's exit, came Steve Davis who completely dominated the Snooker scene in the eighties. He claimed six world titles, narrowly missing the seventh one against Dennis Taylor on a black ball in the decider. He was still in the pink of his health when Stepehn Hendry rocked his citadel with his arrival. In fact, the two living legends were very active in the professional circuit. Their encounter evokes awe and scintillating stuff worthy of the two great champions. Steve Davis met this writer several times during his sojoum to India, and expressed a keen desire to win the World Crown in the nineties. He said, "in the eighties winning the titles became a sort of a habit, but to win in the nineties, has special place and pride for me. For then you are confronting hordes of talented youngsters, ready to unleash their claws on you. It is eventually a triumph of mind over matter". Though he claimed Benson & Hedges, U.K. Championship and had a classic more than ones, but he could not claim the world title in the nineties. But, he is still holding his head high in the midst of younger players. He performed a rare hat trick of Benson & Hedges triumphs by trouncing Ronnie O'Sullivan 10-8, in the final to pick up the cheque of pound135,000. He also has the distinction of making the first televised 147 maximum in a classic tournament in 1982. It is an irony that earlier when John Spencer made the maximum of 147, the TV crew had gone for the tea and refreshments! But Steve Davis biggest disappointment came in 1985 World Championship's final against Denis Taylor when he missed an easiest of an easy black pot in the decider. Both the players cannot forget this moment – one for the agony (so near yet so far)and the other for ecstasy (miraculous gift).

Jimmy White pitched in with telling effect and the fierce competition existed between three mercurial cueists but with contrasting styles.

Steve Davis, when came to India In 1980, was not the Steve Davis we all know. His style has not changed but his approach to the game has undergone a drastic change. He was a happy go lucky person, who used to win a few and lose some. After he crossed the shores of India, he became a ruthless player who administered decimation of his opponent in Snooker game with clinical precision. With sheer tenacity and doggedness he ascended to the top of the world.

Jimmy White, on the other hand, was a swashbuckling and immensely entertaining player. He was known not to give any respite to a player, no matter what the situation of the frame and the lead be. He has destroyed many an almost invincible leads of his opponent. His stunning and incredible long pots was a sheer joy to behold. He was six times the bride but never the groom at the Crucible Theatre! His was a case of 'so near yet so far', not once but many a times. He lost in the quarter-final of Embassy 2000. His last chance to don the grooms dress went awry, much to the chagrin of his legion of fans which are swelling in numbers day by day. They want him to win the World Crown somehow or the other. Barring the glorious uncertainties associated with this game, the chances are that Jimmy White will continue to keep his fans on tenterhooks. There is every possibility that this perhaps is the last appearance to have a crack at the world title for this highly talented youngster.

Stephen Hendry, the magician, enthralled the Snooker world by winning an incredible five world titles in a row from 1989 to 1993. It is known as “Hendry era' in the Snooker World. He broke all the existing records with impunity. It is during this era that Stephen Hendry was nearly unseated by Sonic Multani at 555 International Invitation Tournament at Taj Palace Hotel, New Delhi. What the most professional players could not accomplish in the life time, Multani had almost done and that too in his very first attempt. After having been extricated from the jaws of defeat. Hendry was shaking like a leaf. Perhaps it was too hard to believe that he was winner when he was almost trounced by an unknown player. However, Stephen Hendry is in the habit of performing the impossible. His opponents are known to have butterflies in their stomachs when confronted with their redoubtable opponents. One such classic instance that comes to my mind was of 1997 Liverpool Challenge Cup where he was trailing by six frames against the redoubtable Ronnie O'Sullivan. Thus began the one of his many magnificent fight back in the history of the game. He drew levels and then, cool as a cucumber, chalked out a masterly run of 147.

What a victory and a climax to the event! As if annihilation of the almost unsurmountable lead was not enough, the victory cake needed the masterly icing with the recording of the maximum break in the game.

He then prevailed over Stephen Lee 9-8, after losing the first five frames. These narrow escapes gave him back his lost belief, which hold him in good stead while in arrears.

Then came the piece de resistance when he clinched 1999 World Title for the seventh time, beating all the existing record by a fair degree of margin by claiming the “Magnificent Seven” titles at the Crucible Theatre. Every single vote goes to the invincible and impregnable Stephen Hendry, rating him as the Greatest Snooker player ever lived. Not only for the records, but he has established that he is a complete player, and would be hard to equal. Future generation will refuse to believe that such a player walked on the surface of the earth, with the golden cue!

YASHBIR SHARMA

2001 • 2004 • 2008 • 2012 • 2013

Ronnie O'Sullivan

"SULTAN OF SNOOKER"

He is snooker's child prodigy in the real sense of the world. He was barely ten when he rattled his first century! Few onlookers hailed him as the future world champion. His touch was astonishing, his cue ball contact already cultured. In fact, he was so tiny that it was impossible for him to put the blue ball on the spot. He won his first pro-am title, at the age of twelve. He astounded the whole world by amassing the maximum 147 in English Amateur Championship in 1991 at the age of 16. The name of the sensational child prodigy is Ronnie O'Sullivan.

I distinctly remember his heroic exploits in Bangalore during the World Under-21 Championship. The moment he fired his first century, he became the toast of the Snooker crazy fans of Bangalore. He played stupendous snooker, his play was very crisp and his potting very refreshing. The Bangalore people further recall the awesome talent in this ambidextrous lad.

Once he was waiting for a scooter at the MG Road and I was passing through the MG road. I halted my scooter there and asked him to hop in which he promptly did. He quipped, "How do you manage to sit in that box?" He could only understand the language of snooker. Potting alone was not his forte, he could make or break a snooker with hawk-like eyes, subtle wrist work and very alert mind. One could not easily visualize that he was going to be the greatest player of all times.

He turned professional at the age of sixteen and made a terrific impact. He won his first 38 matches in a row, 74 out of 76 ! The champion has finally arrived. He qualified for the Crucible but soon after received a severe jolt which shattered his social structure and mental peace. His father in a fit of rage stabbed a man in a drunken brawl at the bar. He was awarded imprisonment for eighteen years. Ronnie O'Sullivan's world shattered completely. Perhaps, that was only the initial shock. At first, this trauma did not affect his career as he won several titles including the U.K. Championship beating the legendary Stephen Hendry in the final.

Now the prodigy was turning into a man. It is a difficult transformation which can make or mar many a careers. It was difficult to sustain the excellence which he showered to the world of snooker. In a magnificent burst of sheer talent he made a stunning break of 147 in five minutes and twenty seconds in the Benson & Hedges Master in 1995. Ronnie missed several tournaments in 1998, suffering from 'mental and physical exhaustion' but today he is a rejuvenated man after claiming the Embassy World Snooker 2001.

There have been strings of controversial incidents. He was summarily stripped of the Irish Master Title in 1998 when a random drug test revealed traces of cannabis. He was also fined 20,000 pounds for assaulting an official at the Embassy World Championship. He is moody, whimsical and temperamental.

He knows that things have taken a turn for the betterment. He has the world at his

feet. Throughout his professional career, he was striving for the coveted World Championship. He got it after eight years of turmoil and sheer doggedness. It will not act as a tonic to his already magical play but also to his behaviour. He is the youngest player to compile 200 centuries in the professional circuit. Out of 29 appearances in the final, he came out victor 21 times and thus holds an enviable record. He is a sheer raw genius in the classical mould of Alex Higgins and Jimmy White.

A week after his epic triumph, he did maul Stephen Hendry in U.K. Premier League Final to win 60,000 pound which swelled his earning this year to £6,84,130. Only Stephen Hendry, with £7,40,194 in 1995 and £6,94,056 in 1991 has pocketed more pound sterling.

If Ronnie had been granted one extra wish, it would have been to have his father with him. He eloquently said, "Dad is proud, very proud of what I have achieved and hopefully I will get to see him as soon as possible. I will take the trophy to the prison. "Peter Ebdon, beaten by O'sullivan in their semi-final, says he is nothing short of a genius. He is snooker's equivalent of Mozart, "said Ebden.

"The 108 break he made to level things against me in our semi-final was magical, class personified. You couldn't better it-it was poetry in motion" John Higgins hailed him as the greatest in the game. Ronnie's problem is that he is too good, said Clive Everton, the BBC snooker commentator. Anything less than brilliant has been regarded as a failure by Ronnie. He has had to learn to accept not playing his best all the time.

I could barely envisage in my wildest dreams that the boy whom I gave lift in Bangalore will become the Sultan of Snooker.

YASHBIR SHARMA

SHYAM SHROFF

Seven Times National Snooker Champion

Seven times National Snooker Champion Shyam Shroff, whose death we even mourn today, belonged to the era of Snooker when Billiards was the hog brother. In fact, he was basically a Billiards player who used to play a bit of Snooker! His death sent shock waves to the Billiards and Snooker fraternity throughout India. Former World Billiards Champion Wilson Jones, hailed him as Snooker player of exceptional merit and recalled the meritorious services that he had rendered for this game.

I met Shyam Shroff recently in the National Sports Club of India, Mumbai and photographed him in profusely. He was looking perfectly fit and trim for a man of 63 years of age. We started the conversation over a glass of beer when Shyam Shroff went in a reminiscent mood. He cited the reason for switching over from Billiards to Snooker on account of the dominance of Wilson Jones in the World scene. He further said, "Michael Ferreira was pestering him and that too closely, therefore, it was impertative for me to make the transition from Billiards to Snooker".

He further said, " People consider Wilson Jones to be a Billiards Player. But he was very crafty in Snooker as well. Five National Titles bear testimony to that. Then there was Tony Monterio, a brilliant and dashing player and most dreaded opponent according to me". On Arvind Savur he elaborated, "He did not understand the game at that time. In fact, I did not loose a single game to him before my injury in Dublin where I had gone to participate in the World Snooker Championship. Arvind learnt the intricacies of the game much later".

Shyam Shroff filled up another glass and asked for a sandwich as his lunch, while I ordered a full meal. I noticed that he became an exceptionally poor eater, thriving mostly on sandwiches or pizzas. That was the only sign I noticed in him about his vulnerable health. But I did not give it much thought then. After he finished his little morsel of food, he continued talking. "the biggest disappointment in my career that I could not excel in the World Championship, in my four attempt, I reached that last eight stage twice. I was comfortably leading 4-2 against Max Williams of Australia in 1969 when the catastrophe struck. I got a kick on green and that was that. Williams went on to win the remaining frame. He lost in the final against Denis Taylor 11-10".

I vividly remember Shyam Shroff telling me during the course of an exhibition match in 1979 which yours truly organized on behalf of the Delhi Billiards and Snooker Association at Maurya Hotel, New Delhi on being confronted why he does not make big breaks, he had said, "After crossing the seventy mark I used to become complacent. My job is to win the frame and having achieved my objective, I tend to miss easy shots. A break of 70 or 147 can win you only one frame". He further added that "big breaks are essential from making a player attuned in a better frame of mind for the next frame. The satisfaction you drive in making a century break or a clearance, is immense. It is a triumph of mind over matter. But it is only academic" on being asked why we are not churning out world class players, he elaborated, "it is the system. When a youngster is trying his hand in this game he is confronted with one basic hurdle – how to negotiate with half ball, it is a simple thing but there is nobody to tell the youngster. He then fades away. In Cue Sports it is imperative to coach them young."

About the present lot of Snooker he evaluated that only Yasin and Alok understands the game. According to him they are the best Snooker players in the country. Tony Monterio was very dogged and later on O.B. Agarwal emerged as the finest Snooker player of the country. I am not saying that because he won the world title but you should see him playing. He had lively stance and silken smooth cueing. On his comeback trail Shyam Shroff evinced a desire to participate in the National in Bombay in 1998 but was denied a direct entry. He was asked to play in the qualifying rounds. I remember him saying "after winning seven national titles, I was even asked to start all over again". He not only qualified buy reached the semi-final that year.

About the future of this game in this country he contended, "The picture is quite dismal. No new talent seems to be emerging. You have mentioned Manan Chandra and Pankaj Advani but I have not seen them. Therefore, I cannot comment on them. There is nothing like match practice and now there is a paucity of tournaments. The Billiards and Snooker Federation does not seem to be knowing how to market this game".

We then proceeded for a photo session in the Billiards Room of NSCI Club, Mumbai, which was on the second floor. On reaching there we were told that the lift will be functioning after a few minutes. There I had a taste of Shyam Shroff's impulsiveness. He decided to use the stairs much against my wishes. He had the same immaculate stance of a panther. His eyes lit up on seeing the Snooker balls. Here I was watching the maestro for the last time in action. I photographed him in action. I photographed him in a magnificent Billiards Room and in the splendid lobby of NSCI, where I bade him good bye. He said, "I'll come tomorrow as races will be on". But Shyam almost lost the race of his life. He could never come. "I am not feeling well" his shrill voice on Telephone. Soon he was Snookered by God.

YASHBIR SHARMA

THE ROMANCE OF BEING

ARVIND SAVUR

Aligarh Muslim University organized the 1971 nationals which attracted cream of talent across India, to include Michael Ferreira, Satish Mohan, Shyam Shroff, Tony Monterio, Arvind Savur etc. Since Aligarh was very near to Delhi, H. S. Satara of Chelmsford Club had thrown the doors open for gladiators to perform, the kind of which Delhi had hitherto not seen before. Everyone gave a sterling show and the audience was in raptures through out the exhibition. One thing which caught the imagination of people was the hurricane speed which Arvind Savur used to impart towards his game. I tried to replicate his speed only to find the balls going helter- skelter on the table. There is one and only one Arvind Savur. According to me he is one of the finest snooker players this country has produced.

I saw him after a gap of seven years and found him even faster around the table. He was seen wearing rubber sole shoes so that he can run faster across the table. He possessed enormous weight and girth to be nick named as "Tornado Fats". Only one international player who could hold at candle in front of him was hurricane Alex Higgins.

Some of the famous players fell like nine pins before the might of burly Arvind Savur.

His finest moment came in 1979 Calcutta nationals when in final he led 5-0 against the 17 years world champion Jimmy White. The match was best of 11 frames and had to be abruptly stopped by B.S.F.I. because of T.V. crew came late. Arvind Savur was in

an irresistible form and had been stopped a hand shaking distance from an otherwise famous victory.

The T.V. crew arrived and so was Jimmy White in a new avtaar. He slowly started gathering pebbles and threw at the Indian Champion, teasing him all the way. He demolished him 6-5, winning six frames in a row.

This incidence aroused anger and turmoil which wrecked this huge frame. He directed his ire at B.S.F.I. which was understandable. After this fiasco he regained his composure and started hitting the balls of the yore. Then came the 1982 nationals at Madras where TV Gupta, in a titanic struggle got better of Arvind Savur. This apparently hurt the giant. It was a typical hare and tortoise race where you need not be a Sherlock Homes to know the results.

This had a physiological bearing on the mind of Tornado fats. Slowly, he became a shadow of his glorious past. His biggest contribution to Indian Cue Sports is how he trained and sharpens Pankaj Advani to become a force to reckon with in the green baize game. Pankaj was 12 years old boy, who came to Orchid House, the abode where Arvind Savur lives like a lord, to fire his first salvo on his personal billiards table. He was particularly fond of Jyotsna Savur's terrific cooking. She possessed around 5000 cookery books and the count is still on! I am glad to add one of my cookery book towards her bulging and impressing tally.

What Arvind Savur could not achieve in his life time, he is getting the satisfaction of seeing his ward getting in abundance. He is a bitter and forlorn man in the evening of his life. He feels that he did not get due recognition from federation and Government. As crow flies across the Orchid House, Arvind Savur, in a reminiscent mood may be still thinking on a elusive one frame from Jimmy White. He knows that frame might have changed the destiny of Arvind Savur and Indian Cue Sports. It was not to be.

YASHBIR SHARMA

Wizard of Cue Sports

Pankaj Advani

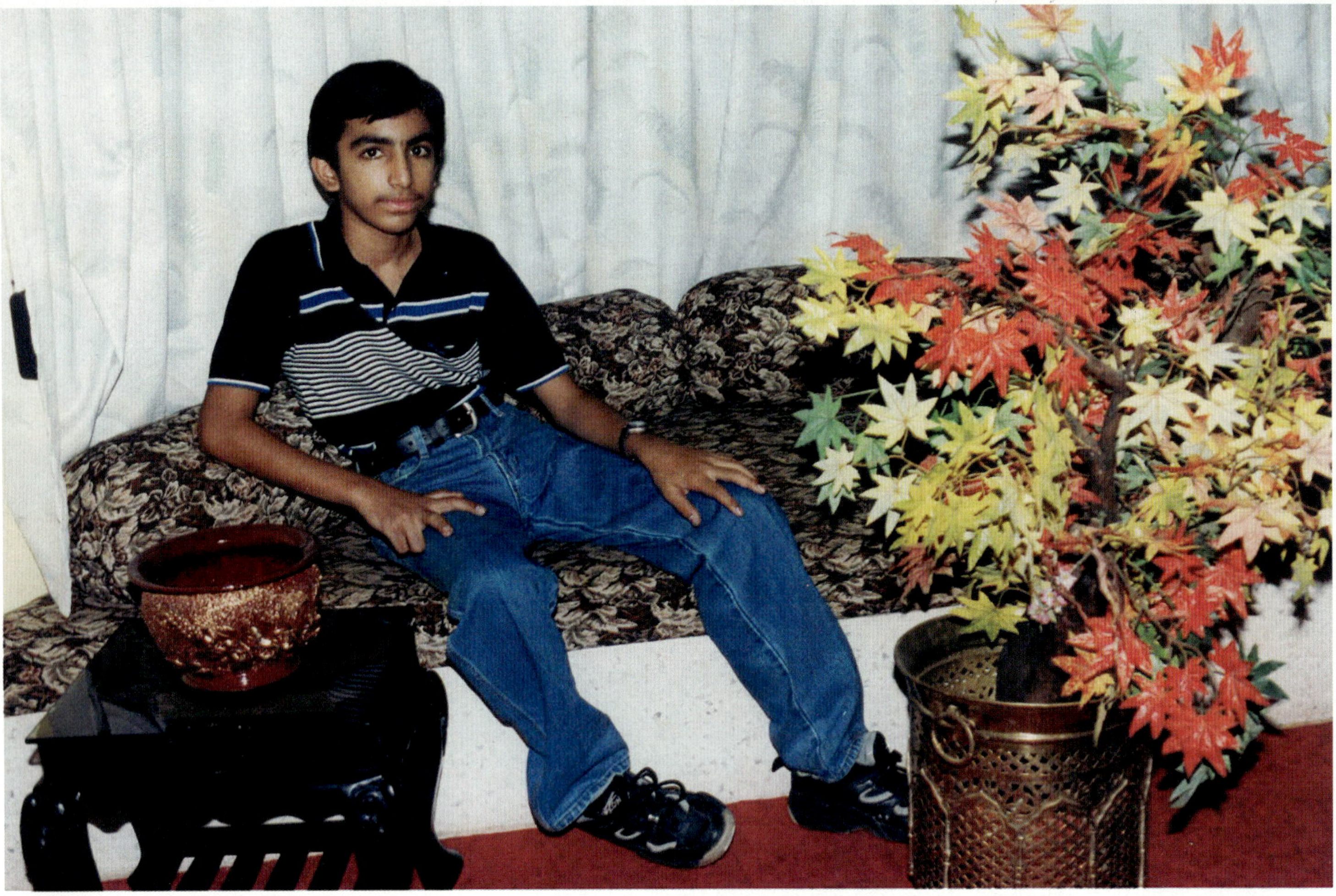

For them he is the wrestler who can floor anybody in a hand shaking distance. He is poised to become a world champion in Billiards but there is an impediment in his way. His propensity towards studies is a clear cut hindrance. He is in three minds: Snooker, Billiards and studies, in this order. He has to select only one if he has to make a niche in this world. At present, to me, it looks as if Billiards may triumph over the other two. India's coach and four times world champion concurred with me when he said in his characteristic style, "Pankaj has to select his priority between Snooker and Billiards. I hope it is Billiards".

It is not an easy decision. Pankaj while elaborating said, "I can certainly choose between Billiards and Snooker without much ado. But to choose between games and studies is sort of a predicament which I cannot answer right now. I have to consult my coach, mom and friends."It is certainly not as easy as it sounds. He can clearly see one bird in an open field and it is regulation catch. What he desires is to catch a few more in his hands. It does not sound plausible. There are several others who play these two games with aplomb. Ashok Shandilya, Devendra Joshi, Alok Kumar, Rafat Habib and Rupesh Shah, who have excelled time and again in the national and international championships. Geet Sethi sailed in two boats for year together. In fact he dazzled in Snooker briefly having executed a mammoth run of 147 at Guntur Nationals in 1987. Soon, wise counsel prevailed upon him and he stuck to one game, which paid rich dividends to him and his country. What a prolific career he has made for himself!

Pankaj can take a leaf out from Manan Chandra's book, who has shunned studies and Billiards from his repertoire. He has a

definite chief aim in Snooker. Like Pankaj, he too has a gift of the God. He wants to utilize the showering and blessings of the Almighty to the hilt. Anyway, why not Pankaj Advani should take this sagacious advice from his well-wishers!

There is one flaw in his cueing which surprisingly no one had noticed before or failed to correct. When playing a stun shot, he lunges forward, which in Saloon parlance is described as "Body Side"? But for a player knocking at the international circuit doors, it is a serious flaw.

I asked his mentor and coach, Arvind Savur and he replied, "When Pankaj started playing, he was so small that the height of the table was too much for him. He had to make an effort in order to reach on the top. This anomaly is the result of that eventually".

This is a serious defect. How can you move while executing a shot ? You have to remain straight. When I asked Michael Ferreira, he just shrugged his vast shoulders and said, "Yes, it is very much there. I have to correct it but not before a major tournament."

He played the game of his life against the Asian Champion Yasin Merchant, with a spectacular clearance in the decider at the Yashwant Club. He was tipped to win the finals but Devendra Joshi was too good for the youngster on that day. After the loss he was the least unruffled. He took the things in his stride. Incidentally, he had lost in two finals within a month. He was unperturbed and flashed a broad smile, 'You can't have your way every time." But with patience his time will come. Amen!

He was extremely popular in the Yashwant Club. People used to throng the Billiards room there, to see this young boy, destined to be a World Champion, in flesh and blood. When Joshi took an unassailable lead, the silence of the younger generation crowd was an indication on whose side they were.

He should see the World Billiards Trophy as clearly as a day light. At the moment, there is a cloud and haze enveloped around it. He should mentally set his mind towards his goal. He can get rid of all the encumbrances. Then and only then, we will have another World Billiards Champion in our midst. His coach should act like a priest and perform his sacerdotal duties. It is a bliss to acquire these winning traits. The biggest sinner in the world is a person who failed to convert his god given gift into a reality. We keenly await your decision Mr. Pankaj Advani!

Farah Khan, was one of the greatest woman champion in cue sports, who claimed the title four years in a row before going for greener pastures abroad. With this background she wrote the following letter in cue sports.

I did manage to get the June copy of CUE SPORTS and the article on Pankaj Advani caught my eye. I was pretty stunned to read the matter and pardon me if I sound rude but I thought it was pretty harsh on him. I have known him since the very first day he started playing at the KSBA and as I am sure, many in the circuit will vouch for his humility. He has achieved a considerable amount of success in a very short period of time and at a very young age. Considering the above, I personally feel he is anything but arrogant. Rather, he is an epitome of modesty for a kid of his age and for the amount he has achieved and I'm sure he will be a role model for many youngsters in the years to come.

After reading the article, I felt he deserved more credit and encouragement which any upcoming player expects from people who make a difference to the sport in the country, such as you.

I would strongly suggest that we, on behalf of the CUE SPORTS, get our facts right since they were wrongly interpreted in that particular article. I do not intend to criticize what you have written but in the interest of the future of this game in the country and internationally, we need to encourage this particular young boy since I have seen him mature into a perfect teenager with a great desire to attain glory for our country.

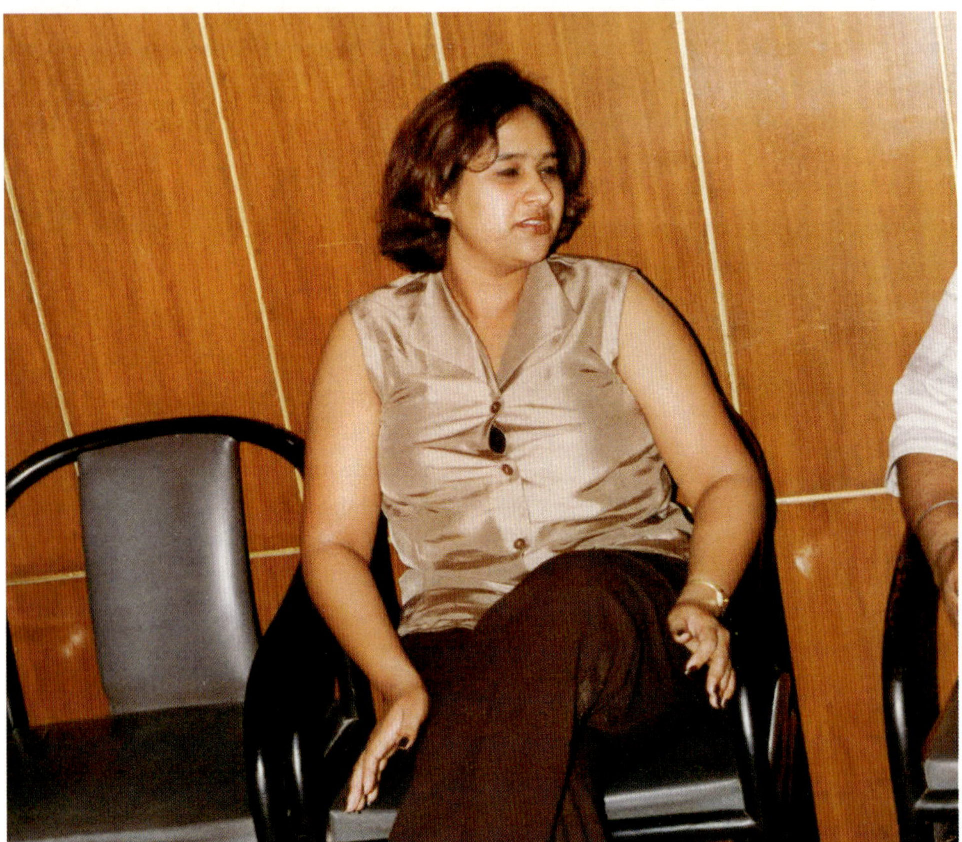

Another point I would like to make is that the Press in Karnataka have seen this little boy win several tournaments and has seen him rise to State No.3 in the seniors from nowhere which by any measure is an incredible feat; we do not see this in every State. There are a few exceptions and Pankaj is one of them. The Press does not hype him unnecessarily, he deserves it! It is their way of encouraging him.

I would like to bring to your notice that I am not being biased, merely comment on something that I read. I know this family and the way he has been brought up and he is truly a gem. And, Mr. Sharma, you can perhaps quote me some day in the future, that I am saying now, that Pankaj will be a World Champion sooner than we expect, and note, with this same humility and modesty.

Please do not take this in any other sense other than what is implying. No hard feelings.

I look forward to reading the next edition and I hope the magazine is getting a healthy response.

With best wishes,

Yours sincerely,

Sd/-

Farah Khan

I hope, trust and pray that Farah Khan's words about Pankaj Advani will become a gospel truth in the near future.

It will be a matter of great happiness if he attains the World Crown. However, his immediate task should be to prepare and win the under 21 World Snooker Championship on his home ground. I wish the boy all the very best.

Yashbir Sharma

To reach moon you don't require stairs, but a giant leap. Pankaj Advani has already landed there and he is eyeing for star at 29, he has achieved a cueist aspire for.

Pankaj Advani was born in Pune and came to Bangalore via Kuwait learnt the final points of the game from India's ace Arvind

Savour. He was barely 12 years old when he won the state junior Championship for everybody to look this boy in zest, wonder and awe. He is not child prodigies to bask in past performance as the later events proved it beyond doubt.

The next year he lifted the state Snooker championship and went on to claim the Indian Junior title three years in a row and recorded the resounding double in 2003. In a same year startled whole world by annexing IBSF world Snooker Championship. In 2005, Pankaj at last shed is milk teeth to become the first player to annex the world title in both formats of timed and points, and thus put the stamp on world billiards while he was still a teenager.

After that a plethora of world, Asian and National titles keeps on flowing kitty faster than you can wink. In 2006 he got an Asian Gold Medal, 2008 he repeated 2005 performance by claiming both timed and point format as well Asian Billiards Championship. In 2009 he put his stamp on Billiards professional titles and repeated the act of annexing Asian Billiards Championship. After that he won that championship before next two years as well. In fact, he won five national titles in a row, a World record. In 2012 he once again won the coveted world title. In 2014 he claimed world 6 - Red Snooker Championship and than record winning World titles in both billiards and Snooker. These world and Asian Titles are only for statistics. Pankaj is striving much more than – the love and affection of his countryman. The day is not very far when you need a calculator to record the achievements of a boy wonder from Bangalore. Hopefully, he will turn into a man by than!!

Pankaj Advani was sipping coffee in the lounge of Chelmsford club during RKG Snooker Championship in a relaxed atmosphere. I asked him as to how come he has relinquished the world professional circuit. Pankaj replied "in a professional circuit if you lose in a very 1st round then we have to sit ideal for about 2 weeks or so". Pankaj is a vegetarian, teetotaller and doesn't have even minor vises. Though he had a fair clip of success but apparently he was not getting any headway plus he was getting home sick. Pankaj further said that "Now I will concentrate on the national scene which hitherto neglected." The National scene will now start getting hectic and readily embrace the maestro. Now there will be a fight for the second spot!

He was on course of winning the RKG crown and was compiling a mammoth break of 134 when I was giving commentary for Doordarshan. The billiards room was rather small and my voice traveled to Pankaj ears when I uttered that he was playing with a break neck speed. Pankaj smiled and later on told me that he has heard that word several times in the past, when you used to describe my play in your articles. Pankaj defeated Kamal Chawla in the Final with consummate ease.

Pankaj was staying in hotel Janpath which is about 500 meters from the venue. The organizer made a faux pass in not providing him the vehicle. The world champion covered the distance with a cue in his hand without raising his eyebrows. He was on time to play his next match. The next day I came to know this incident from R.B. Ganesh, the chief referee of the championship. This is the hallmark of true world champion and great human being.

YASHBIR SHARMA

The Genius from Mumbai

Aditya Mehta

The 2003 S.Chand & Co Invitational Snooker Championship was the highest prize money tournament in India organized by Mr. Ravindra Kumar Gupta. It evoked great response from snooker fraternity to get selected in it was a great singular honour for any player. Out of 16 invited to play, 12 selected themselves. For the remaining, there was a great tussle which almost got settled on the eve of championship.

A tall, lanky and ultra slim young boy, with a suitcase and cue in hand, entered lobby of NSCI Delhi at the stroke of mid-night. He introduced me as Aditya Mehta from Mumbai. He expressed a fervent desire to play in the championship, with a firm voice. His expression was boorish and curt. I pondered over the issue for a while and expressed my inability with utmost reluctance. He stood transfixed for a while and left for the airport.

This was my biggest mistake which I rue even to this date. "I turned down one of the biggest snooker wizard in the history of India for a place in the last sixteen. Who knows that my refusal must have played a part in Aditya Mehta's ascendancy to the top?

He is an introvert, shy and reticent young man, who believes in putting extra hard work during practice. In fact, his ability to churn out big breaks is phenomenal, which stood him in good stead in future. His efforts bore fruits in 2011, he earned the scalp of celebrated Mathew Steven. His real time came in 2012 Asian Games Snooker championship, when in a tense and thrilling encounter he overcame Indian star Pankaj Advani by 7 frames to 5. This victory gave him personal satisfaction by annihilating the best in business. Aditya Mehta came alive for Indian fans.

After getting the Gold Medal in the world Games, he was in an irresistible form in 2013 India Open at Le-Meridien Hotel in New Delhi. Since this was the first ranking tournament in this country, he wanted to have his imprint on Indian Soil.

In the very first match he compiled a great run of 127 to tarnish the hopes of snooker star Peter Ebdon, eventually winning 4-3. After that tense match he had an easy outing against Hammad Miah 4-1 but ran into two Times World Champion Mark Williams. Before his all important match he was quietly sitting in a corner of a coffee shop, when brushed aside his fans wanted to open conversation with him. Thereafter the margin of his victory over Mark Williams even surprised him.

Then came a match which snooker fans of Delhi was eagerly waiting for. It was a clash between two biggest names in Indian Snooker- Pankaj Advani and Aditya Mehta. It was ding dong battle for supremacy in which Aditya Mehta scored a hairline victory against his traditional foe. This win gave him necessary impetus and fill up for a great future. He went passed Stephen Maguire 4-3. A laboured win considering he was leading 3-0 at one stage in the match and his victory was a foregone conclusion. He eventually won 4-3 to reach the final. A great excitement ensued in the finals which turnout to be damps quipped for the legion of his admirers. Beaten fair and square, he was beaten comprehensively by five frames to nil. Ding on that day was simply unstoppable.

Then came the moment - break of 147 which he compiled in Paul Hunter Classic in 2014. Snooker player waits for the entire life for a break of 147. You simply cannot make it even if you try hard, it comes accidently with a fair degree of luck. But to get to this coveted mark is the life time ambitious of snooker player. Ronnie O'Sullivan has reached this magical mark 500 times in practice and match play. Call it luck or pluck, choice is yours.

In May this year he had a dream run in RKG Snooker at Chennai. Big names of Indian Snooker stars started falling like ninepins. In the final where he met the talented star from Kolkata, Brijesh Damani, he raced to an invincible lead of 5-0 and was leading 40 points with two red left on the table. He missed not too difficult pink in the centre. He clenched his fist, slightly tapped his cue and looked heaven wards. Such kind of killer instinct is rarely seen in the Indian Cue Sports players. Brijesh Damani very sportingly shook hands with him and Aditya Mehta lifted RKG Trophy.

Someone asked me – who after Pankaj and Aditya. The silence was deafening.

YASHBIR SHARMA

Tournament Records

2014 World Games - Gold Medal

2013 Indian Open - Runner-Up

2012 Asian Snooker Championship - Winner

2012 Bombay Gymkhana All India Snooker Tournament - Semi Finalist

2012 Justice Sivasubramaniam Memorial All India Snooker Tournament - Winner

2012 79th Indian National Snooker Championship - Winner

2011 78th Indian National Snooker Championship - Winner

2011 Asian Snooker Championship, Indore (India) - Runner-Up

2011 CCI Invitational Snooker Tournament - Quarter Finalist

2011 Shyam Shroff Memorial - Khar Gymkhana Invitational Snooker Tournament - Winner

2010 Guangzhou Asian Games (Snooker Individual) - Bronze Medal

2010 Guangzhou Asian Games (Snooker Team) - Silver Medal (Partners - Yasin Merchant, Brijesh Damani)

2010 77th Indian National Snooker Championship - Rank 4

2009 VIP MATRIX All India Invitation Snooker Championship, Chennai - Winner

2009 IBSF World Snooker (Men) Championship - Top 32

2009 3rd Indoor Asian Games Snooker Team - Gold Medal (Partners Manan Chandra & Brijesh Damani)

2009 76th Indian National Snooker Championship - Rank 7

2009 Shyam Shroff Memorial - Khar Gymkhana Invitational Snooker Tournament - Runner-Up

2009 Otters Club Amateur 9 Ball Pool Championship 2009 - Round 16

2008 World Pro Snooker - 2009 Honghe China Open - Round 3

2009 Nahar Group-MIG Club Invitation Snooker Championship - Winner

2008 World Pro Snooker - 2008 Maplin UK Championship - Round 1

2008 75th Indian National Snooker Championship - Rank 6

2008 75th Indian National Billiards Champion - Top 16

2008 World Pro Snooker - 2008 Royal London Watches Grand Prix - Round 3

2008 World Pro Snooker - 2008 Shanghai Masters Trophy - Round 1

2008 World Pro Snooker - 2008 Northern Ireland Trophy - Round 1

2008 SangSom 6-Red International Snooker Championship - Pre-Quarter Finalist (Top-16)

2008 3rd PCL-Manisha Invitation Snooker Championship - Semi Finalist

2008 24th Asian Snooker Championship - Runner-up

2008 Fifth R.K. Gupta Memorial - Alexander Club (Meerut) Billiards Tournament - Semi Finalist

2008 Fifth R.K. Gupta Memorial - Alexander Club (Meerut) Snooker Tournament - Runner-Up

2008 Shyam Shroff Memorial - Khar Gymkhana Snooker Tournament - Runner-Up

2008 Yasin Merchant Classic Doubles Snooker Tournament - Participated (Partner :: Geet Sethi)

2007 74th Indian National Snooker Championship - Runner Up

2007 74th Indian National Billiards Champion - Top 16

2006 Doha Asian Games (Snooker Team) - Bronze Medal (Partners Yasin Merchant, Rupesh Shah)

2006 Indian National U-21 Snooker Championship - Winner

2006 Quarter Finalist in Asian U-21 Snooker Championship

2005 Quarter Finalist in Asian U-21 Snooker Championship

2004 Quarter Finalist in World U-21 Snooker Championship

2004 Bronze Medal in Asian U-21 Snooker Championship

Laughter, Merriments & Tragedy

(O.B. Agarwal)

1982 Nationals at Bankipur Club, Patna to the lusty cheers from the crowd outside club when the convoy three rikshaw arrived there. Each was occupied by Michael Ferreira, Arvind Savur and myself. In Patna rickshaw's are so compact that it is difficult for two mortal men to sit comfortably. I decided to get down at least 100 yard from entrance in order to escape butt of jokes from Billiards player.

Two heavyweight champions were expected in Billiards and Snooker respectively. Arvind Savur was supposed to crush everybody on the floor with his sheer weight he was playing great snooker when somebody gave him terrific jolt. He was decimated by swashbuckling O.B Agarwal in the Final. It was sunset to someone and sunrise for the inevitable.

We were strolling on street of Patna when O.B. Agarwal brush aside a young man who at once took out a pistol from his hip pocket. A panic ensued among those present. We were almost terrified to say anything. But It was to the credit of Arvind Savur that he separated the two gentlemen then someone told the trigger happy man that he was just been crowned Snooker National Champion and is a sports man. After that he relented, put the gun back in his hip pocket and kept muttering to himself "Yeh Snooker kya game hota hai" and left reluctantly.

In 1994 national O.B. Agarwal got wild card entry in snooker. During a semi-finals a celebration with crackers and bombs were going on outside the playing arena when suddenly a loud noise came. O.B. Agawal was lying supine on the floor, we were so petrified that he has been shot, we raced towards him and O.B. Agarwal immediately got up smiling. It was prank and spectator were laughing. After that he went on to win the Finals and got and entry in the Dublin for the World Championship.

There was a meeting headed by C. Kapoor of secretary of BSFI to take stern action against O.B. Agarwal. Matthew Mundadan pleaded with everyone that he must let off with stern warning. After that reprieve O.B. Agarwal was a rejuvenated man. He created history when he went on to win World Championship for his country. He was given a rousing welcome at Santacruz Airport by the officials of Maharashtra Snooker and Billiard Association.

Unfortunately A brilliant career was cut short due to cancer. I went to see him at his residence in Bandra alongwith several reporters. He was enable to speak and was replying the query of us with a pencil and a pen. Someone asked him in a feeble voice "Sir, will you be Snooker player in your next birth" he gave a sheepish smile and said " its very difficult as you need lots of practice" after that he gestured everybody to leave the room. In the end he was snookered behind cancer.

YASHBIR SHARMA

The Day Geet Sethi Made 147

Winter was at its zenith, so was Geet Sethi in Billiards. He scaled the summit in 1985 by beating veteran Bob Marshall at Taj Palace, Delhi. I along with Tarun Chandra and the mastro went to another Billiard player K.D. Singh's shop at Jorbagh. Allow me to dwell about Tarun, who is the father of modern Snooker star Manan Chandra. Tarun shot into prominence when he stunned O.B. Agrawal 4-0 at Calcutta Nationals in 1979.

K.D. Singh very generously donated 3 copies of an autobiography by world professional Snooker champion Steve Davis to us. I invited them for lunch at Taj Mansingh, which was just a mile away from Jorbagh.

At the table I and Tarun were attacking the Chinese delicacies while Geet Sethi was immersed in the book. He was particularly glaring at that chapter where the writer had described his escapades with several 147. How can any one pot 15 reds, 15 blacks, yellow, green, brown, blue, pink and black, said Geet, with wide eyes in bewilderment. We paid scant respect to his uttering and continued to do justice to the delectable fare dished out. We all know Geet is a Spartan eater but he ate very little on that day. We bade him goodbye at the airport as he was going to Guntour Nationals.

He played his first Snooker fixture against Latif Bux from Kerala, made him a pedestrian and made a resounding 147 in January 1988. He potted 15 reds, 15 blacks, yellow, green, brown, blue, pink and black. This is indomitable Geet Sethi for you.

YASHBIR SHARMA

THE TEMPERAMENTAL GENIUS

He is moody, whimsical and at the same time a temperamental genius. His panther like stance reminds me of Satish Mohan one of the all-time greats, who toyed with the Billiards balls in the past. He had the same kind of frail physique, hawk like eyes and casual approach to the table. He got fame and adulation at a relatively young age. His brush with billiards and Snooker started in 1988 and within couple of years he won the Ahmedabad Junior titles in both the events. He grabbed the senior titles in no time. His name is Sonic Multani, the pride and joy of Gujarat.

He shot into international fame in an international tournament where world's top professional Snooker players were in attendance. Amongst them was a fellow called Stephen Hendry, the greatest cueist of his time. Indian stars Yasin Merchant and Alok Kumar declined to take part due to fracas with the authorities which paved way for Sonic Multani. As luck would have it, he was pitted against the legendary Stephen Hendry. It is the story of David and Goliath. This was in the autumn of 1991.

There were not many spectators for this match and those few who had gathered came only to watch the World No.1. But they were in for a surprise. When David started climbing the mountain, slowly, steadily and surely, the atmosphere became electric and tense.

Sonic Multani was leading by 22 points in the decider having potted the last red was poised for the pink which was slightly difficult but not impossible. He had a sliced cut in the center. There were many things going in youngster's mind that he was about to knock out the world champion and was heading for international accolades.

He paused for a fraction of second and went for the elusive pink which could have possibly given him the frame and the match. The ball wobbled for a couple of times and stood there much to the chagrin of the audience which by that time started swelling in numbers seeing that epic battle. Every heart missed a bit and were eyeing the pink ruefully.

Stephen Hendry had no intentions to give a second chance to his adversary and made a spectacular clearance. He immediately embraced the young Indian.

I was covering the event for Hindustan Times when Steve Davis came rushing to the press room and was clearly gasping for breath. I asked him instantly, "What do you think of Sonic Multani?" He replied without batting an eyelid, "He is Super Sonic". That tag struck to him and was pasted on his name forever. Even after 18 years of hibernation, he is still called Super Sonic.

YASHBIR SHARMA

The crusader who has not called it a day as yet

Amir Ali Merchant always wanted his son to be an accomplished snooker player at the same time to excel in his studies. The senior Merchant was staying with me in Hotel Satkar during 1982 Patna Nationals when he was raving about his son's prowess in cue sports. Contrary to popular public opinion Yasin Merchant was initially a billiards player who uses to dabble in snooker occasionally. Wiser counsel prevailed on him to concentrate only in snooker. The transformation helped him to blossom all time great players of this game in the country.

In 1989 Asian Snooker Championship New Delhi, press billed Geet Sethi much higher than him. The rueful rabbit hogged the limelight and he went on to claim the Asian title trouncing Udan Khemukh in the finals. Geet Sethi was summarily beaten in the semis. That was Yasin's finest hour and he basks in the glory of accolades and honour, the Delhi press bestowed on him. He had a shy on Asian Snooker titles in 1991 but unfortunately lost narrowly in the finals.

He got the coveted national snooker in the same year but he took him 9 years to regain it again in 2000 and subsequently in 2001. His finest moment came in 2002 Busan Asian Game when he won gold medal with Rafat Habib as his partner. He tried his hand in the world professional snooker circuit and attained ranking as high as 65.

In Yasin Merchant's case statistics do tell a lie. He was the most feared opponent during his hey days, when he could gulp any player. He retired from the game when still alive and kicking too. His sudden retirement stunned the snooker scene but his opponents heaved, sigh of relief.

In Shyam Shroff memorial snooker tournament in 2002 he fought grueling battle of attrition and wits with Alok Kumar at the stroke of mid-night, when his mother was fighting the battle of life in ICU. Though he lost in the decider but won hearts of legion of his admirers in his hour of adversity and turmoil.

He is playing a crucial role in the current RKG Snooker Tournament with his acumen foresightedness about the welfare of fellow snooker players. He looks younger than his age of around 50. He is so immaculately dressed up most of the times that it looks that he has come straight from dry cleaners shop.

YASHBIR SHARMA

MARCO FU

Marco Fu Ka-chun is a professional snooker player from Hong Kong. He is best known for winning the 2007 Grand Prix, beating Ronnie O'Sullivan in the final, and for being runner-up in the 2008 UK Championship and the 2011 Masters. He also won the 2013 Australian Goldfields Open and was runner-up in the German Masters and 2013 International Championship. In addition, Fu reached the semi-finals of the 2006 World Championship, equaling the best result for an Asian player in the World Championship along with Ding Junhui and James Wattana. Fu's career high world ranking is sixth, achieved in 2013. As a prolific break-builder, Fu has compiled more than 300 century breaks in professional competition. He currently resides in Happy Valley.

Fu started playing snooker at the age of nine, but did not start playing regularly until he was 15. Fu was born in Hong Kong and emigrated to Vancouver, Canada with his parents at the age of 12. After his high school graduation at age 18, Hong Kong Billiard Sports Control Council Co. Ltd President Joseph Lo invited him to return to Hong Kong to begin his career as a professional snooker player. Before turning professional, Fu won the World Amateur and World Under-21 Championships, both in 1997.

In 1998, the year he turned professional, Fu reached the final of the Grand Prix, beating Ronnie O'Sullivan (5–2) and then Peter Ebdon (5–3) in the process. An in-form Stephen Lee proved too strong for Fu in the final, defeating him 9–2, but Fu nevertheless rose dramatically through the rankings, reaching number 15 in the world for the 2000/01 season. When he first turned professional, he was ranked 377th in the world. During the rest of the 1998/99 season, Fu qualified for four more ranking tournaments, including the World Championship, winning four qualifying matches before losing to James Wattana 8–10 in the first round of the main draw.

He was voted WPBSA Newcomer of the Year and WSA Young Player of the Year in 1999. Tipped by many pundits as a potential champion of the game, Fu's subsequent performance was disappointing, and he slid back down the rankings.

In the 1999/2000 season, with Fu now ranked 35 in the world, he received automatic entry into the main draw of most of the ranking tournaments. Although he failed to repeat the success of reaching the final of the Grand Prix, he made a credible run to the quarter finals before losing to Allister Carter. Other achievements of note include reaching semi finals of the Malta Grand Prix and the Scottish Open.

In the 2000/2001 season Fu was ranked 15th in the world, his first appearance in the top 16. However, a succession of defeats in the last 16, and a first round defeat in the World Championship to Chris Small, saw him fall out of the top 16 for next season. In the 2001/02 season Fu's his best result was a last 16 appearance at the LG Cup. He failed to qualify for three ranking events, including the World Championship, and, as a result, his ranking fell to 27 for the following season, his lowest in two seasons.

The 2002/2003 season brought better luck for Fu, although prior to the Welsh Open his best result was reaching the third round of the UK Championship in December

2002, where he was defeated 9–7 by Ronnie O'Sullivan. However, at the Welsh Open in February 2003, he produced a run to the semi finals. Fu whitewashed Stephen Lee 5–0 in the second round and beat Ronnie O'Sullivan 5–3 in the quarter-finals, before losing his semi-final 6–4 to Stephen Hendry, who went on to win the title.

Going into the 2003 World Championship three months later, after first round losses at the European and Scottish Open suggested he would not go far in the tournament, particularly as his first round opponent was world No. 1 and runaway favourite Ronnie O'Sullivan. Fu reached the first of his two World Championship quarter-finals to date. In what Snooker Scene magazine described as "one of the greatest upsets in the history of the game", the unseeded 25-year-old overcame the odds to defeat O'Sullivan in their first round clash. Fu dominated this match from the outset, opening up a 6–3 overnight lead; and although O'Sullivan made four centuries (including a maximum 147 break), Fu never looked to be in trouble and won 10–6. Fu subsequently eliminated Alan McManus 13–7 in the second round before losing 7–13 to Stephen Lee in his quarter-final match.

In 2003, Fu also won his first title since turning professional in the invitational Premier League, beating Mark Williams 9–5 in the final in Sunderland. This was the first time the title went outside of the British Isles.

Fu is a prolific break-builder. He is the tenth player in history to have produced more than 300 competitive centuries and is currently ranked as No. 6 in the all time centuries list. He achieved his highest break of 147 at both the 2000 Scottish Masters together with 2012 World Open qualifying stage. Fu once held the record for the longest frame in the history of televised snooker. The record of 77 minutes held with Mark Selby was played out during the decisive final frame during the four quarter-final match at the 2007 UK Championship held in Telford, England. Fu eventually lost the match 7–9. However, the record was then broken by Shaun Murphy and Dave Harold in a match at the China Open later in the same season. The new record is 93 minutes. Since his initial breakthrough in 1998, Fu has not won the titles his talent deserves because he has struggled with his technique for large periods of his career.

Non-ranking wins: (4 titles)

- Premier League Snooker – 2003
- World Champions/Asia Stars Challenge – 2004
- Thailand Masters – 2007
- Championship League – 2010

Amateur wins

- IBSF World Under-21 Championship – 1997
- IBSF World Amateur Championship – 1997

They also made us Proud in the realms of Cue Sports

(SNOOKER)

Ashok Shandilya

Another player who missed the world title in 1990 World Championship in Bangalore having led in three of the four sessions. Before he was piped to the post

by Manoj Kothari. Though he won the World Billiard title in 50 up format, he could not have a crack at the time format in future. He is also a great exponent of snooker and pool, having won a couple of national titles.

His conduct in organizing Railway Tournament is exemplary. I have seen Ashok Shandilya and Ajay Rustogi carrying the billiard slate perched on their shoulders from a truck. After all the preparations, he successfully don the mettle of a player, representing Western Railway. I could never imagine that railway national could be that interesting. There is always a fierce fight amongst player to attain supremacy in the team event. The fight is too realistic to believe. In all he begged three national titles in billiards. Recently he is busy on a coaching assignment in Indonesia.

Chitra Magimairaj

Chitra Magimairaj is born on 7th April 1973 in Bangalore. She is an Indian professional player of snooker, English billiards, and pool. Magimairaj was educated

at St. Anne's Girls High School, and graduated from Teresian Collage, Mysore. She started playing cricket and field hockey at a young age.

She is a two-time World Ladies Billiards and Snooker Association World Champion (2006, 2007), a two-time national pool champion, and more recently the World Women's Senior Snooker Championship (2014)

She is the First Indian woman cueist to qualify to participate in two Asian Games and three Asian Indoor Games. First Indian woman cueist to win a medal in Asian Games and Asian Indoor Games. First Indian woman to have won two World Billiards Champion (women's division) titles (2006 and 2007). First Indian to win an Australian Open Women's Snooker Championship (2008) . First Indian woman to win a medal in the IBSF World Snooker Championships (Team & Individual, women's division) in the same year.

Kamal Chawla

A prodigy from Bhopal, Madhya Pradesh, Kamal Chawla is born on 22nd July'1979. He won 2014 Asian Team Snooker Championship – Gold, 2011 H.K. Jafri All India Open 6Red Snooker – Winner, 2009 Shyam Shroff Memorial - Khar Gymkhana Invitational Snooker Tournament – Winner 2008 John W. Roberts Invitation Open Snooker Tournament - Winner 2007 Mohali Club 9Ball Open Pool Champion 2006 Islam Gymkhana All India 9Ball Pool Champion 2006 BHEL All India Open Snooker Champion- 2006 PCL Manisha All India Open Snooker Champion 2003 Indian # 8 in National Snooker Championship- 2002 Indian # 4 in National U-21 Billiards Championship- Highest Break Prize in National Snooker Championship 2006 in his illustrious career.

Mohammed Faisal Khan

He was born on 6th October'1985 in Mumbai/New Delhi.In 2014.He won Asian Team Snooker Championship – Gold, 2009 Islam Gymkhana All India Open 9Ball

Pool Championship – Winner, 2008 Inter-Railway Cue Sports Championship (9Ball Pool) – Winner, 2008 3rd PCL-Manisha Invitation Snooker Championship – Winner. 2005 Delhi State Sr. Snooker Championship - Winner- 2005 Delhi State Jr. Snooker Championship - Winner- 2004 Delhi State Jr. Snooker Championship – Winner.

He also played Cricket League Matches for DDCA.

Lucky Vatnani

Lucky Vatnani is born on 23 December 1985. He is an Indian former professional snooker player. He is from Hyderabad, India,[1] but was based in Sheffield, England during his snooker career.

Vatnani, a graduate from Sheffield Hallam University in Business Administration, showed promise in his amateur career, with a 6–5 loss to Pankaj Advani in 2010 Indian Championship, as well as a run to the last 16 of the IBSF World Snooker Championship in 2009 and winning the gold medal in the British University Snooker Championships during the same year.

In 2011, he won a place on the World Snooker Tour for the 2011/2012 season. However, he missed several events due to visa issues and would struggle and only won two matches, both in the qualifying stages of the Welsh Open and with three consecutive defeats to Adam Duffy in the first round of the World Open, China Open and World Snooker Championship ensured

he was unable to reach the top 64 and therefore dropped of the tour at the end of the season.

Vatnani competed as an amateur in the preliminary rounds of the 2013 World Snooker Championship, but lost 5–3 to Paul Wykes. He also attempted the regain his place on the tour via the Q School in 2012, 2013 and 2014, but was unsuccessful on each occasion.

Judy Walia

Leading the women's snooker brigade in Karnataka, Judy Walia has bagged the state women's snooker title for a record of 11 times. Known for her fluent strokes, she became India's first women's snooker champion when she won the crown in 1989.

She won her second national title in 1997.

Judy Walia is 'married' to snooker. The cue sport caught her fancy fifteen years ago and even now she continues to fall in love with it every time she sees the green baize.

Arantxa Sanchis

Arantxa Sanchis is an Indian female professional Billiards and Snooker player. She won the Gold medal in the Women's Team event at the inaugural IBSF World 6-Red Snooker and Team Snooker Championship in Carlow, Ireland on 6 Oct, 2013.It was a historic first Gold Medal for Indian Women's Snooker at a World Championship. Prior to this she has won ten National and two State Maharashtra State titles. She has created history and a record by winning four titles at single Nationals (Indore 2008). No Indian male or female cueist has accomplished this feat. She won the National Senior Women's Billiards title in 2012 and in 2015 and the National Six Red Snooker titles in the year 2012.

At 17 years of age she represented India at the World under 21 Snooker Championship 2007 held at Goa and was a Semi- Finalist. She also represented India at the WPBSA World Billiards Championship 2012 at Leeds, UK, IBSF World Snooker Championship, Bulgaria,Nov 2012,IBSF World Snooker Championship 2013 at Daugavpils Latvia,IBSF World Team Snooker and Six Red Snooker Championship 2013 at Carlow, Ireland, IBSF World Team Snooker and Six Red Snooker Championship 2014 at Sharm El Sheikh, Egypt,IBSF World Snooker Championship 2014 at Bangalore, India.

The balls range from 2.25 inches (57.15 mm) in diameter to 2.375 inches (60.33 mm) in diameter. Under theWPA/BCA (see below) equipment specifications, the weight may be from 5.5 to 6 oz. (156–170 g) with a diameter of 2.25 in. (57.15 mm), plus or minus 0.005 in. (0.127 mm). Modern coin-operated pool tables generally use one of three methods to distinguish and return the cue ball to the front of the table while the numbered balls return to an inaccessible receptacle until paid for again: the cue ball is larger and heavier than the other balls, or denser and heavier, or has a magnetic core.

Modern cue sticks are generally 58.5 inches (148.6 cm) long for pool while cues prior to 1980 were designed for straight pool and had an average length of 57.5 inches (146.1 cm). By comparison, carom billiards cues are generally shorter with larger tips, and snooker cues longer with smaller tips.

EIGHT-BALL

In the United States, the most commonly played game is eight-ball. The goal of eight-ball, which is played with a full rack of fifteen balls and the cue ball, is to claim a suit (commonly stripes or solids in the US, and reds or yellows in the UK), pocket all of them, then legally pocket the 8 ball, while denying one's opponent opportunities to do the same with their suit, and without sinking the 8 ball early by accident. In the United Kingdom

the game is commonly played in pubs, and it is competitively played in leagues on both sides of the Atlantic. The most prestigious tournaments including the World Open are sponsored and sanctioned by the International Pool Tour. Rules vary widely from place to place (and between continents to such an extent that British-style eight-ball pool/blackball is properly regarded as a separate game in its own right). Pool halls in North America are increasingly settling upon the World Pool-Billiard Association International Standardised Rules. But tavern eight-ball (also known as "bar pool"), typically played on smaller, coin-operated tables and in a "winner keeps the table" manner, can differ significantly even between two venues in the same city. The growth of local, regional and national amateur leagues may alleviate this confusion.

NINE-BALL

Nine-ball uses only the 1 through 9 balls and cue ball. It is a rotation game: The player at the table must make legal contact with the lowest numbered ball on the table or a foul is called. The game is won by legally pocketing the nine ball. Nine-ball is the predominant professional game, though as of 2006–2008 there have been some suggestions that this may change, in favor of ten-ball. There are many local and regional tours and tournaments that are contested with nine-ball. The World Pool-Billiard

Paul Newman

Association (WPA) and its American affiliate, the Billiard Congress of America (BCA), publish the World Standardized Rules. The European professional circuit has instituted rules changes to make it more difficult to achieve a legal break shot.

The largest nine-ball tournaments are the independent U.S. Open Nine-ball Championship and the WPA World Nine-ball Championship for men and women. Male professionals have a rather fragmented schedule of professional nine-ball tournaments. The United States Professional Pool Players Association (UPA) has been the most dominant association of the 1990s and 2000s. A hotly contested event is the annual Mosconi Cup, which pits invitational European and U.S. teams against each other in one-on-one and scotch doubles nine-ball matches over a period of several days. The Mosconi Cup games are played under the more stringent European rules, as of 2007.

THREE-BALL

A variant using only three balls, generally played such that the player at turn continues shooting until all the balls are pocketed, and the player to do so in the fewest shots wins. The game can be played by two or more players. Dispenses with some fouls common to both nine- and eight-ball.

ONE-POCKET

One-pocket is a strategic game for two players. Each player is assigned one of the corner pockets on the table. This is the only pocket into which he can legally pocket balls. The first player to pocket the majority of the balls (8) in his pocket wins the game. The game requires far more defensive strategy than offensive strategy, much unlike eight-ball, nine-ball, or straight pool. Most times, accomplished players choose to position balls near their pocket instead of trying to actually pocket them. This allows them to control the game by forcing their opponent to be on defense instead of taking a low percentage shot that could result in a loss of game. These low percentage shots are known as "flyers" by one-pocket aficionados.

BANK POOL

Bank pool has been gaining popularity in recent years. Bank pool can be played with a full rack (can be a long game), but is more typically played with nine balls (frequently called "nine-ball bank"). The balls are racked in nine-ball formation, but in no particular order. The object of the game is simple: to be the first player to bank five balls in any order (eight balls when played with a full rack). Penalties and fouls are similar to one pocket in that the player committing the foul must spot a ball for each foul. This must be done before the incoming player shoots.

CUTTHROAT

Cutthroat is best played with 3 or more players. Cutthroat (also known as Elimination) is a popular game in social situations, rather than for serious competitive play. The object of the game is to be the last player with at least one ball still on the table. The player with a ball(s) still on the table, when all the other groups' balls are legally pocketed, wins the game.

Famous Po

ol Players

EFREN REYES

World's best Pool Player

Efren Reyes, fifty, was born in poverty, the fifth of nine children, in a dusty little town in the Philippines without electricity or running water. When he was five, his parents sent him to live with his uncle, who owned a pool hall in Manila. Efren cleaned up the pool hall and watched. He was fascinated by the way the players made the balls move around the table and fall into pockets—and by the way money changed hands after a game.

At night he slept on a pool table and dreamed of combinations. He had mastered the game in his head before he finally picked up a pool cue, at the age of eight. He stood on a pile of Coke crates to shoot, two hours in the morning and two hours at night. At nine he played his first money game, and at twelve he won $100; he sent $90 home to his family. Soon he was the best pool shooter in Manila. His friends would wait for him in the pool hall after school, hand him his cue when he walked in the door, and back him in gambling games. He was the best pool shooter in the Philippines when he quit school, at fifteen. By the time he was in his twenties, no one in the Philippines would play him any longer, so he toured Asia. He wrote down in a notebook the names of the best pool shooters in the world, and proceeded to beat them one by one. He became a legend. People who had seen him play recounted the impossible shots he had made. They called him a genius, the greatest pool shooter who had ever lived. Even people who had never seen him play, including many in the United States, soon heard the legend of Efren Reyes, "the Magician."

Gambling from a young age, Reyes played three cushion billiards in the 1960s and 1970s. After establishing himself as a winner, he was discovered by promoters. This gave him the opportunity to compete in big time tournaments.

During the 1980s, when Reyes was considered a top-class player in his homeland but not yet internationally recognized, he

went to the U.S. tohustle. Popular legend claims that Reyes earned US$80,000 in a week; this feat made him a folk hero back home.

Reyes began winning a number of tournaments in the U.S., Europe and parts of Asia. Thus, he started to gain attention and recognition worldwide. At the start of his career, he used aliases to hide his identity so he would be allowed to compete. By the mid-1990s, he had become one of the elite players of the Philippines, alongside Jose Parica and Francisco Bustamante.

Reyes' fame began when he won the US Open Nine Ball Championship in 1994 by defeating Nick Varner in the finals. He was the first non-American to win the event.

Two years later, Efren Reyes and Earl Strickland were chosen to face each other in an event called the Color of Money, named after the movie. The event was a three-day race-to-120 challenge match of 9-ball. It was held in Hong Kong, with a winner-take-all prize of US$100,000. Reyes won the match 120-117. This was the largest single-winning purse in a pool event.

Although Strickland was the first to win the WPA World Nine-ball Championship, Reyes, in 1999, became the first to win while it was broadcast on television. This tournament was not recognized at the time by the WPA, but Reyes was later retrospectively acknowledged as the winner of one of two world championships held in 1999. Nick Varner won the "official" world title. The two tournaments were merged for the following year, with both men listed as the champion for 1999. At the time, the Matchroom Sport-organised event in Cardiff, Wales, was called the World Professional Pool Championship (despite the

entry of many non-professional players).

Efren Reyes posing with fan after he won a historic US$200,000 at the 2005 IPT King of the Hill Shootout.

In 2001, Reyes won the International Billiard Tournament. The event was held in Tokyo, with over 700 players and a total purse of ¥100M ($850K). Reyes dominated the event and beat Niels Feijen in the finals 15-7 and earned the ¥20M ($170K) first prize. At the time, this was the biggest first prize in a pool tournament.

In 2002 he won the $50K winner-take-all International Challenge of Champions, defeating Mika Immonen in a deciding rack after both players split sets.

Near the end of 2004, Reyes beat Marlon Manalo to become the first-ever WPA World Eight Ball Champion. With the win, he became the first player in WPA history to win world championships in two different disciplines.

In December 2005, Reyes won the IPT King of the Hill 8-Ball Shootout. Reyes won a record-breaking $200K for first place by beating fellow Hall of Fame member Mike "the Mouth" Sigel two sets to none (8-0 and 8-5).

In 2006, Reyes and Francisco Bustamante represented their country as Team Philippines in the inaugural World Cup of Pool. They defeated Team USA, Earl Strickland and Rodney Morris, to capture the title.

That same year, Reyes won the IPT World Open Eight-ball Championship over Rodney Morris 8-6. He earned $500K which was the largest prize money tournament in the history of pocket billiards. Unfortunately, due to IPT's financial problems, he has not been able to claim much of this money as of 2007.

In 2009, the Filipino tandem of Efren Reyes and Francisco Bustamante beat the German pair of Ralf Souquet and Thorsten Hohmann by a grueling 11-9 score to take their second championship title. This, together with the semifinal finish of the other Filipino team of Ronato Alcano and Dennis Orcollo, was the best performance by a host nation in the tournament's history.

In 2010, Reyes clinched his fifth title in the 12th annual Derby City Classic as the overall champion, making him the most successful player in the tournament's history.

He has topped the AZ Billiards Money List five times: in 2001, 2002, 2004, 2005 and 2006. In 2006, he set a record by earning $646K in a single year.

Numerous fellow professional players have credited Reyes with being the greatest living player in the world. During ESPN television commentary on a semi-finals match between Reyes and Mika Immonen at the 2000 Billiard Congress of America Open 9-Ball Championship, veteran professional Billy Incardona stated that Reyes was "indisputably the best player in the world—especially when you consider all games—he can play any game as well as anyone, maybe better than anyone.... In my opinion we're watching probably the greatest player in my lifetime and I've been watching pool for the better part of forty years."

In 1995 Billiards Digest Magazine named Reyes the Player of the Year. The following year, when Reyes was ranked number one on the U.S.'s Pro Billiards Tour, the June 1996 issue of the magazine featured a poll of "billiard cognoscenti"—pro players, billiards writers, industry insiders and the like—to pick the best in billiards in various categories. Billiards' own elite named Reyes the best one-pocket player of all time. The magazine wrote, "While a bevy of one-pocket geniuses abound, Efren Reyes, whose prowess in one-pocket is sometimes obscured by his 9-ball stardom, was the popular pick. Is there anything Bata can't do?"

In 2003, he became the first Asian to be inducted into the Billiard Congress of America's Hall of Fame.

Reyes was appointed Philippine Sports Ambassador of the 2005 South East Asian Games alongside some of the Philippines' greatest athletes (Allan Caidic, Rafael Nepomuceno) to promote the event throughout the country.

Titles and Achievements

- 2014 MP Cup Gensan International Open 10-Ball
- 2014 Smokin' Aces One-Pocket Shootout
- 2014 Derby City Classic One-Pocket
- 2012 Chuck Markulis Memorial One-Pocket Division
- 2011 World Mixed Doubles Classic (with Rubilen Amit)
- 2011 US Open One Pocket Championship
- 2010 Spanish Open 2010
- 2010 Predator International Ten-Ball Championship
- 2010 Derby City Classic Master of the Table
- 2010 Derby City Classic Fatboy Challenge 10-Ball
- 2010 Derby City Classic Nine-Ball
- 2010 Asia vs Europe Challenge Match
- 2009 World Mixed Doubles Classic (with Rubilen Amit)
- 2009 Galveston World Classic One Pocket
- 2009 World Cup of Pool (with Francisco Bustamante)
- 2007 Derby City Classic Master of the Table
- 2007 Derby City Classic One-Pocket
- 2006 San Miguel Asian 9-Ball Tour (Indonesia Leg)
- 2006 IPT World Open Eight-Ball Championship
- 2006 World Cup of Pool (with Francisco Bustamante)
- 2006 San Miguel Asian 9-Ball Tour (Vietnam Leg)
- 2006 Derby City Classic One-Pocket
- 2005 IPT King of the Hill Eight-Ball Shootout
- 2005 San Miguel Asian 9-Ball Tour (Indonesia Leg)
- 2005 All Japan Championship
- 2005 Derby City Classic Master of the Table
- 2005 Derby City Classic Nine-Ball
- 2005 Derby City Classic One-Pocket
- 2004 WPA World Eight-Ball Championship
- 2004 On Cue 3: Intercontinental Conquest
- 2004 San Miguel Asian 9-Ball Tour (Singapore Leg)
- 2004 San Miguel Asian 9-Ball Tour (Vietnam Leg)
- 2004 San Miguel Asian 9-Ball Tour (Taiwan Leg)
- 2004 Derby City Classic Master of the Table
- 2004 Derby City Classic One-Pocket
- 2003 Billiard Congress of America Hall of Fame
- 2003 World Classic Billiards Tournament
- 2003 Las Vegas Nine-Ball Open
- 2003 San Miguel Asian 9-Ball Tour (Manila Leg)
- 2003 Mid-Atlantic Nine-Ball Championship
- 2003 All Japan Championship
- 2002 Asian Games Eight-Ball singles (bronze)
- 2002 World Pool League
- 2002 Cafe Puro Challenge of the Masters
- 2002 Shooters Labor Day Weekend Open Nine-Ball
- 2002 ESPN International Challenge of Champions
- 2001 World Pool League
- 2001 Tokyo Open 9-Ball
- 2001 US Masters Nine-Ball
- 2001 International Billiard Tournament
- 2001 Accu-Stats Eight-Ball Invitational
- 2001 The Color of Money II (vs Earl Strickland)
- 2000 U.S. Open One-Pocket Championship
- 2000 PBT World Eight-Ball Championship
- 2000 Camel Pro Eight-Ball Championship
- 2000 Pennsylvania State Nine-Ball Championship
- 2000 USA Billiards Challenger Event 2
- 1999 ESPN Ultimate Nine-Ball Challeng
- 1999 ESPN Ultimate Shootout
- 1999 Sands Regency Open 29 Nine-Ball Championship
- 1999 WPA World Nine-Ball Championship
- 1999 Derby City Classic Master of the Table
- 1999 Derby City Classic One-Pocket
- 1998 World Eight-Ball Championship
- 1998 Camel South Jersey Ten-Ball Open
- 1997 PCA Shooters Challenge
- 1997 PCA Treasure Island Resort Even
- 1996 The Color of Money (vs Earl Strickland)
- 1996 PBT World Eight-Ball Championship
- 1996 PBT Legends of Nine-Ball Championship
- 1996 Camel World Nine-Ball Championship
- 1996 PBT Western Open
- 1996 PBT Florida Flare Up III
- 1995 Sands Regency Open 21 Nine-Ball Championship
- 1995 PBT World Eight-Ball Championship
- 1995 Pro Tour Nine-Ball Championship
- 1995 Maine 14.1 Event
- 1995 Bicycle Club VII
- 1994 U.S. Open Nine-Ball Championships
- 1994 PBT Bicycle Club Invitational
- 1992 International Nine-Ball Classic
- 1992 World Nine-Ball Open (Tokyo)
- 1990 World Cup (Taipei)
- 1988 PBA McDermott Masters Nine-Ball
- 1986 Sands Regency Nine-Ball Championship
- 1985 Sands Regency Nine-Ball Championship
- 1985 Red's Nine-Ball Open
- 1985 Tar Heel Open
- 1985 Willard's Open
- 1985 Chicago Billiard Cafe Open

DARREN APPLETON

Darren Appleton (born 8 February 1978 in Pontefract, West Yorkshire, England) is a British pocket billiards player, nicknamed "Dynamite". He won the first WPA World Ten-ball Championship in 2008 against Wu Chia-ching, the former world champion in both nine-ball and eight-ball from Taiwan. With the victory, he became the second male player from Britain to win a world championship after Daryl Peach who won the world nine-ball title a year earlier.

Appleton, who started playing pool at age 12, was formerly the world ranked no. 1 player in British-style eight-ball pool.He was

twice runner-up in the WEPF Eight-ball Pool World Championship. In 2006, he joined the International Pool Tour's standardised eight-ball competition. That year, he also won the Straight Pool Challenge at the Derby City Classic.

On 5 October 2008, Appleton claimed an upset victory in the inaugural WPA World Ten-ball Championship over Wu Chia-ching, 13–11, winning the US$100,000 top prize: "I've waited 16 years for this and have to enjoy the moment. I had mixed feelings and I was looking back at my disappointments in the past. I was ranked first (earlier in the decade) in the world but I have never won a world championship... It was a dream come true for me and I'm happy to win the title here in the Philippines."

In May 2009, Appleton challenged Dennis Hatch of the United States in a three-day race-to-100 challenge match of ten-ball. Hatch, however, came out the victor with a score of 100-83. In the same year, he won the World Pool Masters tournament by defeating Nick van den Berg.

Darren Appleton also won the 2010 U.S. Open 9-ball Championship against Corey Deuel of the United States in a match that went into extra racks.

Appleton was a member of the victorious European team in the 2010 Mosconi Cup. He was named MVP for the tournament with a 5-1 win to loss ratio.

In 2012, Appleton won the WPA World Nine-ball Championship, subduing China's Li He-wen in the finals with a score of 13-12.

In 2013, he won the nine-ball tournament at the World Games 2013, beating Chang Jung-lin 11–10 in the final.

In 2014, he won the World Straight Pool Championship, beating Shane Van Boening in the final.

On 2 February 2015, Darren Appleton won the 2015 Chinese Pool World Championship, defeating Mark Selby 21–19 in the final.

RALF SOUQUET

Ralf Souquet (pronounced soo-kay) (born 29 November 1968 in Eschweiler, Germany) is a German professional pool player. His nicknames are "The Kaiser" and "The Surgeon." Since 1981, he has won more than 250 tournament titles, including 41 German Championship titles and 34 European Championship titles.

He began playing billiards at the age of six in his parents' pub, practicing up to five hours per day. He won his first German Championship title at the age of fourteen in the juniors division. In 1985, Souquet co-won his first European Championship team title with the National Team, and in 1986 won his first individual title at the European Championship (juniors division). In 1997, he received the Silberne Lorbeerblatt (Silver Laurel Leaf), the highest official distinction awarded to sportspeople by Germany, which was presented to him by German President Roman Herzog.

In 1996, Souquet won the WPA World Nine-ball Championship where triumph over Tom Storm of Sweden. He also reached the finals of the same event in 2001 and 2006, only to be bested by Mika Immonen and Ronato Alcano.

Souquet also won the US Open Nine-ball Championship in 2002 by defeating Alex Pagulayan who would also win the event in the next three years.

In 2008, Souquet won his second world title at the WPA World Eight-ball Championship with a victory over Ronato Alcano (Alcano was also a winner of this event). Souquet won the $ 60,000 championship prize, with 13-9 final score.

TITLES

- WPA World Eight-ball Championship (2008)
- World Pool Masters (1994, 1996, 2000, 2002, 2006)
- WPA World Nine-ball Championship (1996)
- US Open Nine-ball Championship (2002)
- International Challenge of Champions (1996)
- US Open 14.1 Championship (2000)
- BCA Open Nine-ball Championship (2003, 2006)
- All-Japan Pool Championship (2004)
- Derby City Nine-ball Classic (2004, 2006, 2008)

MIKA IMMONEN

Mika Immonen (born 17 December 1972) is a Finnish professional pool player, nicknamed "the Ice Man."

He won the WPA World Nine-ball Championship in Cardiff, Wales in 2001. That same year, he was the runner-up to Corey Deuel in the US Open Nine-ball Championship.

In 2002 he won the UPA International Ten-ball Championship.

He has represented Team Europe on thirteen occasions in the Mosconi Cup, most recently in 2013. During the 2008 event Mika was crowned MVP, forever banishing bad memories of a costly miss in the final game of the 2006 event.

In early 2009, Mika was awarded the title of Player of the Year. Subsequently, he also claimed that title for season 2009 and was awarded early 2010.

Mika was born in London, England, and is also an extremely accomplished snooker player, having amassed more than 100 century breaks.

Mika is a two-time Men's Division title-holder of the US Open Nine-ball Championship, where the worlds top professional billiard players compete in Chesapeake, Virginia. In 2009 Mika won 14 straight matches, finishing with a close 13-10 victory over Ralf Souquet in the finals. On October 26, 2008, Mika claimed a 13-7 victory and pocketed the first-place prize of US$40,000 against runner-up Filipino Ronato Alcano, who settled for $20,000.

Immonen nearly won his second world title at 2009 World Straight Pool Championship, but was defeated in the finals by Stephan Cohen of France. Also in 2009, Immonen bested Darren Appleton to win the International Challenge of Champions, a tournament where he once reached the finals in 2002 but lost the sudden-death rack to Efren Reyes.

In Late November 2009 Mika finally won his second World Title in Manila at the WPA World Ten-ball Championships. He Dominated the Philippine hope Lee Van Corteza in the finals 11-6.

TITLES

2000 Sudden Death Seven-ball Champion

2001 WPC 9-Ball Champion

2002 LG Flatron Challenge Champion

2002 UPA International Ten-ball Champion

2003 On Cue; Philippines vs. Europe

2003 Philippine Open Champion

2004 Atlanta Open Champion

2004 UPA Pro Tour Champion

2005 Atlanta Open Champion

2006 Norway Open Champion

2006 Weert Open & invitational 7-ball Champion

2007 Derby City Straight Pool Champion

2007 Korean Pro Tour Champion

2008 US Open 9-Ball Champion

2008 IPT Pro-Am Champion

2008 Mosconi Cup MVP

2008 All Japan Champion

2009 Galveston World Classic 10-ball Champion

2009 US Open 9-Ball Champion

2009 World 10-Ball Champion

2009 Mezz Classic 10-Ball Event

2009 Blackpool Open

2009 Joss NE 9-Ball Tour Stop

2009 Tri State Tour Stop

2009 Predator Tour Stop

2009 Joss NE 9-Ball Tour Stop

2009 The Challenge of Champions

2009 Qatar International Open Champion

2010 International Challenge of Champions

2010 Ozone 10-Ball Championships, Louisiana

2010 Poison Doubles 8-ball Championships with Rodney Morris, Louisiana

2010 Mezz Tour stop in Skyline Billiards

2010 Mezz tour stop in Atlantic City Billiards

2012 World Cup of Pool champion (Doubles with Petri Makkonen)

2013 Ultimate 10-Ball Championship Men's Division (Champion)

2014 BCA Hall of Fame inductee

NIELS FEIJEN

Niels Feijen (born 3 February 1977) is a professional pool player, from in the Hague, Netherlands. His nickname is "the Terminator".

In 2001, Feijen reached the finals of a nine-ball tournament in Tokyo, Japan. The event had a field of more than 700 players and offered the largest prize money at that time. However, he lost to Efren Reyes. In 2004, he won the inaugural Skins Billiards Championship with prize money of US$42,500. Feijen has won the European straight pool championship four times. In 2005 he was the winner of the Big Apple Nine-ball Classic, held in Queens, New York, an event with 128 of the world's best players. He represented Europe in the 2001, 2004, 2005, 2007, and 2008 Mosconi Cup events.

ACHIEVEMENTS IN 9 BALL:

In the year 2001, Feijen managed to reach the final of a major tournament in Tokyo, Japan. This prestigious event was the largest prize money available at that time however in spite of quality field of more than 700 players, Feijen put up a brave fight in the final before seemingly inevitably succumbing to the magic of Efren Reyes.

In 2004, Niels Feijen succeeded in winning the Skins Billiards Championship which carried prize money of $42.5K. Impressively, Feijen has managed to win the European straight pool championship on 3 occasions in 2002, 2003 and 2004.

In 2005 he won the Big Apple 9 ball Classic, which was held in Queens, New York - an event with an impressive field comprising 128 of the world's best players .Feijen pocketed $10,000 for the 13-11 win. Also in 2005: Dutch Open 9 ball pool Champion and 2005 Belgium Open 9 ball pool Champion. In 2005, Niels was chosen to represent team Europe in the Mosconi Cup event.

In 2007 Feijen won the $50K winner-take-all International Challenge of Champions when he managed to defeat Lee Van Corteza in the final. Also in 2007 Feijen managed to reach the position of being ranked number two in Europe and WPA number one in the world.

Overall, Niels Feijen has proven himself to be a consistently good tournament player even though he has yet to win a major title.

More recently, Feijen won the 2007 $50,000 winner-take-all International Challenge of Champions by defeating Lee Van Corteza. In 2008, Feijen won the World Straight Pool Championship with a victory over Francisco Bustamante in the finals. On October 5, 2008, he received the 3rd prize of $25,000 in the inaugural WPA World Ten-ball Championship. Niels Feijen has been under contract with cue manufacturer Longoni for several years. In 2010, Feijen reached the finals of the WPA World Eight-ball Championship but ended up in 2nd place losing to Karl Boyes of Great Britain.He would reach the finals of that same tournament again the next year, only to be defeated by Dennis Orcollo of the Philippines.

SHANE VAN BOENING

Shane Van Boening (born 14 July 1983) is an American professional pocket billiards (pool) player from Rapid City, South Dakota, currently ranked No.1 in the U.S. Rankings published by the UPA Tour.

Van Boening is hearing-impaired and uses a hearing aid, but it has not limited his pool ability. He has received praise for his attitude towards the sport, partially for his behaviour during matches, and for eschewing alcohol.

Van Boening's family has a strong pool background. His grandfather, Gary Bloomberg, was a trick-shot artist; his grandmother, Jeanne Bloomberg, a VNEA national champion; his mother, Timi Bloomberg, a BCA national champion; and his aunt, Gari Jo Bloomberg, a three-time VNEA national champion.

Van Boening defeated Hungarian Vilmos Foldes at the International Pool Tour qualifier in 2006, and was one of several players to earn a bonus of US$5,000 for breaking and running six consecutive racks in tournament play. Shane was one of only 10 players to earn their IPT tour card by finishing in the top two spots of one of five qualifiers. Shane won the second stop held at the Pool Room in Atlanta, Georgia. He has been ranked number one in the world by AZBilliards.com. When he is not competing professionally, he can be found practicing in downtown Sioux Falls at Lucky Billiards, where he is the house pro and co-owner.

Van Boening is a three-time VNEA national amateur eight-ball champion. In 2007, he made it to the final of the BCA Open Nine-ball Championshipbut lost to Dennis Orcollo. Days later, he dominated the inaugural World Ten-ball Championship to become the first-ever world champion in that discipline of pool.

Shane has been declared by some as the next-in-line and heir-apparent to the throne of being the best Pool player in the US by Inside POOL Magazine.

Van Boening captured the hot seat in the World Summit of Pool on June 16, 2007, giving 2004 WPA Men's World Nine-ball Champion Alex "the Lion" Pagulayan an 11–4 defeat. The last day, all matches were shortened races to 7 because they were being recorded by ESPN. Alex Pagulayanplowed through Francisco Bustamante and Warren Kiamco and faced Van Boening in the final. Despite Pagulayan leading 4-1, Van Boening recovered to tie the score 5-5 before veteran Pagulayan won the next two games to claim the victory, 7 to 5.

The Billiards Congress of America Pool League owner Mark Griffin recognized his talent and decided in 2007 to sponsor him as he advances his professional career.

On October 20, 2007, he won the 2007 (32nd annual) US Open Nine-ball Championship, defeating Filipino Champion Ronnie Alcano in the finals, 13–10. Van Boening remained undefeated in the double-elimination format of the championship, held in Chesapeake, Virginia.

At the Reno Open Nine-ball Championship, held on December 9, 2007, Van Boening and Johnny Archer were in the double-elimination finals. Archer was up to that point undefeated, and Van Boening had to beat Archer twice; Van Boening won the first set, and 83 minutes later, claimed the championship.

As a capstone to his record year, for 2007 he was declared the male Player of the Year by all three of the major pool publications, Billiards Digest, Pool & Billiard Magazine, and Inside POOL Magazine (in each case with Allison Fisher as his female co-recipient of the honour), and also ranked #11 in the P&B 'Fans' Top 20 Favourite Players" poll for that year.

TITLES AND ACHIEVEMENTS

- 2007 Reno Open 9-Ball Championship
- 2007 U.S. Open 9-Ball Championship
- 2007 Predator World Ten-ball Championship, Jacksonville, Florida
- 2007 Inside POOL Magazine Player of the Year
- 2007 Billiards Digest Player of the Year (male)
- 2007 Pool & Billiard Magazine Player of the Year (male)
- 2007 Pool & Billiard Magazine Fans' Top 20 Favorite Players, #11
- 2008 World Cup of Pool - 9 Ball [With Rodney "the Rocket" Morris]
- 2008 US Bar Table Championship - 10 Ball Division
- 2008 UPA Pro Players Championship
- 2009 Derby City Classic 9-Ball Division
- 2010 Players Championship
- 2010 Ultimate 10 Ball Championship
- 2011 Derby City Classic Master of the Table
- 2011 Steve Mizerak Championship
- 2011 US Open 10 Ball Championship
- 2011 Turning Stone Classic XVIII
- 2011 2011 Pool Ocho Open
- 2012 U.S. Open 9-Ball Championship
- 2012 Derby City Master of the Table
- 2012 US Bar Table Championship - 10 Ball Division
- 2012 US Open One Pocket
- 2012 Players Championship
- 2013 US Open 8-Ball[18]
- 2013 US Bar Table Championship - 9 Ball Division
- 2013 U.S. Open 9-Ball Championship
- 2014 U.S. Open 9-Ball Championship
- 2014 World Pool Masters
- 2007 Inside POOL Magazine Player of the Year
- 2007 Billiards Digest Player of the Year (male)
- 2007 Pool & Billiard Magazine Player of the Year (male)
- 2007 Pool & Billiard Magazine Fans' Top 20 Favorite Players, #11

DARYL PEACH

Daryl Peach (born 8 March 1972 in Castleford, West Yorkshire, England) is a British professional pocket billiards (pool) player. Nicknamed "Razzledazzle" and "the Dazzler," he defeated the Philippines' Roberto Gomez in 2007 to become the first British male to win the WPA World Nine-ball Championship (the woman's world championship having been won by Britain's Allison Fisher). His tournament nearly ended prematurely when his match against Filipino Francisco Bustamante had to be suspended, after Bustamante fluked the a 3-9 canon to clinch the match. After over 20 minutes of examining replays of the shot by referees and tournament officials, it was shown that the cue ball had hit the 9-ball fractionally before the 3-ball, and was thus a foul. Despite the furore, Peach held his composure to win the match.

Due to his success in the World Championship he was called up into the 2007 Mosconi Cup in Las Vegas, Nevada, where he took part in a controversial match against American Earl Strickland, whose constant disruptive behavior lead Peach to brand the American "The scum of the Earth" in his post-match interview.

LIST OF TITLES

- 1995 Mosconi Cup
- 1995 World Pool Masters
- 2007 Eurotour German Open
- 2007 Mosconi Cup
- 2007 World Nine-Ball Championship
- 2009 Eurotour Portugal Open
- 2009 Lugo International Nine-Ball Open
- 2010 Eurotour Italian Open
- 2010 International Open 8-Ball
- 2010 World Team Championship
- 2012 Eurotour German Open
- 2012 Longoni Benalux Open
- 2013 Zagreb Open

THORSTEN HOHMANN

Thorsten Hohmann (born 14 July 1979 in Fulda, Germany) is a German professional pool player, nicknamed "the Hitman." He has been described as having a steely demeanor, and being a very precise player.

Hohmann first made a name for himself in 2003 by winning the WPA World Nine-ball Championship at the expense of Alex Pagulayan, 17–10, becoming the third German to become World Champion after Oliver Ortmann (1995) and Ralf Souquet (1996).

Months later, reached the finals of the World Pool League but lost to Rodney Morris, 8–3.

In 2004, Hohmann signed on to be managed by US- and South Korea-based event promotions company Dragon Promotions, who transplanted the German-resident champion to Jacksonville, Florida, as a base of practice and preparation for US competitions. Hohmann then signed with Florida-based sponsors Lucasi Cues

and Universal Smartshaft as their official representative and spokesperson. He remains a German citizen, but a US permanent resident. Thorsten has since been featured on the cover of many pool magazines.

In 2004, Hohmann reached the finals of the US Open Nine-ball Championship. However, he was lost to Gabe Owen, 3–11.

The year 2005 was his most successful to date as he dominated a number of tournaments, including the BCA Open Nine-ball Championship, the Sudden Death Seven-ball event and the World Pool League.

In 2006, he won the inaugural World Straight Pool Championship by defeating Thomas Engert 200–80. Later, he defeated Marlon Manalo 8-7 to win the IPT North American Open Eight-ball Championship with a first prize of US$350K. The IPT prize set a record as the largest first prize ever won in a pool tournament at that time. However, Efren Reyes beat the record shortly afterwards winning $500,000 in the 2006 IPT World Open Eight-ball Championship, the second major IPT event. But because IPT had financial difficulties, 200 players including Reyes were not able to collect their money thus Hohmann is still on record as the biggest purse winner in billiards history to actually get paid, as of early 2007.

Hohmann won the 2005 USA Sportsman of the Year for Pocket Billiards as well as the 2005 Best Dressed Player. Pool & Billiard magazine made Thorsten the cover feature for 2007 and honored him as the 2006 Player of the Year.

TITLES

2015 Archer Cup Champion

2014 Champion of Champions

2014 Manny Pacquiao Cup Champion

2014 WPBL Bonus Ball Champion

2013 World 14.1 Tournament Champion

2013 WPC World 9-Ball Champion

2013 Maryland 14.1 Challenge Champion

2011 World Cup of Pool Champion

2011 World 14.1 Tournament Champion

2011 Philippine Open Champion

2010 All Japan Championships Champion

2009 China Open Champion

2008 Asian 10-Ball Champion

2008 Accu-Stats 14.1 Invitational

2008 Lucasi Hybrid 14.1 Champion

2007 European 9-Ball Champion

2006 IPT North American Open 8-Ball Champion

2006 World 14.1 Champion

2005 Silver Medal World Games

2005 World Pool League Champion

2005 Sudden Death 7-Ball Champion

2005 BCA Open 9-Ball Championship

2004 German 9-Ball Champion

2003 German 14.1 Champion

2003 WPA World 9-Ball Champion

2003 New Jersey State 14.1 Champion

2003 German 9-Ball Champion

Glamour

# of Pool

EWA MATAYA LAURANCE

"The Queen of trick shot shows, Ewa is the Grace Kelly of cue sports!"

Ewa Mataya Laurance is one of the most visible superstars in the history of pocket billiards. Known as The Striking Viking, she took the billiard world by storm since she moved to the US from her native Sweden.

Following her childhood dream of becoming the best in the world, she continues to be a dominant presence on the international billiard scene. Ewa is the current International and World Cup Trick Shot Champion, the holder of multiple World and US Open 9-ball titles, and has also won the Swedish, European and US National Championships in her incredible career. A former # 1 ranked player in the world, Ewa has received Player of the Year honors, been named WPBA Sportsperson of the Year, and in 2004, was inducted into the prestigious Billiard Congress of America Hall of Fame.

This dynamic champion made an historic appearance on the cover of the New York Times Magazine and has been featured in numerous national publications, including People Magazine, Sports Illustrated, Forbes, Glamour, Golf for Women and Cigar Aficionado. Ewa is also a frequent guest on television shows such as Late Night with David Letterman, The Today Show, The Early Show, Current Affair, LIVE with Regis and Kelly, Entertainment Tonight and The Best Damned Sports Show, Period.

When not competing, Ewa serves as the ESPN Color Commentator. She also co-hosted GSN's popular game show "Ball Breakers."

Ewa is on the Board of Trustees of the Billiard Education Foundation and the South Carolina chapter of the Make-A-Wish Foundation. She is a frequent participant at various celebrity golf tournaments around the country. On tour, Ewa is sponsored by Brunswick Billiards.

Ewa Mataya Laurance has fashioned one of the great careers in the history of pocket billiards. The first truly international superstar in the sport, The Striking Viking brought media attention and focus to the game in a way no one before ever had, and continues to this day to embody the best competitive and entertainment aspects of the sport she loves.

Ewa started playing pocket billiards in her native town of Gavle, Sweden at the age of 14, after following her older brother Mats into the local billiard room. She fell instantly in love with the game and practiced six to ten hours per day, doing her school homework between shots. Excelling at a rapid pace, Ewa went on to compete

in her first major tournament that same year, where she finished in fourth place. The following year she captured her first Swedish 9-ball title, and two years later, after having qualified to play in the European Championship by winning the Swedish 14.1 Championship, she was crowned European Champion in Bern, Switzerland. As a result Ewa was asked to represent Europe at the World Championships in New York City.

With a dream of becoming a professional pool player, the 17-year old made the decision to stay and make the United States her home. Since then, she has not only been successfully competing on the Women's Professional Tour, with consecutive years as the #1-ranked player in the world, but has also become widely recognized as one of the great international ambassadors for the sport, promoting pocket billiards worldwide.

Ewa is a two time Player- of- the- Year, a recipient of the "WPBA Sportsperson of the Year Award," "The WPBA PR Award" and the "Billiard and Bowling Institute of America Industry Service Award." She was instrumental in launching the WPBA Classic Tour, and has spent numerous terms as a member of the Women's Professional Billiard Association Board of Directors, including three terms as President, working to organize and promote women's pocket billiards. Ewa writes a monthly column for "Pool and Billiard Magazine," and is the author of three of the sport's most popular books, "The Ewa Mataya Pool Guide," "The Complete Idiot's Guide to Pool and Billiards," and most recently, "Quick-Start Guide to Pocket Billiards."

When not playing, Ewa is the Color Commentator for ESPN Championship Billiards and recently hosted GSN's billiards game show "BallBreakers." She has been sponsored on Tour by legendary Brunswick Billiards since 1988, and continues to be their Professional Player Representative and Spokesperson.

Besides playing on the WPBA 9-Ball Tour, Ewa is the current International Trick Shot Champion, a member of the championship World Cup of Trick Shots team, and is known as the world's premier female trick shot artist. She spends a great deal of the year performing trick shot exhibitions across the U.S. and around the world. An avid golfer, Ewa can also be seen at numerous celebrity golf charity events around the country.

Ewa currently resides in Myrtle Beach, SC with her husband Mitch, daughter Nikki and their menagerie of dogs, cats and horses.

PROFESSIONAL CAREER

In 2005, Ewa Mataya Laurance bested three of her peers, WPBA tour members Allison Fisher, Dawn Hopkins, and Gerda Hofstatter, at the Women's Trick Shot Challenge held at the New York Hotel Casino in Las Vegas, Nevada, pocketing US$25,000 as the grand prize. Animated and expressive, she played to the audience and the cameras, "a true showperson in her element and a wonderful example to all trick shot artists." Ewa has won numerous major women's pool title, including the WPA World Nine-ball Championship, US Open Nine-ball Championship, WPBA National Nine-ball Championship, International Trickshot Championship and the Swedish and European 14.1 Championships.

TITLES

2012 WPBA Masters Champion

Current World Cup Trick Shot Champion

Current International Trick Shot Champion

WPA World 9-Ball Champion

US Open Champion (twice)

WPBA National Champion

World Open 9-Ball Champion (twice)

World 8-Ball Champion

International 9-Ball Champion

National 10-Ball Champion

European Champion

Swedish National 9-ball Champion (twice)

Swedish 14.1 Champion

Swedish Mixed Doubles Champion

ESPN Team Challenge Champion

Brunswick Boston Classic Champion

Nordic Masters Champion

Houston Open Champion

Cleveland Open Champion

Sands Regent Classic Champion

Rocket City Invitational Champion

East Coast Classic Champion

Two Time Ladies Pool Circuit Champion

ALLISON FISHER

"To me success is... producing your best game"

Allison Fisher (born February 24, 1968) is an English professional pool (and former professional snooker) player. She won her first world title at the age of 17. To date, she has won over 80 national titles and 11 world titles in total. She even entered the Male Snooker ranking, but never progressed into the sport's upper levels. Feeling that she didn't receive the respect which the male players had, she moved to the US to play on the pool circuit where women receive greater respect.

Fisher did not take long to make her mark in the world of pool, winning only the second tournament that she played in. She has an unequaled record, winning 50 WPBA titles, which includes 4 world 9-Ball championships. Since her move, she has also been the highest-earning player on a number of occasions, which takes into account male and female players. Matchroom sports invited her to play in the Matchroom snooker league, and she was also invited to play in the Mosconi Cup 1994, when Europe lost 16:12 against Team USA.

Fisher was nicknamed "the Duchess of Doom" and gained similar formidability to that of the thirteen-time darts world champion Phil "The Power" Taylor and snooker players Joe Davis, Steve Davis and Stephen Hendry in the 1930s and 80s–90s, respectively. Her greatest season was the 2000/2001 season when she won 8 consecutive major pro pool tournaments. In the 2005 season, Fisher was the highest earner, winning £111,000.

For 2007, she was declared the female Player of the Year by all three of the major pool publications, Billiards Digest, Pool & Billiard Magazine, and Inside POOL Magazine (in each case with Shane Van Boening as her male co-recipient of the honor), and also ranked #1 in the P&B "Fans' Top 20 Favorite Players" poll for that year. She has been the BD female Player of the Year for 11 of the 12 years spanning 1996–2007, including 6 in a row, 2002–2007.

TITLES AND ACHIEVEMENTS

* 2013 Ultimate 10-Ball Championship, Women's Division (Runner Up)

* 2013 WPBA Masters (3rd)

* 2012 WPBA US Open 9-Ball Championship

* 2011 WPBA US Open 9-Ball Championship

* 2011 Ultimate 10-Ball Championship Women's Division

* 2008 WPBA San Diego Classic

* 2008 WPBA Great Lakes Classic* 2007 US Open Nine-ball Championship (women's division)

* 2007 WPBA Classic Tour National Nine-ball Champion

* 2007 Florida Classic

* 2007 Billiards Digest Player of the Year (female)

* 2007 Pool & Billiard Magazine Player of the Year (female)

* 2007 Pool & Billiard Magazine Fans' Top 20 Favorite Players,

* 2006 WPBA Classic Tour National Nine-ball Champion

* 2006 WPBA Great Lakes Classic

* 2006 Billiards Digest Player of the Year (female)

* 2005 Amway Cup

* 2005 WPBA BCA 9-Ball Championship

* 2005 WPBA Carolina Classic

* 2005 WPBA Great Lakes Classic

* 2005 WPBA Midwest Classic

* 2005 WPBA U.S. Open

* 2005 Billiards Digest Player of the Year (female)

* 2004 ESPN Ladies Challenge of Champions

* 2004 WPBA Delta Classic

* 2004 WPBA Midwest Classic

* 2004 WPBA San Diego Classic

* 2004 Billiards Digest Player of the Year (female)

* 2003 WPBA Delta Classic

* 2003 WPBA Midwest Classic

* 2003 WPBA National 9-Ball Championship

* 2003 WPBA San Diego Classic

* 2003 Billiards Digest Player of the Year (female)

* 2002 Amway Cup

* 2002 Tournament of Champions

* 2002 WPBA Midwest Classic

* 2002 WPBA Players Championship

* 2002 Billiards Digest Player of the Year (female)

* 2001 Amway Cup

* 2001 Tournament of Champions

* 2000 BCA U.S. Open Straight Pool Championship

* 2000 Long Fong Cup

* 2000 Tournamnent of Champions

* 2000 UCC World Ladies Pro 9-Ball Tournament

* 2000 WPBA California Classic

* 2000 WPBA National Championship

* 2000 WPBA Villa Park 9-Ball Challenge

* 2000 WPBA Virtual Pool 9-Ball Challenge

* 1999 Billiard Congress of America Pro Open

* 1999 ESPN Ultimate 9-Ball Challenge

* 1999 ESPN Ultimate Shootout

* 1999 WPBA Arizona Classic

* 1999 WPBA Detroit Classic

* 1999 WPBA National Championship

* 1999 WPBA Players Championship

* 1999 WPBA U.S. Open

* 1998 ESPN Ultimate Shootout

* 1998 Tournament of Champions

* 1998 WPA World 9-Ball Championship

* 1998 WPBA Bay Area Classic

* 1998 WPBA Dallas Classic

* 1998 WPBA National Championship

* 1998 WPBA Philadelphia Players Championship

* 1998 WPBA San Diego Classic

* 1998 WPBA Twin Cities Classic

* 1997 ESPN Ultimate 9-Ball Challenge

* 1997 WPA World 9-Ball Championship

* 1997 WPBA Detroit Classic

* 1997 WPBA Los Angeles Classic

* 1997 WPBA New York Classic

* 1997 WPBA Philadelphia Players Championship

* 1997 WPBA Phoenix Classic

* 1997 WPBA Twin Cities Classic

* 1996 WPA World 9-Ball Championship

* 1996 WPBA Honolulu Classic

* 1996 WPBA Los Angeles Classic

* 1996 WPBA Nashville Classic

* 1996 WPBA National 9-Ball Championship

* 1996 WPBA New York Classic

* 1996 WPBA Orlando Classic

* 1995 WPBA Orlando Classic

KELLY FISHER

"My most thrilling game moment was: winning the San Diego Classic!"

Kelly Fisher (born 26 August 1978) is a British professional pool and snooker player. She currently holds the Embassy Ladies` Snooker World Champion title, although this event was last held in 2003. She has reached the final of every European Ladies` Championship, losing just once to former World Champion Karen Corr. In 2003 Fisher won the first IBSF World Ladies` Championship.

Disillusioned by the lack of ladies` events in the UK ,and the lack of financial reward in ladies` snooker, she switched to pocket billiards (pool), joining women's snooker pros Allison Fisher and Karen Corr in the Women's Professional Billiard Association (WPBA) nine-ball tour.

In August 2008 after being in the top 10 women for the past two years and winning the San Diego Classic for 3 years running (2004-2007) Kelly achieved the No1 Ranking in World Womens Pool and won the US Open Championship.

SNOOKER ACHIEVEMENTS

Snooker

- Connie Gough Memorial – 1994, 1999
- James Brooks Classic – 1994, 1997
- Academy Fork Lift – 1995
- Halstead Ladies Classic – 1995
- M-Tech Ladies Classic – 1995
- Bailey Homes – 1996
- Ladies Regal Scottish – 1996, 1998, 1999, 2002
- Ladies Regal Welsh – 1996, 2002, 2003
- Applecentre Classic – 1996
- Grand Prix (Ladies) – 1998
- Embassy World Ladies Snooker Championship – 1998, 1999, 2000, 2002, 2003
- Ladies British Open – 1999, 2000, 2001, 2002
- Ladies UK Championship – 1999, 2000, 2001, 2002
- National Championship – 1999
- Connie Gough National – 2000, 2001, 2002, 2003
- Consultex Belgium Open – 2000
- Ladies Regal Masters – 2000
- European Ranking Event – 2001, 2002
- LG Cup (Ladies) – 2001, 2002
- Scottish Ladies Championship – 2002

Amateur

- EBSA European Ladies Championship – 1996, 1997, 1999, 2000, 2001, 2002, 2003
- IBSF World Ladies Championship – 2003
- Home Internationals – 2002, 2003 (with team England)

English Billiards

- Embassy World Ladies Billiards Championship – 2001, 2003

Pool

- WPBA West Coast Classic – 2005, 2006, 2007
- US Open Nine-ball Championship – 2008
- WPBA Pacific Coast Classic – 2008
- 2009 International Tournament of Champions
- 2011 Yalin World 10-ball Championships
- 2012 Women's World 9-ball Championships
- 2013 International Tournament of Champions
- 2014 International Tournament of Champions

KAREN CORR

"To me success is... Picking up the trophy"

Karen was born November 10th in Ballymoney, County Antrim, N. Ireland and lived near Maghera, County Derry. At the age of 8, her parents moved to England where she eventually joined a club and began her career in snooker at the age of 14.

Karen was 15 when she entered her first woman's event in Leicester, England. In 1990, she won her first World Snooker Championship and she continued on to win additional World titles in '91, '95, and '97.

In June of 1998, Karen moved to the U.S. and began playing pool. She was curious to see how she would do at pool. After winning 10 qualifying events in a row, she was able to enter WPBA pro events.

By the end of 1998, Karen was ranked # 24. At the end of 1999, she soared through the rankings, all the way to # 4. By the end of 2000, she was ranked 2nd in the world.

Karen won her first WPBA Classic Tour title, "The 2000 Cuetec Cues Players Championship" in Valley Forge, Pennsylvania. She completed that year with two more Classic tour titles. She also won the "All Japan Open Championship" held in Osaka, Japan. She placed second in the "WPA Women's World Championship" and in the "UCC World Ladies Championship" held in Tokyo, Japan.

In 2001, Karen became the first person to win all 6 WPBA Classic tour events since they began. She won the silver medal at the World Games and placed 2nd at the World Championships. Before 2001 ended, Karen found herself at the top, the No. 1 ranked player in the World and remained there for 2 years.

Karen continued her form in 2002 by winning three ranking events and placed in the top three in all other events to maintain her #1 ranking.

2003 was a great year winning the Joss North East 9-Ball men's tour event. She is the only woman to win an event on the Joss Tour. She defended her BCA event in May and won the US Open in Albuquerque, New Mexico and the Canadian Classic. Karen was part of the European team that won the World Team event in Taiwan.

In 2004, Karen had consistent top finishes winning the BCA Championship for the third year in a row and went on to complete the year with a win in the Nationals in Oregon.

2005 was a dryer year with one event win in Florida at the Hard Rock Casino and second place finish in the BCA trying to win it for the fourth year in a row and a second place finish at the US Open in New Mexico.

Karen made 2006 a brilliant year with 3 WPBA wins and her first win in the Tournament of Champions. She was one of the hottest players on the WPBA tour, winning the first event in North Carolina, a second place finish at the Viejas Casino in San Diego, a second win at the Florida Classic, and a third win at the Midwest Classic.

2007 got off to a slow start, but picked up momentum in May when Karen won The EnjoyPool.com championship. She then won the New Jersey State Championship in July and has been a dominant force on the 2007 Joss Northeast Tour. In August, she finished 5th at the Turning Stone Classic IX in Verona, NY.

In October, Karen successfully defended her WPBA Midwest Classic title. Karen successfully defended her Tournament of Champions title in November.

The WPBA season got off to a late start in 2008 due to a schedule change for the Carolina Classic. In the meantime, Karen played well at Turning Stone IX and won the Joss Northeast Tour stop in Providence while finishing 3rd-4th twice in San Diego and Michigan City as the WPBA season got underway in April. The big highlight of the year was a sudden-death victory in the Tournament of Champions over Ga Young Kim. She also opened a new chapter in her life with a move to Goodlettsville, Tennessee.

ACHIEVEMENTS

2008

Tournament Champion - Tournament of Champions

2007

Tournament Champion - Tournament of Champions

Tournament Champion - WPBA Midwest Classic

Tournament Champion - Enjoypool.com World 9-Ball Championship

2006

Tournament Champion - Tournament of Champions

Tournament Champion - WPBA Midwest Classic

Tournament Champion - WPBA Florida Classic

Tournament Champion - WPBA Carolina Classic

2005

Tournament Champion - WPBA Florida Classic

2004

Tournament Champion - Nationals

Tournament Champion - BCA Open

3rd place - WPA World 9-Ball Championships

2003

Tournament Champion - BCA Open

Tournament Champion - Valley Forge, PA

Tournament Champion - US Open

Tournament Champion - Canadian Classic

2002

Tournament Champion - Nationals

2nd place - WPA World 9-Ball Championships

Tournament Champion - BCA Open

Tournament Champion - WPBA Spring Classic

2001

Pool & Billiard Magazine's Player of the Year

Billiard Digest Magazine's Player of the Year

WPBA's Sportsperson of the Year

World Games - Silver Medalist

Tournament Champion - WPBA Nationals

Tournament Champion - WPBA Midwest Classic

Tournament Champion - WPBA Alburquerque, NM

Tournament Champion - WPBA Charlotte, NC

Tournament Champion - WPBA Spring Classic

Tournament Champion - WPBA Valley Forge, PA

2nd place - WPA World 9-Ball Championships

2000

N.E. Woman's Tour Player of the Year

Tournament Champion - WPBA Valley Forge, PA

Tournament Champion - Baltimore Shootout

Tournament Champion - LA Expo

Tournament Champion - All Japan Championship

2nd place - WPA world 9-Ball Championships

1999

Billiard Digest Magazine's Rookie of the Year

N.E. Woman's Tour Player of the Year

World English Billiards Champion

1998

N.E. Woman's Tour Player of the Year

World English Billiards Champion

European Snooker Champion

1997

World English Billiards Champion

World Snooker Champion

1995-1996

World Snooker Champion

1990-1991

World Snooker Champion

Certified BCA instructor

First woman qualified through the World Snooker Association to coach snooker

SHANELLE LORAINE

"Glamorous Beauty of Pool..."

Shanelle Loraine, who is one of the bright new faces of the billiards world, is an up and coming female pool player on a journey to become a world class billiards artist. Since her debut in the billiards world in Korea, Shanelle Loraine made headlines by defeating Jeanette Lee live on national television! You've read right, friends! It happened at the Dragon Promotions Women's World Pool Cup!

Shanelle Loraine then finished second place only to Ga Young Kim in the MBC ESPN Women's Ultimate Trick Shot Challenge, besting a field of players that included top players Miyuki Sakai, Yu Ram Cha, Isabelle Krafczyk, and Jeanette Lee. People immediately started to search for more information on this glamorous beauty from Guam – quickly becoming the most searched topic online in Korea for days!

Shanelle Loraine plays with a Poison Arsenic Pool Cue - the Poison AR6, and uses Poison Cues' VX 2.9 Jump Break Cue – all with the Uni-Loc Bullet joint. She is currently coached by Charlie Williams and Wayne Catledge of Orlando. Moreover, Shanelle has had instruction with billiards legends such as Mike Massey, Mika Immonen, and the great 3 Cushion master Semih Sayginer. And her wins against that formidable group of pool players just goes to show Shanelle Loraine is not just about good looks! She is definitely a pool player to reckon with!

With the upsurge in popularity of female pool players, I decided to make a regular posts on the women of our favorite sport - billiards. And without further ado, here are some pictures of the beautiful Shanelle Loraine, who is managed by Dragon Promotions and Predator Cues – Poison Billiards line.

Shanelle is an up and coming pool player who's on a journey to become world class. She is currently sponsored by Poison Billiards, the most sophisticated pool cue at its price range, benefiting from Predator engineering and designed for pool players just getting into the game.

JEANETTE LEE

"My most thrilling game moment was: the first time I ran over a 100 balls and then later it was when I won the gold medal in the 2001 World Games... One for personal accomplishment, one for the prestige of it.'"

Jeanette Lee, known throughout the world as "The Black Widow," has enjoyed one of the most illustrious careers in billiards history. Repeatedly recognized by Billiards Digest as one of the sport's most powerful people, Lee has claimed more than 30 national and international titles. Formerly ranked as the #1 player in the world, she was named the "WPBA Sportsperson of the Year" in 1998 and has earned Player of the Year honors from both Billiards Digest and Pool & Billiards Magazine. In 2001, Jeanette was the Gold medalist for the United States at the World Games and has also captured Silver twice at the World Championships during her 14-year professional career. In 2004, Jeanette won the World Trick Shot Championships and BCA Open. In 2005 Jeanette won the China Invitational and more recently in 2007 won the World Team Cup, Empress Cup, and the International Skins Billiard Championship with her doubles partner and husband, George Breedlove.

Born on July 9, 1971, Jeanette was raised in Brooklyn, NY. At the age of thirteen, Jeanette was diagnosed with scoliosis, a disorder in which there is a curve, often S-shaped or C-shaped, of the spine or backbone. To alleviate the progression of the debilitating condition, Jeanette underwent scoliosis surgery. The surgical procedure involved techniques to fuse or join the vertebrae along the curve of her spine. Metal rods and other instrumentation were attached to her spine in order to hold her vertebrae together during the months after her surgery while the bones in her spine eventually fused together. Such instrumentation was left in her body where they remain today. Scoliosis surgery is one of the longest and most complicated orthopedic surgical procedures performed on children due to the long operation time and hospitalization for recovery. Her surgery at the time was thought to be a success, but Jeanette's affliction with scoliosis was not yet at an end.

As an adolescent, Jeanette Lee excelled in scholastics and was accepted into the prestigious Bronx High School of Science. Jeanette expected to attend college and pursue a more conventional career after graduating high school. She completed two years of college while pursuing a Bachelor degree in Early Childhood Development and Elementary Education. However, around this time period in her young life, Jeanette discovered the game of pool, a discovery that would change the course of her life.

Jeanette immersed herself in all facets of the game and began to practice pool incessantly; practicing up to ten hours a day. Additionally, Jeanette began studying literature on the game and even befriended "old-time" pool professionals.

During this time of her billiards immersion, Jeanette suffered immensely from pain caused by the steel rods implanted in her back. Her intense pursuit to perfect her new passion consequently aggravated her spinal condition. Regardless, Jeanette relentlessly continued to exert herself physically and mentally. According to one account, she played pool consecutively for thirty-seven hours, to the point of unbearable pain, physical exhaustion, and literally had to be lifted and carried back home by her friends.

In 1993, Jeanette's hard work and unrelenting pursuit of excellence in the game of pool resulted in her professional debut at the age of 21. She turned pro as a full-time member of the Women's Professional Billiards Association (WPBA) only three years after picking up the sport at age 18. In only her first year as a pro, Lee rocketed into the ranks of the top ten in the WPBA. Less than two years later, at the age of 23, Lee was ranked the number one women's professional pool player in the world.

Jeanette Lee entered the professional pool world with fury. Her reputation grew to legendary proportions as the world came to know her as "The Black Widow," a persona Lee acquired through her ability to overwhelm, almost devour, her opponents in combination with exclusively wearing black attire during tournaments.

Lee's first victory came in 1994 at the Baltimore Billiard Classic, the debut event of the WPBA season. Lee followed up her first professional title with another win at the tour's next event, the Kasson Twin Cities Classic, and went on to claim two more titles at the BCA San Francisco Classic and U.S. Open 9-Ball Championships. She capped off her sophomore season with a win at the

Connelly WPBA National Championships in the tour finale for five victories and was named "Player of the Year" by Billiards Digest.

Lee's success continued in 1995 as she captured titles at the Olhausen Los Angeles Classic and the Brunswick New York Classic, and was nominated by the WPBA for the "Sports Person of the Year" award; a nomination she would receive again in 1997, before winning the award in 1998. Jeanette would claim three more tour stops during the next two seasons, winning the BCA Charlotte Classic in 1996 and posting back-to-back victories at the Hubler Cues Nashville Classic and the Olhausen San Diego Classic in 1997. Lee's spectacular performance in 1997 earned her "Player of the Year" honors by Pool & Billiards Magazine.

In 1998, Jeanette would post three more victories en route to being named the "WPBA Sportsperson of the Year." She claimed another trio of wins during the 1999 season, including the Tournament of Champions. In 2001, Lee not only won the BCA Open Championship, but also took home the Gold medal for the United States at the 2001 World Games. Lee claimed the Tournament of Champions again in 2003 and added two more titles in 2004, with wins at the Cuetec Cues Florida Classic and the Women's Trick Shot Magic World Championship.

Yet, throughout Jeanette's flourishing career and unprecedented success, she suffered from chronic pain, which stemmed from her scoliosis. By August 2005, Jeanette had undergone a total of nine surgeries to the back, neck, and shoulder. In spite of her medical challenges, Lee continues to achieve in the game of pool and other ventures outside of the pro billiards tour. She is celebrated as an inspiring leader and has served as the National Spokesperson for The Scoliosis Association, Inc. for the last decade. She also serves as a trustee or the Women's Sports Foundation.

Lee's beautiful and deadly game, underscored through her nickname "The Black Widow," has attracted attention away from the pool table as well. She has been featured on ESPN's list of Sexiest Female Athletes in the World, in Esquire's Ten Women We Love and among Aloette Cosmetics Dozen Most Attractive Women Athletes. Jeanette has made television appearances on Arli$$, Best Damn Sports Show Period, Entertainment Tonight, Extra!, Hard Copy, HBO Real Sports, Late Show with Craig Kilborn, Today, The Late Show with David Letterman and Live with Regis & Kelly. She was also featured in an ESPN SportsCenter commercial and made a cameo appearance in the Walt Disney Picture The Other Sister.

The combination of Lee's pool prowess, engaging personality, beauty and mystique has led to Lee's renowned reputation as the most famous pool player of her generation. She is unmistakably a fan favorite and continues to dazzles audiences with her pool artistry and arsenal of trick shots. Golf Digest proclaims Lee "an absolute show stopper," noting that "she was the star at our U.S. Open party filled with Donald Trump, Carson Daly and other celebrities."

World champion pool player, celebrity, and philanthropist Jeanette Lee recently announced in March 2007, plans to build the first Black Widow Billiards at Carolina Crossroads. The two-story, 20,000 square foot facility will feature 24 pool tables, a full-service pro-shop, restaurant, VIP rooms. Scheduled to open in 2008, Black Widow Billiards will be equipped for televised tournaments, as well as charity and corporate events.

Jeanette Lee currently resides in Indianapolis, Indiana with her husband George Breedlove, a top ranked men's pro billiards player and owner of Midwest Outdoor Products, their three year-old adopted daughter Cheyenne Lee Breedlove, whom they have had since her birth, and John Kang, a fifteen year-old New York native who they obtained legal guardianship over in February 2007. Morgan and Olivia Breedlove, Jeanette's two step-daughters, are currently attending universities in Indiana.

JASMIN OUSCHAN

"Best words of advice I have received are: That winning is not always everything in life."

Jasmin Ouschan is an Austrian professional pool player from Klagenfurt, Carinthia in Austria. Her first professional competition occurred in 2002, but she did not officially become a professional member of the Women's Professional Billiards Association (WPBA) until 2007. She is currently one of the top-ranked women in the world according to the 2009 prize money list and by the WPBA rankings. At times, she has been ranked as the number one female player in the world. Since 2006, she has been listed among the top-ten women in the annual prize money rankings. Ouschan competes regularly with men on

the EuroTour and in 2008 became the first woman to earn a medal in an open world pool championship.

In international competition she has earned the World Games 2005 gold medal and World Games 2009 silver medal in nine-ball. She has earned a total of nineteen European Championship gold medals (nine in eight-ball, seven in nine-ball and three in straight pool) since 1999, including eight (three in eight-ball, two in nine-ball and three in straight pool) since joining the open Women's division in 2005. She was the Youth European Champion in eight-ball six consecutive years from 1999–2004 and is the current two-time defending Women's European Champion in the event as well as the defending champion in nine-ball.

Ouschan began playing pool at a very early age because her parents owned a pool hall. Although she had a miniature table of her own, she aspired to play on the regulation size table and started playing by standing on a box. She has trained with Michael Neumann since the age of six and continues to train with him to this day. She has a younger brother named Albin. She graduated from high school in 2004 and has since taken coursework to become an accredited pool trainer in Europe.

She has earned eight open European Championship titles in eight-ball (2006, 2008, 2009), nine-ball (2005, 2009), and straight pool (2005–2007) in the women's division. She also won eleven Youth European Championship titles in eight-ball (1999–2004) and nine-ball (1999–2001, 2003, 2004).

In 1996, she entered at a tournament in Austria in which players like Allison Fisher, Gerda Hofstaetter and Franziska Stark participated and placed 4th place behind these three well established players. In 1998, she earned a silver medal in eight-ball and a bronze medal in nine-ball at the Youth European Championship. Starting in 1999 , she won gold medals in both events every year as a Youth until 2004 except in 2002 when she earned a silver in nine-ball.

Her first professional competition was the Florida Classic 2002. In 2002, she had professional earnings of US$1,750 in prize money for taking first place in the 2002 WPBA Amateur Nationals. In 2005, she had earnings of $1,700. That year she became the World Games women's nine-ball champion. She also moved up to the Women's division in the annual European Championships in 2005 and has earned at least one gold medal each year since.

In 2006, she was ranked sixth among women in the prize money year-end rankings with a total of $36,251 in earnings. That year, she won the May 14—20, 2006 BCA Open Nine-ball Championship women's division, defeating the UK's Allison Fisher and earning $20,000. She has competed in what have traditionally been regarded as men's tournaments, especially while participating in the EuroTour. She placed 5th in the men's World Straight Pool Championship in 2006, which was won by Thorsten Hohmann. She also finished 3rd in the women's World Pool 10-ball Championship in Manila, Philippines.

In 2007, she joined the WPBA. That year, she was ranked ninth among women in the prize money year-end rankings with a total of $23,000 in earnings. Her best payday for the year was a second place finish at the WPBA San Diego Classic for which she earned $8,300. She competed again at the Men's World Straight Pool Championship in 2007 but lost to Warren Kiamco in the last 16 to finish in 9th place.

In 2008, she was ranked fourth among women in the prize money year-end rankings with a total of $44,059 in earnings. During the season, she reached the top of the world rankings. Her largest victory that year was the September 14 WPBA Carolina Classic 7–1 win over Jeanette Lee, which earned her $13,500. In 2008, she reached the Men's World Straight Pool Championship semifinal by beating Mika Immonen and defending champion Oliver Ortmann, but then lost against Francisco Bustamante. However, her third place finish resulted in the first medal won by any woman in an open world pool championship.

In April 2009, she won the European Championship eight-ball competition. She was also the world's top-ranked woman in early 2009. On June 21, 2009 she earned $12,700 for winning the WPBA Great Lakes Classic. On July 25, she earned a silver medal after losing to Allison Fisher at the 2009 World games. As of August 3, 2009, her 2009 earnings, which rank fourth on the prize money list, are $23,878.

MONICA WEBB

"What I enjoy most about competing is: the intensity and the other good players."

Born and living in Atlanta, GA, Monica Webb played in her first professional event in 1995 before going pro in 1999. She quickly rose to the upper echelon of the tour despite the lack of a first- or second-place finish. However, she is a former Amateur National champion and also boasts numerous top-five finishes. Monica fell in love with the game of billiards when she was only 8 yrs old. Her father, Johnny, opened a local pool room in her home town of Douglasville, GA. With the help and coaching of top ranked touring pro and US OPEN Champion Helena Thornfeldt, Monica won the 1998 Amateur

Nationals Championship and went on to become the #1 United States player on the Women's Pro Billiard Assoc. Tour (WPBA). Monica has one of the top 3 most consistent top finishing records in pool and that has earned her an impressive amount of T.V. coverage on ESPN, ESPN2 and ESPN CLASSIC. Monica says "Stay tuned, because the best is yet to come!"

original name, the indirect game, is thought to have developed in the 1820s in Britain, it developed out of an older game called the doublet game, that dates to at least 1807. The game is sometimes incorrectly called one-cushion or one-cushion billiards, which is the direct translation of its name into English from various other languages such as Spanish ("una banda") and German ("einband").

The object of cushion caroms is to score cushion caroms, meaning a bounce off of both of the other balls on the table, with at least one rail of the table being struck by the cue ball before the contact with second object ball. Cushion caroms was not played for a number of years, but came back in the late 1860s. Its return was for similar reasons as to why balkline developed. It was frustration of many people with straight rail. The techniques such as nursing that were invented to make scoring much easier, also made the game very boring to watch. Thus, as straight rail lost popularity, cushion caroms was revived for a time. Cushion caroms is rarely played in the U.S., but it still has some popularity in Europe.

Three-cushion billiards

In three-cushion billiards, sometimes called three-cushion carom, three-cushion, three-cushions, three-rail, rails and the angle game, the object is to carom off both object balls with at least three rails being contacted before the contact of the cue ball with the second object ball. Arising sometime in the 1870s, the origin of three-cushion billiards is not entirely known. It is undisputed that the Internal Revenue Collector of the Port of St. Louis, Wayman C. McCreery, made the game popular. At least one publication states he invented the game as well.

The first three-cushion billiards tournament took place January 14–31, 1878 in C. E. Mussey's Room in St. Louis, with McCreery taking part. The tournament was won by New Yorker Leon Magnus. The high run for the tournament was just 6 points, and the high average a .75. The game was infrequently played prior to 1907, with many top carom players of the era saying they did not enjoy it. However, in 1907 after the introduction of the Lambert Trophy, the game became more popular in the U.S. and internationally.

By 1924 three-cushion had become so popular that two very well know players in other billiard areas agreed to play each other in it at a challenge match. On September 22, 1924 Willie Hoppe (last name rhymes with "poppy"), the world balkline champion and Ralph Greenleaf, the world pocket billiards (pool) title holder, played a well-advertised, multiple-day, 600-point match. Hoppe was the eventual winner with a final score of 600–527. The game's decline in the U.S. came about in 1952 when Hoppe, then 51-time billiards champion, announced his retirement.

Wayman C. McCreery, possible inventor of three-cushion billiards. Three-cushion billiards is a very difficult game. Averaging one point per turn at the table is professional-level play, and averaging 1.5 to 2 is world-class play. An average of

one means that for every turn at the table, a player makes one point and misses once. This means that the player makes a point on only 50% of his or her shots. The highest run at three-cushion billiards for many years was 25, set by the American Willie Hoppe in 1918 during an exhibition. As of 2007, the high run record is 31 points, shared between Semih Saygıner of Turkey and Hugo Patiño who is originally fromColombia but resides in the U.S. The best game at the standard 50 points in a tournament is 9 innings by the Swedish player, Torbjörn Blomdahl in 2000, and 4 innings (count: 19-11-9-11) by Korean and U.S. national champion, Sang Lee in September 1992 in a game at SL Billiards in Queens,New York. The highest tournament average is 2.536 by Dick Jaspers from the Netherlands in 2002 at a tournament in Monaco. Raymond Ceulemans from Belgium has won an unmatchable 21 three-cushion billiards world-championships.

Three-cushion billiards is the most popular carom billiards game played in the U.S. today, where pocket billiards (pool) is far more widespread. Three-cushion retains great popularity in parts of Europe, Asia, and Latin America.

The principal governing body of the sport is the Union Mondiale de Billiard (UMB). That organization has been holding world three-cushion championships since the late 1920s. Decades later, the Billiards World Cup Association (BWA) competed with UMB, but faded in the late 1990s due to financial problems. The International Olympic Committee-recognized World Pool-Billiard Association (WPA) cooperates with the UMB to keep their rule sets consistent.

Artistic billiards

In Artistic billiards, sometimes called fantasy billiards or fantaisie classique, players compete at performing 76 planned shots, each assigned a degree of difficulty. Each set shot has a maximum point value assigned for perfect execution, ranging from a 4-point maximum for lowest level difficulty shots, and climbing to an 11-point maximum for shots deemed highest in difficulty level. There is a total of 500 points available to a player. The governing body of the sport is the Confédération Internationale de Billiard Artistique (CIBA).

Each shot in an artistic billiards match is played from a well-defined starting position. In fact, in some tournaments the balls must be placed within two millimeters of a diagrammed position. Each shot must also be done in an established manner in order for points to be awarded. Players are allowed three attempts at each shot. In general, the 76 shots in the game—even the lowest difficulty 4-point shots—require a high degree of skill, much practice and specialized knowledge to perform.

World title competition first started in 1986 and required the use of ivory balls. However, this requirement was dropped in 1990. The highest score ever achieved in world competition was 374, by the Frenchman Jean Reverchon in 1992. The highest score in competition overall is 427 set by Belgian Walter Bax on March 12, 2006 at a competition held in Deurne, Belgium, beating his own previous record of 425. The game is played mostly in western Europe, especially in France, Belgium and the Netherlands.

Heated slate

The slate bed of a billiard table is often heated to about 5 °C (9 °F) above room temperature, which helps to keep moisture out of the cloth to aid the balls rolling and rebounding in a consistent manner, and generally makes a table play faster. A heated table is required under international carom rules and is an especially important requirement for the games of three-cushion billiards and artistic billiards. Heating table beds is an old practice.Queen Victoria (lived 1819–1901) had a billiard table that was heated using zinc tubes, although the aim at that time was chiefly to keep the then-used ivory balls from warping. The first use of electric heating was for an 18.2 balkline tournament held in December 1927 between Welker Cochranand Jacob Schaefer, Jr. The New York Times announced it with fanfare: "For the first time in the history of world's championship balkline billiards a heated table will be used ..."

HISTORY OF GAMES

Straight rail

Straight rail, sometimes called carom billiards, straight billiards, the three-ball game, the carambole game, and the free game in Europe, is thought to date to the 1700s. No exact time of origin is known though. It was called French caroms, French billiards or the French game in early times, taking those old names from the French who made the game popular. The object of straight rail is simple: one point, called a "count", is scored each time a player's cue ball makes contact with both object balls (the second cue ball and the third ball) on a single strike of the cue ball. Winning is achieved by reaching a certain number of points, agreed to between the players to be the winning number.

When straight rail was first invented there was no restriction on the way points were scored. However, the technique of crotching, meaning to have two balls right next to each other on the area of one of the table's four corners where the rails meet—the crotch—made scoring a lot easier. This resulted in an 1862 rule which allowed only three counts before at least one ball had to be sent away from the corner in order to legally score another point. Techniques continued to develop which increased counts greatly despite the crotching ban. One of these techniques is called "nursing", and made scoring much easier. A "nurse" is a series of shots where the balls are kept very close together, allowing a player to score off of them with very soft strokes without changing their positions much, so the scoring can continue. The most important of these nurse techniques, called the rail nurse, involves nudging the balls down a rail, moving them just a few centimeters on each score and keeping them close together and positioned at the end of each stroke in the same or near the same arrangement so that the rail nurse can be repeated.

Professional straight rail in the United States was only seen for six years, from 1873 to 1879. It was followed by a game designed to reduce the use of the rail nurse so that spectators would not be bored by watching it. Today, straight rail play is not very common in the U.S. but it still popular in Europe, where it is thought to be a good practice game for balkline and three-cushion billiards. Europe hosts professional

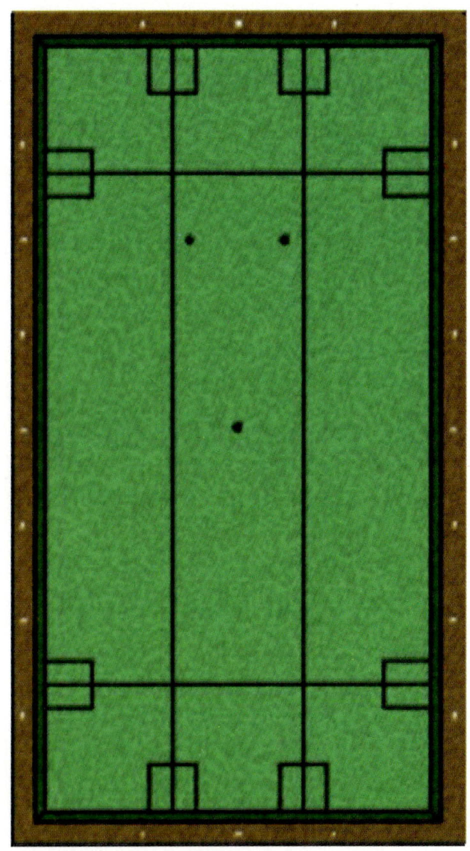

Balkline table with standard markings

competitions, known as pentathlons after the ancient Greek Olympic competitions, in which straight rail is one of five billiards games at which players compete. The other four are called 47.1 balkline, cushion caroms, 71.2 balkline and three-cushion billiards.

The champion's game

A new game appeared in 1879, called the champion's game or limited-rail. The champion's game is considered an in-between game—between straight rail and balkline—and was designed to stop the rail nurse. The game uses diagonal lines—balklines—drawn at the table's corners to indicate that if balls were inside those lines, points could not be scored, thus "cutting off four triangular spaces in the four corners, [taking] away 28 inches [711 mm] of the 'nursing' surface of the end rails and 56 inches [1422 mm] on the long rails." Despite its differences from straight rail, the champion's game only expanded the areas of the table where many points in a row could be scored before the balls had to be moved to a new position. This was not sufficient to stop nursing.

Balkline

Balkline came after the champion's game. It added more rules to stop nursing techniques. There are many varieties of balkline, but all divide the table into marked regions called balk spaces. The balk spaces define areas of the surface of the table where a player may only score up to a certain number of points while the object balls are within that region.

In the balkline games, rather than drawing balklines a few inches from the corners as was done in the champion's games, the entire table is divided into rectangular spaces. This is done by drawing balklines a certain distance across the length and the width of the table. The lines are drawn a number of inches parallel from each rail. This divides the table into eight rectangular areas called "balk spaces". Additionally, rectangles are drawn where each balkline meets a rail, called anchor spaces. The anchor spaces were added to the game to stop nursing techniques that developed especially for the challenges of balkline without them.

Generally, the differences between one balkline game and another are defined by two different things: 1) where the balkines are drawn on the table, and 2) the number of points that are allowed in each balk space before at least one ball must leave that region of the table. Balkline games are named by giving two numbers that tell us about the spacing used and how many points can be scored in the balk spaces. The first number tells us how many inches from the rail the balkine will be drawn. The second number after a "dot", indicates the number of points that can be scored in the balk spaces before the balls must leave it (that number is always either one or two). So, for example, the name 18.2 balkline, tells us that balklines are drawn 18 inches (460 mm) distant from each rail, and only two points are allowed in a balk space before a ball must leave that area.

Over its history balkline has had many variations including 8.2, 10.2, 12.2, 13.2, 12½.2, 14.1, 14.2, 18.1, 18.2, 28.2, 38.2, 39.2, 42.2, 45.1, 45.2, 47.1, 47.2, 57.2 and 71.2 balkline. In its different forms, balkline was the main carom game played from 1883 to the 1930s. After that, other carom games became more popular. This is especially true of three-cushion billiards. Balkline is not very common in the U.S., but remains popular in Europe and the Far East.

Cushion caroms

Jacob Schaefer, Sr. tobacco card, c. 1880s; Schaefer was a dominant billiards player during the 19th century.

Cushion caroms, sometimes called by its

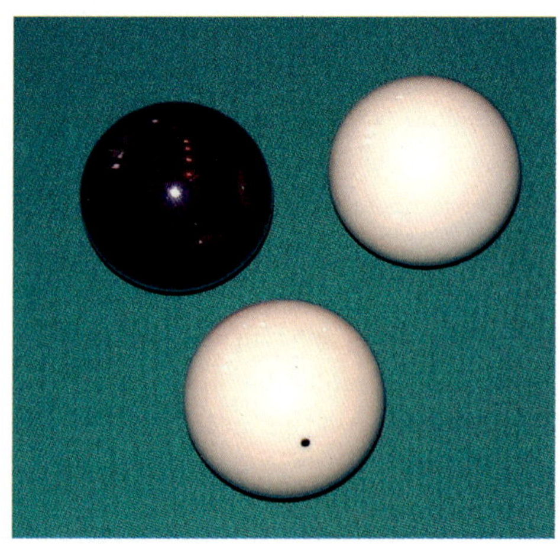

A standard set of carom billiards balls, including a red object ball, a plain white cue ball, and a dotted cue ball for the opponent. Some games use an additional object ball.

Carom Billiards

When imagination run riot on Billiards Table

Carom billiards, sometimes called carambole billiards or simply carambole (and sometimes used as another word for a game called "straight rail") are a family of billiards games played on cloth-covered tables. In these games, the players strike heavy balls with sticks called cues. Carom billiards tables have no pockets or opening where balls are sunk, that snooker and pool tables do have. In its simplest form, the object of carom billiards games is to score points or "counts" by bouncing one's own ball, called a cue ball, off of the other two balls on the table. The date the first carom game was invented is not exactly known. Also, how exactly the games developed and which game was first is not clear. However, carom billiards games are believed to have started sometime in the 18th-century (the 1700s) inFrance in Europe.

There are many different games, each with distinct rules, strategies and objects of play, that are all part of carom billiards. Some of the most well known games are straight rail, cushion caroms, balkline, three-cushion billiards and artistic billiards. There are many other carom billiards games that combine aspects of these games, but that are not as well known. For example, the champion's game was a short-lived game that developed during a transitional period between the invention of straight rail and the invention of balkline. Other games are combinations of these games and other games played on tables with pockets (pool or snooker games), such as English billiards played on a snooker table and its related games, American four-ball billiards, and cowboy pool, played on a pool table.

How the name came about

The word "carom" means any strike and bounce off something. It started being used to describe the pocketless billiard games in the 1860s. It is a shortening of the word carambola, used in Spanish and Portuguese and spelled carambole in French. Carambola was earlier used to describe just the red ball used in billiards games, but later was given to the game itself. Some people who study word origins suggest that carambola was originally the name of a yellow-to-orange colored, tropical Asian fruit, known in Portuguese as a carambola. This was taken from an earlier word, karambal, from the Marathi language of India, also known as starfruit. The accuracy of the fruit origin has been questioned. It has been said to be just a legend, because the fruit does not look very similar to the big red ball that is used in carom games, and there is no direct proof for the fruit explanation.

Cues

Carom billiard cues have specialized refinements making them different from the typical pool cue with which many people are more familiar. Such cues tend to be shorter and lighter overall, with a shorter ferrule, a thicker butt and joint, a wooden joint pin (in high-end examples) and collarless wood-to-wood joint (for a one-piece cue "feel"), a fast, conical taper, and a smaller tip diameter as compared with pool cues. Typical cues are 140–140 cm (54–56 in) in length and 470–520 g (16.5–18.5 oz) in weight—lighter for straight rail, heavier for three-cushion—with a tip 11–12 mm (0.43–0.47 in) in diameter. The specialization makes the cue significantly stiffer, which aids in handling the larger and heavier billiard balls as compared with pool cues. It also acts to reduce deflection (sometimes called "squirt"), which may be defined as displacement of the cue ball's path away from the parallel line formed by the cue stick's direction of travel. It is a factor that occurs every time english (side) is employed, and its effects are magnified by speed. In some carom games, deflection plays a large role because many shots require extremes of English, coupled with great speed; this is a combination typically minimized as much as possible, by contrast, in pool. The wood used in carom cues can vary widely, and most quality carom cues are handmade.

They also made us Proud in the realms of Cue Sports

(POOL)

Mukesh Rehani

He was born on 8th September' 1961 & represented India in World Pool Championship.

First as a player and later as the national pool coach, Rehani connected with everyone involved with the game. A trendsetter, Rehani was the first Indian to reach the knockout stage (Last 64) of the World 9-ball Pool Championship in Cardiff in 2004. The No.2 billiards player in the country also played pro billiards for five years.

The sad demise of Mukesh Rehani on June' 10 2011 was shock for everyone.

Alok Kumar

The seasoned Right Handed Cueist was born on 05th October '1968 in Mandi Govind Garh in Punjab. His highest Sports Qualification is IBSF World Billiards # 2 – 2013, IBSF World Snooker # 3 – 2006 Asian Snooker Champion - 2004

Alok Kumar won India's first ever Asian Games medal in Pool in November 2010. In the year 2011 he created history by beating Sumit Talwar 9-8 to annex his maiden 8 ball pool title and become the first player to win all possible National titles in Cue Sports - Snooker, Billiards, 9-ball and 8-ball pool.

Asian Billiards Champion – 2011 Asian Games Pool Bronze – 2010.

His highest break in Billiards is 398 & in Snooker 142. He won 2014 Asian Billiards Championship - Silver Medalist, - 2013 World Billiards Championship (Timed Format) - Bronze Medalist, 2013 Asian Team Snooker Championship - Gold Medalist, - 2013 Asian Billiards Championship - Silver Medalist, - 2011 Asian Billiards Championship – Winner, - 2011 Asian Billiards Championship – Winner.

Dharminder Lilly

Born on 19th November 1974 in Jallandhar, Punjab. 2014 Asian Team Snooker Championship – Gold. He turned professional in the year 1995 He turned professional in the year 1995 Indian National Champion Carombole.

Lilly is 9 Ball Pool game specialist and in the year 2007 he finished runners-up at Asian 9-ball pool championship. He also won 2001 & 2007 National Carombole Championship.

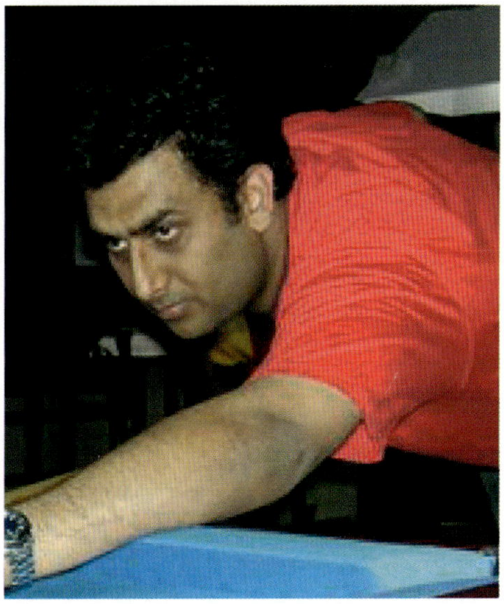

Manan Chandra

Manan Chandra is born on 28 February 1981 in New Delhi. He is an internationally notable Indian amateur snooker and pool player.

Chandra reached the semi final at the 2006 IBSF World Championships in Amman, Jordan, where he was eliminated by Daniel Ward 8-7.

Sumit Talwar

Sumit Talwar is born on 06th February 1983 in Chandigarh, PUNJAB. He won the 2010 Indian National 8Ball Pool Championship. He reached quarter finals of 2006 Doha Asian Games 9 Ball Pool Championship. He was ranked 2nd in 2011 Indian National 8Ball Pool Championship.

Competition disciplines

- **Triathlon:** Straight rail, Balkline and One-cushion or Balkline, One-cushion und Three-cushion (like the actually ANAG Billiard Cup).

- **Pentathlon:** Straight rail, Balkline (47/2 & 71/2), One-cushion and Three-cushion.

BASICS ABOUT THE GAME

There are no pockets on this type of billiard table. The idea is to try to use the white cue ball to hit the other two. What makes this interesting is that there is one more rule: Your cue ball must hit at least 3 cushions before striking the last ball.

To illistrate, imagine a carom billiard table (twice as long as wide with no pockets), where one can locate any point on the table using the Cartesian coordinate system. Let the lower left corner be (0,0) and the upper-right corner (8,4).

The "Diamond system"

The Diamond system is used in 3-cushion billiards find a place to aim the cue ball so that it strikes 3 cushions before hitting any balls.

This system has three steps : First find the natural angle off the cushion that would strike both target balls.

Find the cue position, counting the diamonds differently. Begin near the corner by the target balls, and count by 1/2 the diamonds (or dots) starting at 1 1/2.

Subtract the Natural Angle (Step 1) from the Cue position (step 2). The result is diamond (or dot) that you need to aim at, counting with the same numbering as Step 1, to strike three cushions before the two other target balls.

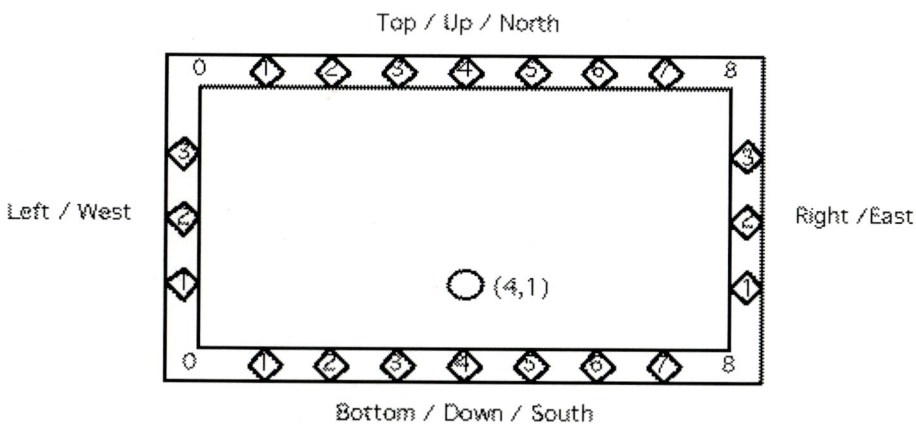

A cue ball at (2,2) needs to be aimed at diamond 4 1/2 on the south cushion so it can strike the other two balls at (5,3) and (5, 2 1/2)

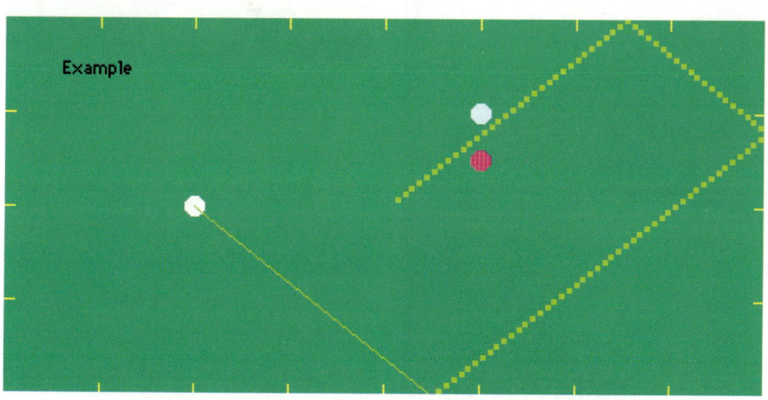

The "Diamond System" is one way to help figure out the correct place to aim the cue ball. In this example we have a cue position of 5, and a natural angle of 1 1/2, so the diamond to aim at is 5 - 1 1/2 = 3 1/2 (counting from the right -- this would be 4 1/2 in the coordinate system, where you always count from the left to the right). This looks complicated until you get the idea of how to count the diamonds..

CAROM BILLIARDS PLAYER OF REPUTE

Nobuaki Kobayashi

Nobuaki Kobayashi (born March 26, 1942) is a Japanese professional three-cushion billiards player and 2-time world champion.

After placing 2nd to Belgium's Raymond Ceulemans three times (1970, 1972 and 1973) in the UMB World Three-cushion

Championship, Kobayashi turned things around and defeated Ceulemans for the world title in 1974. With this win, he ended Ceulemans' 10-year reign as champion. Kobayashi later admitted that he had been taping on camera Ceulemans' performances in a 1969 tournament in Tokyo in order to study the Belgian's playing style.

A decade later, he won it again at the expense of Ludo Dielis. He defended it unsuccessfully the following year, losing to Ceulemans again.

For more than three decades, he has been the only Asian native (not counting Sang Lee who represented the United States at the time) ever to win a World Three-cushion Championship. Two other players

from Japan were close to achieving a world title but both were not very fortunate. This was until Ryuuji Umeda, another Japanese, won the title in 2007.

Kobayashi is a 9-time Japanese Champion. His son, Hideaki Kobayashi, is also a three-cushion billiards player. His highest run documented is 15.

Dani Sánchez

Daniel Sánchez Gálvez (born 3 March 1974 in Santa Coloma de Gramenet), and best known as Dani Sánchez is a Catalan Spanish professional carom billiards player. He first reached the finals of the UMB World Three - cushion Championship in 1996, but finished 2nd to Christian Rudolph. He successfully took the title in 1998, defeating 14-time World Champion Torbjörn Blomdahl. He won it again in 2005 against Jean Paul de Bruijn.

Sánchez is a winner of the CEB European Three-cushion Championship twice (1997 and 2000) and is a 31-time Spanish national Champion. He also won the gold medal twice at the three-cushion event of the 2001 and 2005 World Games, defeating Dick Jaspers on both occasions.

Semih Saygıner

Semih Saygıner (born November 12, 1964, in Adapazarı, Turkey) nicknamed Mr. Magic and the Turkish Prince, is a Turkish professional carom billiards player.

He won the 1999 CEB European Three-cushion Championship by defeating Dion Nelin of Denmark. He nearly won it again the next year but lost to Daniel Sánchez. He was the first from his country to win that tournament. A second player named Murat Naci Çoklu won it five years later.

Dick Jaspers

Dingeman Jacobus Johannes "Dick" Jaspers (born 23 July 1965) is a Dutch professional carom billiards player who specializes in the three-cushion event.

Jaspers became a professional billiard player in 1986 after seeing Raymond Ceulemans and Nobuaki Kobayashi on live television during their World Cup final in Valkenburg. Jaspers won two silver medals in the Dutch Championships 1986. In 1987 and 1989 he won the National Championship, and participated three times at the European Youth Championship. He won the gold medal on all of those occasions.

Cricket

ON SNOOKER TABLE

This is one of the most recent games to have appeared, and can be played over two frames or four. As the name implies there is a batsman and a bowler. The batsman pots colours only, and scores the same points as he would in snooker. The bowler pots reds only, and when all these have been potted the frame is over, and the batsman's score is recorded. The table is then re-set, and the game continues with the players reversing their roles. If it is felt necessary to handicap the batsman, the best way is to limit him to two consecutive pots on any spotted ball.

THE RULES OF CRICKET

The game is played with the twenty-two balls of the snooker set.

To begin the game the twenty-one object-balls from the snooker set are placed in a triangle, with the apex ball placed on the Pyramid spot as depicted in the above diagram. The six coloured balls are placed in any order in the centre of the triangle, with the fifteen reds completely surrounding them.

The opening (break) stroke of each frame is played by the bowler, who, playing from the 'D', must cause at least two object-balls to contact a cushion.

The bowler is always 'on' the reds. If he causes the cue-ball to contact a coloured ball before a red, it is a foul.

No red balls are ever re-spotted.

If the bowler makes a foul stroke, then as in Snooker, the relevant points are added to the score of his opponent.

The batsman is always 'on' the colours. If he causes the cue-ball to contact a red before a colour, it is a foul.

If the batsman makes a foul stroke, the bowler may remove any red ball of his choice from the table.

The batsman scores points by potting the coloured balls. which have the same value as they do in Snooker.

After a coloured ball has been potted, it must be replaced on its own spot; but if its spot is occupied, then as in Snooker it must be placed on the highest spot available.

If the cue-ball is potted, it is a foul; and the next player must play from the 'D'.

Each frame is over when the last red is potted, or removed from the table, as in Rule 8. The winner is the player who scores most points during his turn as batsman.

Shuffle Pool

Shuffle Pool Rules apply to the game of "Shuffle Pool" which is generally a billiard game played solely as a means to gamble. Shuffle Pool can be played by any number of players, and the order of play may be dictated by any method. The red balls are arranged in a hollow triangle.

The object of Shuffle Pool is to first "qualify" to play for the colored balls. This is done by potting at least two red balls. According to Shuffle Pool rules, touching a colored ball with the cue ball before potting the requisite red balls is a foul. The penalty for this foul is the addition of one more red ball to the total of two that must be potted to qualify.

When a player qualifies, he or she selects from a blind draw box to determine which ball will be the object ball. The blind draw box shall contain tokens or slips of paper representing the balls numbered two through seven. (Yellow through Black.) The shooting player is not required to inform the other players of which ball has been drawn. The game ends when a qualified player first pots their drawn object ball in one of the corner pockets. Any qualified player may pot any colored object ball in any of the corner pockets. Being the first player to qualify in Shuffle Pool, therefore, has many strategic advantages.

If a player who is late to qualify finds that their drawn ball is no longer on the table, they may call "dead" to the other players after potting one more red ball. However, that player is not required to declare "dead" and may attempt to clear other colored balls to prevent others from winning. Any qualified player may pot any red ball in any pocket. If a foul is committed after the offender has qualified, he or she must pot a red ball before they may return to shooting for colored balls.

A game of Shuffle Pool ends when either a qualified player pots their drawn ball, or when only one qualified player is at the table and all red balls are gone. All players who need to pot more red balls than are present on the table are required to withdraw from the game. It is not permitted to lay a snooker to any players who are attempting a red. If a snooker is laid in such a situation, the incoming player places the ball at a position on the table from which at least one colored ball is visible. For the purposes of the rules of Shuffle Pool, a snooker is defined as a position on the table from which no part of the ball-on is visible. If just one side of the ball is playable, the ball is not considered snookered.

Players may use one colored ball to pot another as long as the player is qualified. Players may not use a red to pot another colored ball, regardless of whether or not they are qualified. Coloured balls are returned to play on the table only if it is potted by a player who is not qualified, or if it is potted by a qualified player who is on a foul and must pot a red first. If a ball is to be returned, it is placed against the center of the top cushion. Shuffle Pool Handicapping is normally done by increasing the number of reds which unqualified players must pot.

These are the base rules, and the Shuffle pool rules tend to change from pool room to pool room. As usual, be sure to clarify the rules before play, and keep them consistent.

Slosh Pool

These Slosh Pool rules explain the very popular snooker game played quite frequently in India. According to Slosh Pool Rules, points may be scored via in-offs, cannons, and pots. The game is played similar to snooker, and the six colors are placed as they are in snooker. That is one red ball in the direct center of the top cushion, and one white ball in the direct center of the bottom cushion. The game is played by two players, each of which whom use the same cue ball. The cue ball used is generally the spot white ball from a billiards set. The following list breaks down some scoring and general Slosh Pool rules.

Slosh pool begins with the first player striking the black ball. If a cannon or a valid pot or in-off results from that shot, the beginning player continues at the table. If the shooting player fails to score, fails to hit the black ball first in the shot, or commits a foul, the player's inning is over and the incoming player is up. All Slosh Pool players have to strike the black ball first with their opening shots at the table. Should they fail to contact the black ball they shall continue toward this goal, however, each failed attempt constitutes a foul. Once the shooting player successfully strikes their black ball, they may play for any ball in each consecutive turn. If a player should foul at any time during the game, they must complete the aforementioned striking of the black ball. Slosh Pool can be played on either a time-limit or a high score limit.

- In Slosh Pool rules, to pot the black ball or to make an in-off from the black ball is worth seven point. These shots, however, can only be made in the top pockets.
- Any pot or in-off shot that is not made in the proper pocket is assessed a foul. The minimum foul assessed is four point, and higher fouls may be assessed for infractions involving higher value balls.
- Six points can be attained by potting the pink ball or performing and in-off from the pink ball. These shots may be made in any of the four corner shots. The blue ball may only be shot in to either of the two center pockets, the brown ball may be shot in to only the two bottom pockets, the green balls may be shot in to only the bottom left pocket, and the yellow ball may be shot only in to the bottom right pocket. To pot these balls would yeild the standard snooker point values for the balls, which are seven, six, five, four, three and two respectively.
- When shooting, and potting a ball from an in-off, the shooting player returns to, and plays from, within the D. All potted balls are replaced to their respective spots on the table. Any time a player is playing from in-hand, they must strike a ball out of the baulk, or strike a cushion outside of the baulk prior to contacting any ball resting inside the baulk. If this Slosh Pool regulation is not met, a four-point foul shall be assessed.
- To pot a red ball in-off is worth 30 points to the shooting player. However, if the red ball is struck directly, and a pot in-off does not result, a foul is assessed with a penalty of 30 points. After shooting the red ball, the cue ball may not strike any other ball in the same shot. Should this occur, a foul is assessed with a penalty of 30 points.
- Potting the white ball, or performing an in-off via the white ball is worth 15 points. Other conditions are identical as those with the red.
- Any shot off of the red ball or the white ball may be made in any pocket.
- Cannons may be made off of any balls except for the red and white balls. All cannons are worth two points, and only three consecutive cannons are allowed. Beyond three consecutive cannons, the player must play a pot, or an in-off. There are no restrictions on the amount of pots or in-offs a player is allowed.
- Combination pots, cannons, and in-offs are all scored as in billiards, with appropriate adjustments to the ball's values.
- If the break shot concludes with the player failing to score, his or her score is added to their previous total score. If the break shot concludes with the player committing a foul, that player loses all points scored during the inning, and the value of the foul is either deducted from the offending player's total or added to the other player's total score.

Slosh Pool rules are fairly simple, but you'll never really learn how to play Slosh Pool unless you get out there and hit the tables.

Skittles

This game is very interesting part of Cue Sports.
The general rules of the game are as follows

Game of Skittles

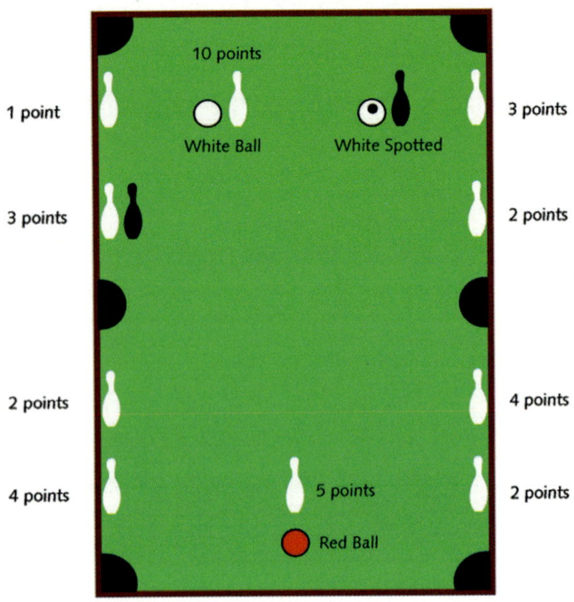

GENERAL RULES

- This game is played with three billiard balls and twelve pins (ten white and two black), all of which are placed on the table, according to the diagram.
- The game is thirty-one up. The white pins are number 1 - 10 and 2 black.
- The rotation of the players is decided by numbered counters drawn from a basket, one by each player; and each player has one stroke alternately, according to his rotation.
- Any persons who knocks down a black pin (after making his stroke) with a ball, cue, his sleeve, or in any other way and has to take a fresh cheque and the points he made stands cancelled.
- Any pin or pins having been removed by a player must be replaced before the next player makes his stroke.
- No pin is considered to be down unless it is entirely off its spot, or leaning against the cushion.
- Foul strokes are made by the following means, viz: By knocking down a white pin without striking a ball first, or before the bails have ceased running, by playing out of turn; when all the pins are not in their places, or the three balls are not on the table, or by knocking down a white pin in any way before or after playing a stroke. Running into the pocket or jumping off the table is not foul. Anyone making a foul stroke cannot score.
- A player has to make 31 points minus the counter he gets from the basket, i.e. if he gets the counter of 16 then making 15 points to win. There are 1 – 16 counters in the basket.

Michaela Tabb

First Woman Referee

PROFESSIONAL RANKING SNOOKER TOURNAMENT

Michaela Tabb (born 11 December 1967, Bath, England, UK) is the world's leading female snooker and pool referee. A former eight-ball pool player, she was a member of the Scottish Ladies' Pool Team from 1992–2003, and has also won the UK and European women's pool championships.

POOL PLAYING CAREER

Introduced to the game by a former boyfriend, Tabb started playing pool competitively in 1991 and was selected for the Scottish Ladies' Pool Team in 1992. In 1997 and 1998, the team achieved two consecutive "Grand Slams," accomplished by winning the Nations Cup, European Championships, and World Championships in the same season. Tabb captained the team during both Grand Slam wins, and remained on the team until 2003. Her sister Juliette Tabb also played on the Scottish ladies' team between 1996 and 2008.

As an individual competitor, Tabb won the UK women's singles title in 1997. The following year, she won the European Women's Pool Championship in Gibraltar.

POOL REFEREEING CAREER

Tabb became involved in refereeing in the mid-1990s, when she and her husband, professional pool player Ross McInnes, began running their own amateur eight-ball and nine-ball pool tournaments. Her husband subsequently encouraged her to pursue refereeing at a professional level.

Tabb made her professional refereeing debut at the St. Andrew's Cup nine-ball pool tournament in September 1997. She refereed on television for the first time the following year, when the 1998 St. Andrew's Cup was sponsored by Barry Hearn's Matchroom Sport and broadcast on Sky TV. Tabb went on to become one of pool's top officials, and has refereed at the WPA World Nine-ball Championship, the Mosconi Cup, and other premiere events.

Tabb has been involved in several controversies, often involving the fiery American nine-ball pool player Earl Strickland. The two were at loggerheads for much of Strickland's 2003 WPA World Nine-ball Championship match against Steve Davis, with Strickland at one point telling Tabb to "shut up" when she reprimanded him for his confrontational attitude toward Davis's supporters. Strickland later presented Tabb with flowers to apologize for his unruly behaviour. At the 2007 Mosconi Cup, she was forced to intervene when Strickland repeatedly heckled and taunted the reigning nine-ball world champion Daryl Peach, to the point where the two almost came to blows.

SNOOKER REFEREEING CAREER

In 2001, Jim McKenzie, then chief executive of the World Snooker Association, recruited Tabb to snooker, openly admitting that he wanted the 33-year-old to transform the dowdy image of the sport's referees. Dispensing with the customary five-year apprenticeship, he placed Tabb on a fast-track towards refereeing ranking tournaments, a move that, as Tabb acknowledges, generated some resentment among other officials and fellow referees.

Tabb qualified as a Class 3 snooker referee in September 2001 and made her ranking tournament debut on 23 January 2002 at the Welsh Open, refereeing a first-round match between Ken Doherty and James Wattana. On 19 April 2003, she made her World Snooker Championship debut at the Crucible Theatre in Sheffield when she took charge of a first-round match between Mark King and Drew Henry.

In July 2003, the World Snooker Association abruptly terminated the contracts of Tabb and Dutch referee Johan Oomen, stating that dwindling sponsorship revenue had forced them to cut the number of tournament referees from ten to eight, and that Tabb and Oomen had been removed on a "last in, first out" basis. However, the WSA soon reversed its decision to dismiss Tabb. She signed a new contract in September 2003.

On 18 February 2007, at the Welsh Open in Newport, Monmouthshire, Tabb became the first woman to referee a world-ranking snooker final, presiding over Neil Robertson's 9–8 defeat of Andrew Higginson. On 20 January 2008, she refereed the final of the sport's second-most prestigious tournament, the Saga Insurance Masters at Wembley Arena in London, as Mark Selby defeated Stephen Lee by 10 frames to 3 to claim his first major snooker title. On 5 April 2009, Tabb took charge of the 2009 China Open final in Beijing, where Peter Ebdon beat John Higgins by 10 frames to 8.

On May 3 and 4 2009, she became the first woman to referee a World Snooker Championship final, officiating as John Higgins defeated Shaun Murphy by 18 frames to 9 to capture his third world title. During the interval of the final's third session, the BBC broadcast a profile of Tabb, in which she discussed her refereeing career and the pressures of juggling her family life with her busy travel schedule.

CAREER SUMMARY

The world's leading female snooker referee, Michaela Tabb has certainly hit the big time in recent years and is now considered to be one of snooker's leading referees along with Eirian Williams and Jan Verhaas.

It was in another cue-sport where she made her name however as she forged a successful career as a pool referee, starting in September 1997 during the St Andrews Cup as organised by Matchroom Sports. Indeed this proved to be the start of a long association between Michaela and Barry Hearn's company and one that still exists today as she takes time out from her snooker schedule to referee the Mosconi Cup competition.

Michaela chats following day one of the 2007 Mosconi Cup. Her involvement with snooker was to begin in 2001 when her achievements in pool were recognised by World Snooker who approached her with regard to the possibility of refereeing in their competitions. As a snooker fan since she was a little girl, Michaela jumped at the chance and quickly began to rise up the ranks.

Her first major landmark came at the 2002 Welsh Open when she took charge of the round one clash between eventual finalist Ken Doherty and Thailand's James Wattana. Indeed the Welsh event has been a special one to her down the years as five years later she became the first female to referee a ranking event final there as Neil Robertson defeated Andrew Higginson to take his second title.

Michaela lets out a yelp at the 2008 Grand Prix!

Her World Championship bow came in 2003 when she was in charge of the match between Mark King and Drew Henry and since then she has gone on to referee in the semi-finals in 2007 (Murphy/Selby), and 2008 as Ronnie O'Sullivan defeated Stephen Hendry.

Prior to the O'Sullivan/Hendry clash however she had recently taken charge of an even bigger match, the 2008 Wembley Masters final between Mark Selby and Stephen Lee. Unsurprisingly she was the first female to do this and in 2009 was again present at the tournament, though this time the final went to Jan Verhaas.

Early in 2009 it was announced that in May that year, Michaela would take charge of her first World Championship final at the Crucible Theatre, in the process becoming the first woman ever to do so. More importantly for her though it was her first final and thankfully it all went without incident as fittingly she saw fellow Scot John Higgins lift the trophy for the third time.

Patricia Murphy

Most Beautiful Referee

When I refereed Jimmy White and Alex Higgins at an exhibition in Limerick. The venue had a wooden floor and because of the echo of my heels Alex said in front of the whole place "You're like a horse clip-clopping round the table" I didn't know what to say! Thankfully I have never refereed on a wooden floor since!!

- Patricia Murphy

Patricia Murphy is an experienced pool and snooker referee. She honed her craft after years of playing and dedicating herself to the rules that govern cue sports. This dedication started at a young age and moved her to seek guidance from other referees like Michaela Tabb.

Born in Ireland, Patricia Murphy now lives in Lincolnshire and is establishing herself as the most senior female referee in the sport after Michaela Tabb. Although she has yet to referee at the World Championship, since qualifying in 2004 she has been involved with events such as the UK Championship and the World Series, as well as a series of exhibition matches. Notably, one of these exhibitions involved Ken Doherty and the late Paul Hunter in a repeat of their epic 2003 World semi-final, and this was almost as memorable with Ken making a 147 in Dublin!

Hopefully over the next few years she will continue to gain experience and become a more familiar face to the TV viewers, though like Michaela some of you may recognise her from her work with pool.

Most memorable match: An exhibition match between Ken Doherty and Paul Hunter in October 2004 in Dublin, Ken made a 147, it was fantastic to referee.

Most embarrassing moment: When I refereed Jimmy White and Alex Higgens at an exhibition in Limerick. The venue had a wooden floor and because of the echo of my heels Alex said in front of the whole place "You're like a horse clip-clopping round the table" I didn't know what to say! Thankfully I have never refereed on a wooden floor since!!

If you weren't a referee what would you do? I couldn't imagine not refereeing but if I had to choose anything other than that it would be to study sports psychology.

Which is the toughest rule to apply? Probably the miss rule. If a lot of balls are moved from their original positions it can be difficult to replace them.

Which rule would you scrap? At the moment none of them as they are all there for a reason.

What do you carry in your pockets? Two ball markers and a coin.

Where do you get your gloves? Gloves Online. It's a company in America and I get them shipped over.

Interests: Playing poker, boxing, listening to music and spending time with my family in Ireland whenever I get the chance.

Famous Personalities

...light moments with Cue Sports

Three Prime Ministers

Pt. Jawaharlal Nehru, Indira Gandhi and Rajiv Gandhi

Martin Luther King Jr.

Barack Hussein Obama

Playing Pool

Laurel & Hardy

It's the world's most famous game of eight-ball !
With Marliyn Monroe working her charms to utter distraction, James Dean lines up his shot, and competitors Elvis Presley and Humphrey Bogart look on

Kapil Dev

For RAVINDRA KUMAR GUPTA (RKG) ALTRUISM knows no BOUNDARIES

After the rather long stint with Delhi Billiards Snooker Association, having successfully organized in 1981 and 1985 in World Billiard Championships, Ravindra Kumar Gupta decided to dabble in organizing snooker tournaments, kind of which the country had not seen and felt. In the picturesque and salubrious climate of Mussoorie he organized two invitational tournaments at Residency Manor, which was city in itself. For sheer artistic grandeur and opulence, this hotel is second to none. He offered cream of snooker talent to come, stay and play in this outstanding atmosphere. He gave them highest prize money ever in this country to boost. Players mingled with each other and stayed with their families. Besides playing serious snooker, fun and frolic was order of the evening.

They played in this carnival atmosphere led by Geet Sethi, Yasin Merchant, Alok Kumar, Dharmendra Lilly, Sidhartha Roa, Rupesh Shah, Sonic Multani etc. This was during the turn of a century. Thus began the saga of RKG Hospitalities and benevolence.

The world spread and his tournament acquired a certain halo. In the year 2002 players started converging at Jaypee Hotel in Agra, the city famous for artistic marvel, symbol of love – Taj Mahal. Some player from Pakistan also took part and a grand show by the automobile giant Mercedes added to the charm of the tournament. Live gazals sang by famous singers and artists enliven the evenings. Players comfort was paramount in his mind which was eventually reflected on snooker table. Taken to the historical places and other sites almost every day as an when time permitted.

The scene shifted to redolent and historic capital of India to select the sixteen players. It was around mid-night when a tall, lanky and ultra slim young man with a suitcase and cue in his hands approached me for a place in the final 16. With utmost reluctances, I expressed my inability to include him. He waited for a while, showed no remorse and there was hardly any expressions on stoic face. He walked out with gingerly pace and went back to the airport. To select the slot for sixteen players became an arduous and onerous task. To turn down a player of Aditya Mehta's stature and caliber will continue to haunt me forever. It was jig-saw puzzle which try to solve with best of my

ability. But it is a tribute to Ravindra Kumar Gupta that he did not meddle and exerted any pressure on me.

The tournament was a runaway success which was beamed live by Doordarshan. Some extra ordinary performances by Alok Kumar, Pankaj Advani, Mannan Chandra, Yasin Merchant etc., who gave more than 100%. Chief Minister of Delhi Ms. Sheila Dixit and her cabinet were so enamored that they watched the proceeding for entire day with apt interest. The tournament attracted of five lacs of rupees as prize money.

Then there was a defining silence for about a decade vis-e-vie snooker due to personal reasons for almost a decade. He wanted to catch up the lost time by announcing a magnanimous RKG Snooker, which entails prize money of over Rs. 25 Lacs. It was held in Chennai, Delhi, Kolkata & Pune and reached a wild crescendo for a Grand Finale in the Mumbai. A galaxy of players of India and abroad participated to make it a gala affair. The onerous task of organization fell on Yasin Merchant, who did exemplary work.

The Finals between Stephen Lee and our own Pankaj Advani manage to produce a humongous amount of interest amongst the sporting public of Mumbai. It was a kind of pot-boiler one can hope to witness. Nineteen frames of sheer ecstatic and grandeur adorn the entire match. After that gruelling fight and titanic struggle last black separated the winner and runners-up before black played truant for quite sometime. A great pity that someone has to lose.

The recent RKG Snooker championship was a result of long deliberation and prayers. Pankaj Advani, Lucky Vatnani, Aditya Mehta and Brijesh Damani were deserving winners in Delhi, Ahmadabad, Chennai and Kolkata respectively. The grand culmination is at NSCI Mumbai, who deserved kudos for organizing a tournament of such a short notice.

He has seen many snooker players lived in abject poverty. That is how he mooted the big price money tournament. A sagacious advice to the players is to shed all the encumbrance and inhibition to play a game in right earnest. According to him if four or five like minded people can join him his crusade, then we will soon herald Indian Flag at Crucible Theatre.

YASHBIR SHARMA

Your Search for comfort...
...ends here
RKG
DIVINE INN
7 B, Dr. C.V. Raman Road, Near Gurudwara,
New Friends Colony, New Delhi - 110 065
Ph.: 011-45-787878 Fax: 011-45-787888
E-mail: info@divineinn.com
Web: www.divineinn.com
RKG
Divine Inn
...a Boutique Hotel Experience

Exclusive Collection

of RKG's Creative Books !

Uncover Delhi's rich history along with its heritage tourist attractions

RKG

Indraprastha... Dilli... Shahjahanabad... New Delhi

This is a touristic and historical book on Delhi. It covers almost all monumental historic tourist spots from Ancient Delhi to New Delhi with photographs personally conceived & captured and detailed description about them. Also a folded Guide Map about Delhi, placed inside the book. The Historical Map of Walled City is placed at front inside cover in the size of 24 x 48 cms.

- 216 Pages • Size : 23.5 x 24 cms. • Hard Cover **(Coffee Table Book edition)**

ALSO AVAILABLE IN SMALL SIZE

• 272 Pages • Size : 13.5 x 20.5 cms. • Paper Back • Also a folded Guide Map about Delhi placed inside the book. The title opens with a Historical Map of Walled City itself in the size of 20.5 x 26.5 cms.

Delve into Kumaon's enchanting beauty with its history

RKG

KUMAON

The land of God...

Kumaon offers some of the most stunning mountain scenery and perennially snow capped peaks of Great Himalayan range, which are covered in this book. Most of the photographs are self conceived & captured.

- 256 Pages • Size : 13.5 x 20.5 cms. • Paper Back

Discover glorious beauty of World's amazing, alluring places

RKG

Discover Another World

It contains personally conceived & captured approx. 300 photographs from around the World covering U.S.A. (New York, Boca Raton, Miami, Minneapolis), U.K. (London), Czech (Prague), Austria (Vienna), Italy (Sicily), India's Historical Delhi, Jaipur, Himachal Pradesh (Chail & Parwanoo), Nainital, Gangtok, Goa, Sri-Lanka & Singapore.

- 144 Pages • Size : 23 x 28.5 cms. • Hard Cover

Explore Various Tourist Attractions in India & Abroad

RKG

Treasures of the World

Through my Eyes

This travel book covers pictures, conceived & captured personally of the grand historic monuments, picturesque hills, serene nature, shimmering lakes, gorgeous sunsets, elegant heritage architecture, superlative Iceland, mysterious oceans, along with other interesting places from India (Agra, Darjeeling, Gangtok, Nainital, Bhimtal) & Abroad (London, Lake District, Yorkshire, Inverness, Edinburgh, Dublin, Venice, Istanbul, Prague, Reykjavik, Nice, Monte Carlo, Rovaniemi, Helsinki, Stockholm, Bergen, Oslo and Dubrovnik).

- 128 Pages • Size : 23 x 28.5 cms. • Hard Cover

RKG Publishers
CREATIVE PUBLISHING

To buy your copy please contact : 7-B, Dr. C.V. Raman Road, New Friends Colony, New Delhi.
Ph.: 011-45-787878, +91 9891068807 | E-mail: rkghospitalities2007@gmail.com
To buy online visit **www.rkgpublishers.com** or **Amazon**

Several club members enjoying an eveni

It has long been accepted that the game played on a Snooker table w
as an amalgam of various Billiards table games although it has recently become